African Cinema

Blacks in the Diaspora
Darlene Clark Hine, John McCluskey, Jr., and David Barry Gaspar
General Editors

Manthia Diawara

African
Cinema

politics & culture

indiana university press
bloomington & indianapolis

The paper used in this publication meets the minimum requirements of America
National Standard for Information Sciences—Permanence of Paper for Printed
Library Materials, ANSI Z39.48-1984.

Manufactured in the United States of America

Library of Congress Cataloging-in-Publication Data

Diawara, Manthia, date.
    African cinema : politics and culture / Manthia Diawara.
      p.   cm.—(Blacks in the diaspora)
    Includes bibliographical references and index.
    ISBN 0-253-31704-5.—ISBN 0-253-20707-X (pbk.)
      1. Motion pictures—Africa—History.   2. Motion pictures—Social
aspects—Africa.   3. Motion pictures—Political aspects—Africa.
I. Title. II. Series.
PN1993.5.A35D5   1992
791.43′096—dc20   91-24579

    3 4 5 96

contents

acknowledgments

Several people assisted me during the research for this book. African filmmakers were particularly helpful. I learned a lot from Ousmane Sembène, Souleymane Cissé, Cheick Oumar Sissoko, Ben Diogaye Beye, Ngangura Mweze, and Gaston Kaboré. Jean Rouch adopted me as if I were one of his students at the *Musée de l'Homme*. Andre Daventure and her colleagues at ATRIA opened several files to me. I also benefited from discussions and advice from Teshome Gabriel, James Naremore, Mbye Cham, and Jim Pines. Finally I thank Saloum Kamissoko, Mariam Fofana, Gagny Diawara, and Seydou Ly for their unconditional support.

Thanks to the following journals where earlier versions of some chapters appeared: *Jump-Cut* (no. 32, 1987), for "Sub-Saharan Africa Film Production: Technological Paternalism"; *Blackframes: Critical Perspectives on Black Independent Cinema* (MIT Press, 1988), ed. Mbye Cham and Claire Andrade-Watkins, for "Film in Anglophone Africa: A Brief Survey"; *Framework* (no. 37, 1990), for "African Cinema Today"; and *Third World Affairs* (1986), for "FESPACO: An Evaluation."

I would also like to acknowledge the support of the University of California at Santa Barbara for the many fellowships that enabled me to travel to film archives and cinémathèques in Paris, Dakar, and Ouagadougou. Thanks, finally, to Catherine McKinney and Tanika Beamon for clerical and editorial assistance.

introduction

French film historian Georges Sadoul observed in 1960 that while many African countries south of the Sahara had gained their independence, no really African film yet existed, i.e., one produced, directed, photographed, and edited by Africans and starring Africans who spoke in African languages. Rather, only British, French, and U.S. filmmakers had been making documentaries and fictional films in Africa and about Africans ever since 1900, five years after the Lumière Brothers invented motion pictures.[1]

Jean Rouch, father of Cinéma Vérité and founder of the Comité du film ethnographique (Ethnographic Film Committee) at the Musée de l'Homme (Anthropological Museum), noted how this situation changed. At a round table discussion on Africa and film, organized in 1961 by UNESCO, Rouch drew attention to the legacy left by the British Colonial Film Unit in Africa, the Belgian Missionary Cinema, and the Ethnographic Film Committee in collaboration with the French Foreign Ministry. He pointed to the Anglophone Africans trained at the Accra Film Training School and the first Francophone African graduates from the Institut des Hautes Études Cinématographiques (National Film School) in Paris.

Rouch also wanted to get the French government to install partial film production units in the former colonies and to create a Paris-based postproduction center where Francophone African filmmakers could process their rushes and gain access to postproduction services available only in Europe and the United States.[2] Furthermore, Rouch prescribed 16mm cameras as most economically viable for any developing countries.

However, more than twenty years later, Med Hondo, a Mauritanian filmmaker, wrote in *Le Monde,* "Despite the constant efforts of politicians and men of culture, African cinema is tottering."[3] African cinema, to use Ousmane Sembène's celebrated words, is still at the era of "mégotage."[4] Africa lacks film-processing laboratories, sound-dubbing and synchronizing studios, and editing facilities. These problems as well as financial ones force filmmakers to wait years before finishing one film.

Francophone African filmmakers have made more films than their Anglophone counterparts, yet they have not improved the situation under which they do production. Following in the steps of Ousmane Sembène, younger filmmakers such as Souleymane Cissé, Ola Balogun, and Gaston Kaboré have also made films of international acclaim, but Africa has not developed a film industry. Some film historians blame this on the French government's paternalistic attitude and neocolonial practices toward African filmmakers. Victor Bachy explained the oppressive French input in Francophone African film production in this way:

> In the beginning one finds a willingness on the part of the mother country to keep relations of cooperation, exchange, and friendship with its former subordinates; and to ensure, at the same time, the French presence in Africa, condition sine qua non of the continuation of the relationship. On the other hand, the newly independent countries accept this cooperative relationship because it guarantees them protection.[5]

Not only film production but also distribution in Africa has faced a ruthless and monopolistic exploitation by American, European, and Indian distribution companies. The film industry in Africa has no government protection—neither import quotas nor the freezing of box-office receipts. Because of import quotas, France and West Germany, Europe's two most important film producers, have survived the bombardment of their film market by the U.S. Motion Picture Export Association of America (MPEAA).

At the same time that African countries could not control foreign domination of distribution and exhibition, they also have not raised, as have France and Germany, subsidies for national African film production. Furthermore, foreign distributors use block-booking and other monopolistic practices so that African films are often not even seen in their country of origin. To put it in Férid Boughedir's words, "Fundamentally, African cinema does not exist because film distribution is not in Africa's hands."[6]

Clearly, film production in Africa has a complex background. A mere listing of films made by Africans, although helpful, would not clarify the structural and political issues. Nor would I put all the blame on foreign distributors, as French scholars and administrators often do. Rather, I propose to analyze the structures of film production since colonialism and the different stances toward film production promoted by governments and individuals in the colonialist countries and then later in the African nations. The reader will notice the relatively strong emphasis on film in Francophone Africa, because it is the dominant cinema in sub-Saharan Africa. The reader will also see the role played by the Fédération Panafricaine des Cinéastes as well as the new measures taken collectively or by individual countries to liberate African cinema from its colonial trappings. Finally, I will demonstrate how different types of production politics have resulted in certain types of films.

African Cinema

I.

Anglophone African Production

In 1884, the European countries met in Berlin for the "Scramble of Africa." To justify themselves morally, they argued that they had a duty to civilize Africans. Most of the pioneers who introduced film production to Africa used the same argument. They believed that distributing commercial films, such as those by Charlie Chaplin, would harmfully introduce Africans to film's powerful means of persuasion. Such films were held to be technically too sophisticated for African minds and also damaging because they depicted the negative aspects of European and North American lives. In this light, L. A. Notcutt, founder of the Bantu Educational Cinema Experiment, argued the following:

> With backward peoples unable to distinguish between truth and falsehood, it is surely in our wisdom, if not our obvious duty, to prevent as far as possible the dissemination of wrong ideas. Should we stand by and see a distorted presentation of the white race's life accepted by millions of Africans when we have it in our power to show them the truth?[1]

Colonial governments, missionaries, and anthropologists thus tried to give Africans a different cinematic heritage than the mainstream films of Europe and the United States. The British opened the way in 1935 with the creation of the Bantu Educational Cinema Experiment. This was sponsored by the Colonial Office of the British Film Institute and financed by such interest groups as the Carnegie Corporation of New York, the Roan Antelope Copper Mines, the Rholkana Corporation, and the Mufulira Copper Mines, Ltd. The program sought through film to educate adult Africans to understand and adapt to new conditions, to reinforce ordinary classroom methods, to conserve the best of African traditions, and to provide recreation and entertainment (Notcutt and Latham, pp. 27–28).

In economic terms, the Bantu Cinema Experiment was not mandated for "quality production." It got neither 35mm cameras nor equipment for synchronized sound. The unit used 16mm cameras and 12″ discs for sound recording. The team was also lucky to have as its field director Major Notcutt, who "had had African experience and was able to train and direct native actors. He not only wrote most of the scenarios, including those of the story type, photographed most of the films and directed almost all of them, but he had a complete technical knowledge of every detail of the work of producing talkies; and most of the apparatus devised for the experiment was designed, and some of it was actually made, by him or under his direction" (Notcutt and Latham, p. 186).

Notcutt and his team arrived in Tanganyika (present-day Tanzania) where between 1935 and 1936 they produced approximately thirty-five short films with commentaries in English, Swahili, Sukuama, Kikuyu, Luo, Ganda, Nyanja, Bemba, and Tumbuka. Some of the films were designed to teach Africans to adopt European ways: e.g., *Post Office Savings Bank, Tax, Progress*. Others directed farmers toward cash-crop agriculture: e.g., *Coffee under Banana Shade, High Yields from Selected Plants, Coffee Marketing*. Some taught the prevention of disease: e.g., *Anaesthesia, Infant Malaria, Hookworm*. Notcutt even made a film on African folklore, *The Hare and the Leopard*.

Africans participated in the Bantu Cinema Experiment's productions. Notcutt realized that he could considerably reduce the film's costs by efficiently utilizing local personnel. He wrote, "Intelligent young Africans can be trained to do much of the routine work of the darkroom and the sound studios and even some of the semiskilled work" (Notcutt and Latham, pp. 183–84). To their credit, Major Notcutt and the Bantu Educational Cinema Experiment did the whole of film production, including processing and editing, for the first time in Africa. This fact is even more significant and ironic when we compare it to the conditions of production that prevail in Africa now.

At the end of their project in 1937, Notcutt and his colleagues recommended that the British Colonial Office start local film units in the colonies that would cooperate with a central organization in London. Rather than waste money on autonomous production units similar to the Bantu Cinema Experiment, the colonial office was to set up groups, each of which had their "own skeleton film-producing unit, concerned mainly with the photography, and that the highly technical and more skilled work of completing the films should be done at a central organization shared by all" (Notcutt and Latham, p. 187).

In 1939 the British set up the Colonial Film Unit, with branches in different parts of Africa: an East African branch for Kenya, Tanganyika, and Uganda; a Central African branch for Rhodesia (present-day Zimbabwe) and Nyassaland; and a West African branch for Nigeria and the Gold Coast (present-day Ghana). According to Jean Rouch, the British government set up these film units to get Africans to participate in World War II. Rouch added, however, "If the immediate goal of the Colonial Film Unit was to make war propaganda, its organizer, W. Sellers, in fact had in mind a long-range project—establishing a systematic way to utilize film with an African audience" (Rouch, p. 390).

At first, the Colonial Film Unit distributed propaganda films in Africa. For this purpose films made in Europe and America were re-edited and commented on in order to achieve the desired effect with Africans. In 1945, after World War II, this distribution policy changed to one of production. Films such as *Mister English at Home* and *An African in London* were made to demonstrate British etiquette. Films were also produced in Africa and at the Central Bureau in London to sell Western products such as transistor radios *(Lusaka Calling)* or to show the advantages of Western medicine over the African ways of healing *(Leprosy)*. Unlike the Bantu Cinema Experiment, which used 16mm cameras, the Colonial Film Unit shot its films in 35mm.

In 1949, following a report John Grierson wrote for UNESCO, the Colonial Film Unit initiated a film school at Accra, Gold Coast. Grierson decided that films made by the Bantu Cinema Experiment and the Colonial Film Unit never attracted African audiences because Africans could not identify with them. Grierson wrote, "I believe that we'll resolve the problem of cinema in the Colonies not by projecting films from the West, but by colonial people's making films inside the colonies for themselves" (quoted in Van Bever, pp. 16–17).

The school was to train students for a period of six months, after which they would break into small groups and make films. After the first six months the Film Training School moved to Jamaica, then to London. According to Van Bever, the school had encouraging results: "African students were trained in this manner to become excellent assistants to the production teams sent to West Africa by the Colonial Film Unit's central organization in London" (p. 23).

By 1955 the Colonial Film Unit declared that it had fulfilled its goal to introduce an educational cinema to Africans. The colonies were asked to finance their own film production. The Colonial Film Unit changed its name to Overseas Film and Television Centre. No longer responsible for developing cinema in the colonies, the center served as a point for coordinating the autonomous production units in the colonies and for training film and television crews. It was also a place for African filmmakers to buy film equipment and do postproduction work. In other words, Britain no longer had the economic burden of producing films for the colonies, and this policy also assured that the colonies would be dependent on Britain in developing their film production. Jean Rouch said this change in the policy came because the British knew that at any time these colonies would become independent (Rouch, p. 390).

The Effect of the British Colonial Film Unit

The Bantu Cinema Experiment and the Colonial Film Unit were in many ways paternalistic and racist. They wanted to turn back film history and develop a different type of cinema for Africans because they considered the African mind too primitive to follow the sophisticated narrative techniques of mainstream cinema. Thus they thought it necessary to return to the beginning of film history—to use uncut scenes, slow down the story's pace, and make the narrative simpler by using fewer actors and adhering to just one dominant theme. The ideology of these units denied that the colonized peoples had elementary human qualities. And this ideology prevented the British filmmakers from seeing the obvious: their films were boring and clumsy. Critic J. Koyinde Vaughan wrote of this period in 1957:

> Yet African film audiences, daily growing larger, when faced with the choice of seeing the "simplified screen narrative" produced by the "Colonial Film Unit" and the foreign "commercial entertainment film" have overwhelmingly decided in favor of the latter products, in spite of their "complicated technical conventions." In African towns like Freetown, Accra, Kumasi, Lagos, or Nairobi, Charles Chaplin and many popular stars of the screen are already household names.[2]

The British also failed to understand African life and traditions. The Colonial Film Unit treated everything African as superstitious and backward and valorized Europe at Africa's expense, as if they needed to downgrade traditional African culture in order to demonstrate European efficacy (Rouch, p. 392). With these paternalistic and racist attitudes, the British never adequately trained Africans to handle their own film production. In fact, if the colonies could make their own films, the colonials would no longer be needed for this form of national expression. The British understood this and therefore put an end to the Colonial Film Unit in the early fifties in the wake of independence movements in Africa.

However, the Colonial Film Unit had an impact on the current structures of film production in Anglophone Africa. As Frantz Fanon analyzed colonialism in *Sociologie d'une révolution,* "It is the White who creates the Negro."[3] In *Pour la révolution africaine,* Fanon also explains the effect of the colonizer's technological paternalism: the colonizer frames the structure of the behavior of the colonized. By maintaining control over how technology is used, the colonizers achieve "an organized domination of a nation which they have conquered militarily."[4] Fanon's insight sheds light on the determining role played by the Colonial Film Unit in Africa.

Ghana and Neocolonialist Production

After independence, the Anglophone countries, except for Ghana and Nigeria, did not attempt to integrate film into their cultural policy, either as an essential element of development or as entertainment. Most of them stopped film production with the closing of the British Colonial Film Unit. Ghana saw several attempts to keep alive the structures of production inherited from the British. The Ghana Gold Coast Film Unit became independent in 1950, even before the Colonial Film Unit ceased production in Africa. Sean Graham, a student of John Grierson, helped organize the Gold Coast Film Unit, which made films as coproductions with independent British interest groups and with masters of the documentary such as Grierson himself.

Ghana's film unit saw its purpose as making educational and entertainment films to distribute in and outside the country. Rejecting the aesthetic of the Colonial Film Unit, it embraced current narrative styles of fiction films and documentaries. Graham and his team made films about acculturation *(Jaguar High Life);* city life *(The Boy Kumasenu);* and independence movements *(Freedom for Ghana).* Graham's biggest success, *The Boy Kumasenu* (1952), was widely distributed in Ghana and England.

However, Graham and the Ghana Gold Coast Film Unit did not set up a self-contained production unit that could be taken over by Ghanaians at the threshold of independence. It is to Graham's credit that the unit departed from the style of overdrawn narratives, burdened with commentaries, but this very concern with quality narratives also kept Graham from dealing with African economic realities. The unit shot 35mm film stock and processed and edited in London. Thus the Ghana Film Corporation was still dependent upon the Overseas Film and Television Centre in London. More significantly, the students who came out of the Accra Film Training School never had the chance to direct their own films. They remained in the background as Graham's assistants.

In 1957, Graham left Ghana after independence, and Ghana president Kwame Nkrumah nationalized both film distribution and production. This marked a new phase in Ghanaian film production. Between 1957 and 1966, the Nkrumah regime built the most sophisticated infrastructure of film production in Africa, including editing studios and 16mm and 35mm processing laboratories. Ghana did not have its own directors yet, but foreign directors made several newsreels, documentaries, and propaganda films in Ghanaian studios. When Nkrumah was overthrown, the new regime confiscated all the films produced between 1957 and 1966, explaining that the films fed the "personality cult of Nkrumah." To set up new production policies, Sam Aryetey, a graduate of the 1949 Accra Film Training School and a film director and editor, was named head of the Ghana Film Corporation in 1969.

According to the foremost authority on African cinema, Paulin S. Vieyra, when Aryetey took it over, the Ghana Film Corporation had "equipment capable of completing a dozen feature films a year."[5] Aryetey himself boasted, "In Ghana, we possess the best cinematographic infrastructure in tropical Africa."[6] The Ghana Film Corporation could also draw upon the expertise of Ghanaian technicians trained in Accra and London, and there were already ten Ghanaian film directors. Despite this potential technical reservoir, Ghana has produced only twenty films since 1966, out of which fewer than ten are features.[7]

First of all, Aryetey shifted to a policy of coproduction, as he said, to "find distribution outlets outside Africa" (Raeburn, p. 19). In this vein, Aryetey signed with an Italian director, Giorgio Bontempi, to make the film *Impact* (1975), which was a financial disaster and seen by very few people. In a classic move in which colonial government domination is replaced by neocolonialist capitalist domination, Aryetey did not use Ghanaian and African directors but turned to Europeans to make films for Ghana. He thus set back the progress of film production in Ghana to where it had been when the Colonial Film Unit left.

In situations in which African government production units such as the Ghana Film Corporation turn to foreign directors and entrepreneurs to make films, the only hope for an African cinema remains in the hands of independent filmmakers. In Ghana the future of independent cinema depends very much on one director, Kwaw Ansah, whose film *Love Brewed in the African Pot* (1981) enjoyed wide distribution in Ghana, Kenya, and outside Africa. Ansah was able to use the equipment of the Ghana Film Corporation and Ghanaian technicians to produce and direct his films.[8]

Nigerian Cinema

The other significant producer of film in Anglophone Africa is Nigeria, the biggest country in Africa, with more than 100 million people and more than 100 movie theaters. The Colonial Film Unit, which had three offices in Nigeria, left behind 16mm cameras, studios, and laboratories. Furthermore, Nigerian television, created before independence in 1959, has a large audience all over the country. It has an international perspective. With Segun Olusola as its director, Nigerian television has adapted plays by Jean-Paul Sartre, Wole Soyinka, Duro Lapido, J. P. Clark, and Anton Chekhov.

Olusola himself had attempted a career in film production when he coproduced *Son of Africa* in 1970. However, he did this with a group of Lebanese businessmen who own part of the monopoly of film distribution in Nigeria. According to Ola Balogun, Nigeria's foremost filmmaker, Olusola and his associates hastily created a film company, Fedfilms Limited, to produce *Son of Africa* so they could go down in history for "producing the first Nigerian film."[9] Most significantly, under Olusola, *Son of Africa* and all the television adaptations were directed by foreigners. Clearly, Olusola had no solution for Nigerian and/or African media production.

At the same time that *Son of Africa* was made, another important Nigerian film producer came on the scene—Francis Oladele, perhaps the first genuinely independent film producer in Anglophone Africa.[10] Oladele dreamed of making Nigeria an African Hollywood. He founded his production company, Calpenny Limited, with the financial support of North Americans from California, Pennsylvania, and New York—hence the name Cal-Pen-NY. He wanted to produce films that would be successful in both Africa and the West, and thus he thought he needed international film directors, actors, and coproducers.

Oladele's first film was an adaptation of Soyinka's play, *Kongi's Harvest* (1971), directed by a famous U.S. Afro-American director, Ossie Davis, and starring Soyinka himself. His second film, *Bullfrog in the Sun* (1972), was adapted from Chinua Achebe's two novels, *Things Fall Apart* and *No Longer at Ease.* A West German, Hans Jurgen Pohland, directed that film with actress Princess Elisabeth of Toro, who had once been a lawyer in Uganda and then had worked as a model in New York. The film abounds with violent wars and lingers on the issue of cession of Biafra to Ibos, a political issue that makes many Africans find the film in poor taste. As for *Kongi's Harvest,* it was denounced by its own playwright, Soyinka, and Ossie Davis's credentials for directing a film on Africa for Africans were seen as questionable (Balogun, p. 255). Although Oladele still produces newsreels upon request, he has not produced a feature film since *Bullfrog in the Sun.*

Ola Balogun is the director who has revealed the first real promise of Nigerian cinema. Born in 1945, Balogun graduated from the Paris National Film School before becoming a diplomat for his country between 1968 and 1971. Balogun is also known as a novelist and playwright. Back in Nigeria at the end of his diplomatic career, he produced and directed twelve films between 1972 and 1977. Balogun has produced and directed at least one feature film a year, earning the title of the most prolific film director in Africa. Balogun makes comedies and African musicals. These films enjoy a big success in Nigeria, which allows Balogun to recoup his money each time and make new films. He proves that it is possible for a filmmaker in a country the size of Nigeria to survive and continue producing on the basis of local consumption of his films.

Balogun's critical statements in international magazines, coupled with his films' success, have fired an overall Nigerian interest in film. The government has begun to sponsor students to study film abroad. African cinema also played an important role in the 1977 Festival of African Cultures (FESTAC) organized in Lagos. Subsequently a seminar was organized on Nigerian cinema, the proceedings of which are published in a book, *The Development and Growth of the Film Industry in Nigeria* (1979), edited by Alfred E. Opubor and Onuora E. Nwunel. The Nigeria Film Corporation, which took the place of the Colonial Film Unit, has since been reorganized, and the duties of its manager, Alhaji Adamu Halilu, include encouraging national film production by Nigerians. In chapter 8, I discuss Nigerian and Ghanaian film production in more detail.

Problems Faced in Anglophone Africa

Aside from these weak traces of film production in Ghana and Nigeria, cinematographically speaking, Anglophone Africa can be said to be dieting. Film specialists and amateurs alike have given many reasons for the lack of films made here. Some say it comes from the fact that the British did not have an assimilationist policy toward their colonies. Unlike the French, who taught about "nos ancêtres les gaulois" (our French ancestors) to Africans, British colonialism seemed "strictly business and never succeeded or tried assimilation, which was linked to French economic colonialism" (Boughedir, p. 34).

Another argument claims that film was not a priority for developing African countries. Acting out of pragmatism, the Anglophone countries abandoned local production with the closing of the Colonial Film Unit. They directed their energies toward more pressing problems. While they accepted a few documentaries dealing with "reality," i.e., hard facts, they shunned fiction, make-believe, and metaphysics. They were empiricists like their former British masters, with "more practical and pragmatic attitudes inherited from the former British authority."[11]

Others point out that Anglophone Africans have not been exposed to film culture. In Francophone countries, for example, French embassies have cinémathèques where Africans can see contemporary cinema from Europe and the United States and discuss it with a French discussion leader. The British embassies in Africa lack such cultural activities. The British cultural service was more interested in promoting didactic and often boring documentaries. As Michael Raeburn puts it, "Compared to Francophone African countries, the Anglophone African countries lack in cinematic culture" (Raeburn, "Le cinéma piétine," p. 254).

Director Ola Balogun believes that the problem is mainly economic. Taking Nigeria as a case in point, he argues that during the colonial epoch the country consumed products made in Great Britain, including film. Furthermore, and most significantly, Nigeria's political independence was not followed by economic independence.

Today, film distribution in Nigeria remains in the hands of foreign companies (U.S. and Lebanese) that dictate their will in the matter of cinema. Since the distributors benefit more by buying up old U.S., English, and Indian films at a very low price, their policy has consisted in discouraging all attempts to create a national film production (Balogun, p. 252).

Criticisms and Potential New Directions

The experience of Ghana and Nigeria also demonstrates the technological and aesthetic dependence of the African cinema on the West. Both in Ghana and in Nigeria, Westerners are often called upon to direct films intended for Africans. *Coproductions are desirable, but, if possible, they should first be between African nations.* There are many reasons why I assert this principle. First, by using African technicians, the producers will spend less. Secondly, the film, by its double or triple nationality, increases its chances that it will recoup its cost among African audiences. Coproduction among Africans also may save some of the equipment inherited from the Colonial Film Unit from stagnation. Most important, films run less of a risk aesthetically of misinterpreting African cultures when made by African directors.

Furthermore, in analyzing Ghana and Nigeria, we see the need to think about film production in a critical manner. Based on economic realities, these two countries should choose 16mm production rather than 35mm, for example, and make an effort to train Africans in editing and in laboratory skills. Such tactics would have demystified film to technology and made it accessible even to Africa. Let us not forget, after all, that in 1935 Major Notcutt and the Bantu Educational Cinema Experiment had a self-contained unit and that all their films were produced on the spot. This practice was abandoned by the Colonial Film Unit and, unfortunately, not resumed by their independent African countries.

Let me return for a moment to consider the Bantu Cinema Experiment and Major Notcutt's techno-paternalistic approach to filmmaking for Africans. Assuming that Africans could not appreciate quality film images, Notcutt chose the 16mm camera and the most rudimentary conditions of postproduction to make his "African" films. His blindness to African aesthetic tastes also led him to forgo the hiring of foreign experts in cinematography, directing, editing, etc., and to do all this work in Africa helping himself with African manpower.

The point I am making is that Major Notcutt has simultaneously invented two types of cinema: racist and economically liberated. If Anglophone Africans had used his cost-reducing production methods while divesting them of their racist content, the results could have led to an accessible, demystified cinema, similar to the kind made by the Argentine filmmakers Fernando Solanas and Octavio Gettino and called Third Cinema.

Furthermore, the very racist tendency of Notcutt seems to have prevailed in Anglophone African cinema, long after the Colonial Film Unit left. Patterns of racist filmmaking emerge in the work of the most influential African directors and managers of production companies. Sam Aryetey and Alhaji Adamu Halilu, respectively managers of the Ghana Film Corporation and Nigeria Film Corporation, have made and defended this type of cinema. Aryetey's film *No Tears for Ananse* (1970) and Halilu's *Shaihu Umar* (1976) are both "specially" edited, with almost no ellipses, in order not to confuse their African audiences.

Supposedly, Africans prefer these films.[12] However, J. Koyinde Vaughan has demonstrated that African audiences, when faced with the choice, have decided in favor of economically edited narratives "in spite of their 'complicated technical conventions'" (see note 9). In fact, African oral narratives abound in digressions, parallelisms, flashbacks, dreams, etc. Aesthetically in the same tradition, an African film can easily contain all these elements without necessarily disorienting its audience.

The ideology of the directors of the Ghana and Nigerian film corporations is both economically wasteful and racist. Aryetey and Halilu can learn from Ousmane Sembène's *Emitai* (1971) and Gaston Kaboré's *Wend Kuuni* (1982) that motion pictures don't have to be turned back. Here's a clear case of the colonizer "inventing" the colonized, as Fanon put it. Aryetey and Halilu, trained at the Colonial Film Training School in Accra and the Overseas Film and Television Centre in London, represent that first stage of the encounter between Europe and Africa. A more politically and aesthetically critical approach to filmmaking in Anglophone Africa will undo this situation and lead to the real independence of African cinema.

II.

Zairian Production

Belgian colonial film production began much later than production by the British Colonial Film Unit. In fact, the Belgians used the British Colonial Film Unit as a structural model for their own film production in the Belgian Congo (Zaire). Zairian cinema has been determined and hurt by colonial prescriptions similar to the ones seen with the British Colonial Film Unit.

The Belgian government introduced a series of laws in 1936 about cinema in the Belgian Congo (Zaire) so as to forbid unauthorized filmmakers from filming there (Van Bever, p. 56). The Belgian colonial office collected fees from all commercial films shot in the territory, and it controlled the content of anthropological films made about the different ethnic groups there. In 1945, the Belgian government passed another law forbidding anyone to "admit to movie theaters, public or private, people other than from the European and the Asian races" (Van Bever, p. 55).

Following in the ideological footsteps of the British, the Belgians concluded that commercial films were no good for Africans. Pierre Piron, director of the General Secretariat of the Belgian Congo, argued this:

> The study of the reaction of the Congolese spectators, supported by similar studies undertaken in neighboring territories, leads to a disappointing observation: the African is, in general, not mature enough for cinema. Cinematographic conventions disrupt him; psychological nuances escape him; rapid successions of sequences submerge him. (Van Bever, p. 6)

A Belgian board of censors always had to approve how much the Congolese might get involved in film activities. During World War II, the only approved films for the Congolese, who were then called "non-évolués" or "indigènes," were war propaganda films depicting the Nazis as the enemies of the human race, including Africans.

After the war, in 1947 a branch of the Belgian Ministry of Information, the Film and Photo Bureau, set as a policy producing films especially conceived for the Congolese. L. Van Bever, Chief of the Film and Photo Bureau, was convinced that just distributing films from Europe and the United States would not meet the need of providing Africans with their own cinema. Van Bever wrote, "For the great majority of Africans it would be necessary to film with a special technique, simplified to the extreme. We must, therefore, make, ourselves, the largest share of films destined for Africans" (Van Bever, p. 16).

Bureau projects included the production of educational films for Africans, as well as newsreels and documentaries about Africa for the Belgians. The films were shot with 16mm cameras, and most of the postproduction, except for the laboratory processing of rushes, was done on the spot in the Belgian Congo. Van Bever boasted that all the Bureau assistants were Africans because Belgians understood that Africans, as soon as their education improved, would soon replace their educators. Thus, in the Belgian Congo, although the "indigènes" "have not been trained as in the Gold Coast (Ghana) to know all the steps of film production, they have been instructed, each, to perfectly accomplish a determined work: electrician, assistant to the director, assistant to the editor" (Van Bever, p. 23).

Van Bever also mentioned the existence in 1952 of a Congolese ciné-club in Léopoldville (Kinshasa), where Africans were taught how to make films, and he was proud of the fact that one day this ciné-club would be credited with the training of many indigenous filmmakers. He stated that already the students (Mongita, Dokolo, Boumba, Lubalu, Katambwe, etc.) had made a film: *Une Leçon du Cinéma*.

Before proceeding to evaluate the impact of the Belgian colonial cinema on Zairian film production, I must describe another company that was established at the same time as the Bureau in the Belgian Congo. Called the Congolese Center for Catholic Action Cinema (C.C.A.C.C.), it arose from efforts of Catholic missionaries representing the Scheutist Church in Belgian Congo. Here is how Father Alexandre Van den Heuvel, director of the C.C.A.C.C., explained the center's origins:

In 1945, I insisted with the bishops that cinema be utilized for religious propaganda; I contacted the International Catholic Cinema Office (O.C.I.C.), the central headquarters of which was in Belgium. September 23, 1946, the bishops of the Congo, during a plenary conference, inaugurated the Congolese Center for Catholic Action Cinema (C.C.A.C.C.)[1]

The purpose of the C.C.A.C.C. was to convert Africans to Christianity, to raise money, and to use film to earn African sympathy and friendship toward the Belgians and the Church. The C.C.A.C.C. was funded by the Indigenous Social Welfare Fund, an organization whose object was to "repay the Congo for its efforts during the war. It was a big effort which consisted of supplying wartime Europe with rubber, palm oil, food stuff, copper, and most of all, uranium" (Haffner, p. 88).

Under the C.C.A.C.C. there were three major film production centers in the Belgian Congo, Father Van den Heuvel was in Léopoldville (Kinshasa) with the production company, Edisco-Films. Besides his duties as director of the C.C.A.C.C., Father Van den Heuvel produced a series of "animated cartoons for Africans" called *Les Palabres de Mboloko*. These were short 16mm color films, starring "Mboloko the little antelope," and they illustrated vice and virtue according to the ideology of the church. Father Van den Heuvel was credited for his usage of African music soundtrack. His idea about producing African cartoons was also revolutionary for Africa (Haffner, p. 92).

Father Van Haelst, manager of Luluafilms production in Luluabourg (Kanaga), Western Kasai, was the most active among the producer/ members of the C.C.A.C.C. He produced more than fifty short films that were high in quality and successful in synthesizing instruction and entertainment. His silent comedies, the series of *Matamata et Pilipili*, were shorts about a Chaplin-like character, Matamata—"stubborn and slightly pretentious, but extremely kind" (Haffner, p. 92; Van Bever, p. 34).

The last major missionary production unit, Africa Films, in Bukavu and Kivu, was headed by Father De Vloo, reputedly a great director and a sociologist of African traditions. "His profound knowledge of African symbols and culture, together with his perfect mastery of the cinematographic techniques, enabled him to make some remarkable educational films" (Van Bever, p. 34).

In 1960, when Zaire became independent, both the C.C.A.C.C. and the Film and Photo Bureau stopped their African production. The value of the three centers of missionary production had been discussed by many historians of African cinema. Compared to the official Belgian production of the Bureau, the productions of the C.C.A.C.C.

were, in the eyes of some historians, the most significant films made for Africans. Jean Rouch, for example, stated that whereas the films by the Bureau were naive and disarmingly paternalistic, the missionary films were most advanced in quality. Rouch was particularly impressed by the missionary film director's ability to transpose African folktales such as *Les Palabres de Mboloko* to film. This made Rouch wonder, "What would the evolution of missionary cinema have been had the missionary been allowed to continue producing films?" (Rouch, p. 394)

Historians of African cinema, such as Victor Bachy, have even listed the Belgian missionaries as the first African filmmakers. Bachy selected them, out of all the colonial film producers, as the only authentic African filmmakers because he believed that the missionaries understood Africans better. Bachy argued that if Costa-Gavras's *Missing* (1982) was a U.S. (Hollywood) film, why couldn't the missionary cinema be African? The fact that Hollywood has a tradition of absorbing world famous directors and that the missionary cinema was imposed on Africans did not stop Bachy from making up such an imperialist analogy. He said the missionary cinema had an African content because it borrowed materials from the African folktales. And it was loved by Africans. Bachy writes, "The films spoke a simple language which was direct, received, understood, appreciated, and requested" (pp. 23–24).

Another reason why Bachy saw a difference between the missionary films and other colonial films was that the missionaries were not satisfied with the so-called special films for Africans. They created, instead, an "African cinema, which differed from documentaries, ethnographic films and commercial films, and which was cultural and entertaining." Pointing to *Les Palabres de Mboloko* and other films, Bachy stated that the missionaries had left Zairians a cinematic legacy that would be revalorized. "With them [the missionaries], they [Zairians] have discovered THE cinema, one which could be theirs."

Technocratic Paternalism in Zaire

Today, how can we assess the official Belgian cinema of the Film and Photo Bureau and the private productions of the missionaries in terms of their impact on national Zairian film production? What role have they played in determining the future of Zairian cinema? Paulin S. Vieyra revealed that at the time of independence in July 1960, there was not a single Zairian film director prepared to take over after the Belgians. It was Vieyra's discovery that whereas in colonial times an important infrastructure of film activities existed in Belgian Congo (Zaire), no African was involved as producer and/or director in these film activities. Vieyra wrote, "In the private sector, as well as in the government sector, the African remained as an auxiliary for whom one pretended to work" (p. 222).

Ngangura Mweze, a prize-winning filmmaker in Zaire and a professor of film at the National Institute for the Arts, also argues that although the Zairians were unique among many Africans in having a flourishing film industry created exclusively for them, the colonial structures of film production precluded serious African participation. Mweze understood that both Belgian missionaries and officials, under the guise of educating, instructing, and/or evangelizing, were laying the groundwork for total colonial domination. Zairians could not be trusted to make films. And in analyzing the films themselves, as Mweze puts it, "One sees clearly, through the themes they treated, the forms, and the structures of production and distribution, that everything was very colonial."[2]

A look at the Congolese ciné-club, referred to earlier in this study, will prove Mweze right. According to Van Bever, Zairians were trained at the ciné-club and other places in order for them to replace their Belgian educators in film production. However, after independence, all the students of the ciné-club except one, Mongita, turned to other activities. Dokolo became the first Zairian to own and preside over a bank. General Boumba became chief of Mobutu's army. Other students of the ciné-club, such as Lubalu and Katambwe, had also taken up nonfilm activities. As for Mongita, he kept one foot in film and the other in theater. Since independence he has been involved with the making of only one documentary, *Les tam-tams du Congo* (1963).

It was this dispersion of the students of the ciné-club that led Mweze to argue that the Belgians had not adequately trained Zairians to take over as filmmakers. Mweze did not believe that any of the students, including Mongita, were sufficiently trained to become film directors or producers. He suspected that the Belgian instructors really stood in the students' way and prevented them from fully realizing the importance of cinema and from making their own films. It was in this vein that Mweze challenged the directorial role attributed to Mongita and others.

> In the making of *Une Leçon du Cinéma* (1952), *Les Pneus Gonfles* (1953), and *Les tam-tams du Congo* (1963), one never knows exactly the role played by the Belgian instructors and/or advisors and the role played by the so-called Zairian directors. (Mweze, interview)

The point here is that Belgian officials and missionaries were producing a paternalist and racist cinema, and in the process they shut out the Zairians as filmmakers. Colonialists' fetishization and/or mystification of the technological apparatus prevented them from having a person-to-person rapport with Zairians. They treated Zairians as "non-évolués" with lower mental capacities; it would therefore have been contradictory for them to imagine training these Africans to function in unsupervised positions as filmmakers and producers.

No one was, in this sense, as paternalistic as the director of the C.C.A.C.C. and author of the series, *Les Palabres de Mboloko,* Father Van den Heuvel. His rationale behind the making of the animated cartoons *Les Palabres* was that Africans were like children who were not mature enough for regular feature films. In a paper presented at the Rencontres Internationales de Bruxelles: Le cinéma et l'Afrique noire (1958), entitled, "Convient-il de faire du 'Film pour africain,' " Father Van den Heuvel reaffirmed in writing what he implicitly put forth in his films:

> For this audience that we call primitive, we must make films for Africans. The scenario will be simple and will deal with few characters. The characters will be easily distinguishable from one another, and they will each have well-defined habits. The spectator must be able, without great effort, to identify with the heroes whom he will imitate. There is an advantage, thus, of having Congolese actors performing in a Congolese setting.
>
> The technique for such films will generally be analogous to the one used when filming for children. The content will, however, be different. The projection time, as for children's films, must not be long. Fifteen minutes to half-hour screening may be followed by an intermission which will be used to explain what has been shown and what will follow. The scenes will follow each other in a chronological manner; no flashbacks or flashforwards. Dream sequences will be banished. The ideal is a film in which the action takes place in one day. (Haffner, p. 91)

Father Van den Heuvel's metaphor of Africans as children necessarily implied the existence of a permanent father who would provide protection and guidance for them and exercise control over them. At that time during the presentation of his paper, Father Van den Heuvel was called a paternalist by some of his own countrymen. People pointed out to him that the time had come to stop doing things for Africans and to teach them how to do things themselves. As recently as 1978, Father Van den Heuvel defended his views, maintaining that a paternalistic attitude was the most sensible, "considering the evolution of the population at that time" (Haffner, p. 91). Interestingly enough, in 1978

Senegal's leading filmmaker, Ousmane Sembène, saw the octogenarian Father Van den Heuvel in Kinshasa (Zaire) while the old man was repairing a film projector for a church. Haffner reported that Sembène wondered why there was not a Zairian assisting him and learning from him.

One way to answer Sembène's question, and at the same time to shed light on the technocratic paternalism of the missionaries, is that the missionaries saw in the production, distribution, and exhibition of films a way to recruit converts for their religion and to make more money. Training Africans to become filmmakers and producers could have caused the missionaries to lose their audience and/or compete for it. In this light one understands why Father Van den Heuvel and the C.C.A.C.C. were willing to go beyond distributing special films for Africans and to produce "African films." But at the same time, they were never anxious to train Africans to take over film production in Zaire. Their blindness (or must one say their deliberate technocratic paternalism and racism?) ought to be pointed out at the same time that any critic makes a reference to them as establishing "African cinema."

It is no surprise, therefore, that Zaire at independence did not take up film as an integral part of its cultural and political development. In 1957, at the peak of the film activities, the Belgian officials and missionaries reached nine million spectators with fifteen thousand screenings in Zaire (Rouch, p. 394). In 1960 the new Zairian government had very little experience with film exhibition that could enable it to keep at least a portion of this important film industry in operation. The Zairians had films especially manufactured for them. Those Zairians whose involvement was necessary for the production (actors, assistants, and porters) had been treated as assembly line workers and kept from understanding film as an asset for national culture growth. At independence, these so-called assistants had not learned to appreciate cinema as a powerful tool that they could use for an indefinite number of purposes. They turned, therefore, to other activities with more tangible opportunities.

A look at the present situation of film production in Zaire still shows colonial influence. In 1960 when the Belgian Film and Photo Bureau ceased production, a Zairian ministry, the Department of National Orientation, was put in charge of the materials and the structure left behind. This ministry called upon French and Belgians from the private sector to come and manage film production, i.e., newsreels and documentaries. In 1967, film production was relegated to national television; the Voice of Zaire, which had just begun, was augmented in 1973 with a separate department for making educational films, the National Board for Educational and Cultural Productions (RENAPEC).

Despite these changes, the Zairian government made no decision to create a national cinema. Except for the production of a few biographies, newsreels, and political propaganda, Zairian television has so far contented itself with airing foreign productions such as *Dallas*. RENAPEC has not yet made a full use of the important infrastructure left behind by the Belgians. A group of Zairian technicians organized under the name Image of Dawn made a collective film in 1975 called *Le Hasard n'existe pas* (There's No Such Thing as Chance). This is the first authentic Zairian feature film. Unfortunately, Image of Dawn did not receive the support needed from national television to continue collective film production.

On the private side, another religious group, Saint-Paul Audiovisual Editions (E.P.A.), has replaced the missionary production of the C.C.A.C.C. Since 1975, when it began production, the E.P.A. has made religious propaganda, which it exhibits throughout Zaire in the existing channels of distribution left behind by the C.C.A.C.C. The films are shot with Super 8mm cameras and processed in the studios of the Zairian national television. Zairian film directors direct most of the films. So far, two E.P.A. films, *Le bon samaritain* (The Good Samaritan, 1976) and *Soeur Annuarite, une vie pour Dieu* (Sister Annuarite, a Life for God, 1978), have become national successes. *Soeur Annuarite* was coproduced with Zairian television and was directed by a Zairian, Madenda Kiese.

However, the E.P.A. has recently come under attack from the Zairian Organization of Cinéastes (OZACI) because its contracts with Zairian film directors do not include distribution benefits. With *Soeur Annuarite,* for example, Madenda received a small salary to direct the film, coproduced with national television. The equipment and the TV technicians were used for free and the film is now a big success, but Madenda is not sharing in the profits (Mweze interview). The OZACI is also fighting to reorganize the structures of film production in Zaire so as to create an "authentic national cinema."[3] For this purpose its members have asked the Mobutu government to authorize the creation of a National Film Center, which will levy taxes on the distribution of foreign films in Zaire and use that money to promote national cinema. The OZACI has also appealed to Zairian businessmen to invest in national film production.

If the Mobutu regime cooperates with OZACI, one can look forward to the emergence of a national cinema in Zaire, which has not yet produced a single fictional film since the departure of the Belgians. The OZACI already counts among its members many young directors trained in Belgium, in France, and in the cinémathèque of the French embassy in Kinshasa. Such documentary filmmakers as Kwami Mambuzinga, who made *Moseka* (1972), and Ngangura Mweze, who made *Kin Kiesse* (1982), are already known throughout Africa and in Western festivals and European university circles.

One would like to see the Zairian filmmakers put to full use the structures of production, distribution, and exhibition left by the colonial African film producers. However, the Zairians must be sure to rid these colonial tactics of their racist elements. It is good to produce African cartoons, for instance, but for children. The Zairian filmmakers can also learn from the cost-efficient productions of the Catholic E.P.A., which shoots with Super 8.

Meanwhile, until Zaire gets its Centre National du Cinema and Zairian businessmen invest in film, these filmmakers will do the same as their counterparts in other Francophone African countries: depend on France for the production of most of their films. Their prospective coproducers are the French Actualités Nationales (newsreels), which serves French television, the French Foreign Ministry, which is presently the biggest producer of African cinema, and UNESCO.

III.

France's Contribution to the Development of Film Production in Africa

Films directed by Africans in the former French colonies are superior, both in quantity and in quality, to those by directors in other sub-Saharan African countries formerly colonized by the British, the Belgians, and the Portuguese. Eighty percent of black African films are made by Francophone Africans.[1] In 1974, six feature films were made by directors in Senegal alone.[2] In 1982, Francophone Africans made as many as thirty short and feature films, against thirteen made by their counterparts in Anglophone and Lusophone Africa and in Zaire.[3] While Haile Gerima (Ethiopia) and Ola Balogun (Nigeria) are the only internationally known directors outside of Anglophone Africa, such Francophone filmmakers as Ousmane Sembène (Senegal), Oumarou Ganda (Niger), Dikongue Pipa (Cameroon), Safi Faye (Senegal), Med Hondo (Mauritania), and Souleymane Cissé (Mali) are famous for winning awards at film festivals in Ouagadougou (Upper Volta), Carthage (Tunisia), Cannes, Paris, Rome, and Moscow.

For a film historian, it is a complex task to explain the emergence of Francophone African filmmaking. One would have to determine the role played by the French government and individuals in furthering film production in their former colonies in a manner that has not interested other ex-colonial powers such as England and Belgium. One would also have to clarify the extent to which the French involvement is political, and merely reproducing in the domain of cinema, too, the structures of neocolonialism as it has been the case in other areas of the transfer of technology between North and South.

Unlike the British and the Belgians, who had colonial African film units, the French had no policy of producing films that were especially intended for their subjects in Africa. The only decision made by France concerning film in the colonies was the implementation of a law in 1934 called "Le Décret Laval." Paulin S. Vieyra has argued that the development of movie soundtracks in 1928 was what prompted the French government to take measures to control film activities in the colonies, lest the involvement of Africa in these activities become subversive or anticolonialist. Vieyra says that during the silent film era, France was indifferent to the state of cinema in the colonies, but at the end of this era, Pierre Laval, the French minister of the colonies, changed his attitude toward the uncontrollable development of film in Africa.[4]

The purpose of the Laval decree was to control the content of films that were shot in Africa and to minimize the creative roles played by Africans in the making of films. It gave Laval's ministry the right to examine the scripts and the people involved in the production before giving its authorization for filming. It was clearly stated in the law that "any person who desires to make cinematographic images or sound recordings must address a written request to the Lieutenant Governor of the colony where the applicant intends to operate. To this request, which must include all the information about the civil right and the professional references of the applicant, he will add the script of the film or, if he is making slides, the text of the musical accompaniment" (Vieyra, pp. 107–10).

Although historians of African film agree that Laval's decree was rarely applied against filmmakers, they also believe that it had the effect of postponing the birth of Francophone African film. It is in this vein that Rouch argued that "while the rule was practically never applied against French filmmakers, it served as a pretext to deny young Africans, judged to be too turbulent by the colonial administration, the right to film their own countries."[5]

Furthermore, a look at the few times the Laval decree came into action against filmmakers will show France's determination in colonial times to keep cinema from playing a revolutionary and/or evolutionary role in Africa. The first film censored was *Afrique 50* (1950), made by a Frenchman, Robert Vautier. *Afrique 50*, clandestinely filmed in Ivory Coast, is about the French repression of an African liberation movement, Rassemblement Démocratique Africain (R.D.A.). The second time the Laval decree was summoned against a film was in 1955, when Chris Marker and Alain Resnais, two famous French filmmakers of the New Wave, got together to make *Les statues meurent aussi,* which was produced by the famous African publication house, Présence Africaine. Marker and Resnais's film was about African statues that were taken out of context and put in European museums. The film depicts the way the statues lost their meaning and were mummified as soon as they were cut off from their active environment and put in European museums as *objets d'art. Les statues meurent aussi* also pointed out the European aesthetic influence on the newly carved African statues. The violent montage technique with which the film was made to denounce the brutality of colonialism was praised by the critics (Rouch, p. 396).[6] The French government confiscated and held *Les statues* for ten years before releasing it.

During the same time that *Les statues* was censored, permission to film Africa was denied Paulin S. Vieyra, the first African graduate of l'Institut des Hautes Etudes Cinématographiques (IDEHC). In the face of this impossibility to film their own countries, Vieyra and his friends, Le Groupe Africain du Cinéma, resigned themselves to making *Afrique sur scène* (1955), a film about Africans in Paris. The film is cited in history as the first directed by a black African.

The restrictions imposed by the Laval decree were at the root of the postponed birth of Francophone African film production. In the colonial epoch, the French government was as determined to ban Africa from the films of African directors as it was to stop anticolonialists, like Marker and Vautier, from showing their African films. Furthermore, the Laval decree is an illustration of the French colonial system, which had no economic, political, or cultural policy encompassing the majority of its subjects and which was limited to assimilating few Africans, such as Vieyra and Le Groupe Africain du Cinéma, at the top. Thus, in regard to the development of film in the colonies, where one may say that the British and the Belgian colonial film units failed because of racism and paternalism vis-à-vis the Africans, one can also say that the French were opposed to an African cinema.

The Roles of Jean Rouch and Jean-René Débrix

It would be incorrect, however, to give the impression that both Francophone Africans and private Frenchmen waited for the Laval decree to be lifted before raising the issue of African cinema. The Laval decree was denounced throughout the fifties by Vieyra and Le Groupe Africain du Cinéma, who could not make films in Africa. For example, in 1955 they asked their professor, Marcel Griaule, to act on their behalf in order to convince the minister of France Overseas Territories to lift the ban (Rouch, p. 21). Also, in the fifties, Jean Rouch, who is to African cinema what Jean-Paul Sartre was to *Négritude*, was busy in Niger and Ivory Coast, demystifying the techniques of filmmaking, using a portable 16mm camera. Rouch employed his African actors as his assistants, and in the process he discovered and helped two pioneers of African cinema, Oumarou Ganda and Moustapha Alassane. It is also true that, in the fifties, the Laval decree did not constitute an obstacle to Africans who majored in film at French universities and those who learned the techniques of filmmaking at French cinémathèques and the cultural centers of the colonial administration. Finally, one must not forget the criticism of the famous French film historian Georges Sadoul, who denounced France's failure to provide Africans with the opportunities of filmmaking. Sadoul wrote:

> In 1960, sixty-five years after the invention of motion pictures, there hasn't been, to my knowledge, a single feature film that is truly African; I mean a film that stars Africans, is cinematographed, written, directed, edited, etc., by blacks, and speaking, of course, an African language. Thus, two hundred million men have been denied the use of this most advanced of modern arts. Before the end of the sixties, I am convinced that things will change and that this scandalous situation will become nothing but a bad memory.[7]

The collaborative effort of African film students and Frenchmen like Rouch and Sadoul is a factor that influenced France in the early sixties to change its policies toward African involvement in film. The other determining factor is France's intention of forming binding economic, political, and cultural relations with its former colonies. It is therefore interesting that France began its production of African film after most African countries assumed their independence from it. The financial and technical support from the French Ministry of Coopération was serious enough to start in 1963 with the release of Ousmane Sembène's *Borom Sarret,* the emergence of Francophone African film, and to catapult the Coopération on top as the biggest producer of African cinema.

In the postindependence era, France's first cinematic action in Africa began in 1961 with the creation in Paris of the Consortium Audiovisuel International (C.A.I.). The purpose of the C.A.I. was to help the newly independent African countries in the field of communications.

Now that France was willing to support African film production, it was pointed out that film constituted an invaluable tool of development and education for people who, for the most part, were illiterate. Since these people had neither the equipment, the necessary funds, nor the technical expertise, France decided to intervene "by providing, at a shared cost of the newsreels and education programs, the African and Malagachy states with the technological assistance needed."[8] Following, therefore, the example of the British Overseas Film and Television Centre, it was estimated to be too costly to build autonomous production complexes in each African country. Thus a decision was made to install partial production units in Francophone African capitals and the C.A.I. in Paris, where the films were sent for the postproduction phase (Hennebelle, p. 80). By operating in this manner, the C.A.I. and its African production units made 416 newsreels and documentaries each year between 1961 and 1975 (Hennebelle, p. 81).

In 1963, the French Coopération made a second and more important move in African film production. Jean-René Débrix, former adjunct general director of the IDHEC, was named as director of the newly created Bureau du Cinéma at the Coopération. Before Débrix came to the Coopération, the emphasis of France's aid to its former colonies was in the domain of literature, theater, music, and dance. Franco-African cultural relations were highlighted by a branch of the Coopération, the Association pour le développement des échanges artistiques et culturels (ADEAC), which assumed the diffusion of French culture (literature, filmed theater) in Africa and the promotion of African art and artists in France.

When Débrix took over his new post, his first priority was to change the emphasis of the ADEAC from literature, music, and dance to film. He succeeded in convincing people at the Coopération that the best way to help Africans to regain their cultural identity was through "the field of cinema, a predestined means of expression, an ideographic language which is favored by these image-starved Africans" (Hennebelle, p. 79).

Whereas the C.A.I. was geared toward helping African governments produce newsreels and documentaries, the aim of the Bureau du Cinéma was to provide independent African filmmakers with the opportunity to create. Generous funds were suddenly made available to aspiring directors; a laboratory and an editing room in 16mm production were installed at the Coopération to complement the already existing 35mm postproduction facilities at the C.A.I. The editing room of the Coopération, 20 rue de la Boétie, because a Centre d'accueil for

African filmmakers. There they found professional editors such as Bernard Lefevere, Daniele Tessier, Paul Sequin, and Andrée Daventure, who were patient and friendly (Hennebelle, p. 80).

Débrix, who described himself as a student of Abel Gance and André Malraux, wanted to be at the origin of a new cinema created by Africans, sixty-five years after the invention of motion pictures. In his mind, Western filmmakers had reached an impasse because they allow rhetorical and dialectical styles to take over their films, subjecting, in this manner, the art of cinema to Cartesianism and to the precepts of literature and theater. Under the spell of a notion that an African contribution could save cinema by restoring to it the "sorcery," the "magic," and the "poetry" which Débrix thought film had lost in the West, he seized the opportunity offered him by his new job to become the architect of this new cinema. It was in this light that the doors of the Coopération were opened to all the prospective Francophone Africans. To put it in Débrix's words, "Any African director who thinks, as Louis Malle puts it, that he 'has a film in his stomach,' can find the means to make that film in freedom at the Bureau du Cinéma" (Débrix, p. 16).

The growth of African film was assisted by the Bureau du cinéma at the Coopération in two ways. The Coopération could either act as the producer of a film and provide the African director with the financial and technical means, as well as the technicians, or the Coopération could wait until an independent director made the film, then pay for the cost of production in return for some of the distribution rights of the film. In the first case, in which the Coopération assumed the role of producer from the beginning, the filmmaker was required to submit a script with a detailed explanation of the sequences, which were carefully examined by a committee. According to Débrix, the committee's role was limited to determining whether the script was cinematographically feasible or not. Thus, on the level of the content, the directors were free to choose any subject they wanted. The only script that Débrix rejected on the basis of the subject matter was *La noire de* . . . (1966) by Ousmane Sembène (Hennebelle, p. 80). In *La noire de* . . . Sembène equated the way the French Assistance Technique used cheap African labor to a new form of slavery. It is interesting that the Coopération bought the rights of *La noire de* . . . after Sembène managed to produce it independently. Some of the first films for which the Coopération acted as a producer from the beginning were *Point de vue I* (1965) by Urbain Dia-Moukori (Cameroon), *Concerto pour un exile* (1967) by Désiré Ecaré (Ivory Coast), *Cabascado* (1968) by Oumarou Ganda (Niger), and *Diankhabi* (1969) by Mahama Traoré (Senegal).

In the second case, in which the Coopération bought the rights of a film that was finished or almost finished, the filmmaker acted as his own producer and tried to find funds from varied sources. This route was a painful one since African filmmakers had limited resources and could not get help from their own countries where filmmaking was considered an extravagance, a subversive activity, and not a priority. It often took years to finish one film. Sembène rightly referred to this system of production as the "mégotage" (Vieyra, pp. 109–10). Thus, when the Coopération offered its help, either to finish the film or to pay some of the production costs in return for the rights of distribution, the filmmaker always took it as a relief. The first directors to have received this form of aid from the Coopération were Sembène—*Borom Sarret* (1963), *Niaye* (1964), *La noire de . . .* (1966); Moustapha Alassane (Niger)—*Aoure* (1962), *La bague du Roi Koda* (1964), *Le retour de l'aventurier* (1966); and Timité Bassori (Ivory Coast)—*Sur la dune de la solitude* (1964) and *La femme au couteau* (1968).

The aid provided by the Coopération gave many Francophone Africans the opportunity to realize their dreams as filmmakers. Within the first five years of the creation of the Bureau du Cinéma, it contributed to the production of thirty-nine films (mostly shorts) by African directors (Débrix, pp. 16–18). By 1975, 185 shorts and features were made in Francophone Africa, four fifths of which were produced with the financial and technical help of the Coopération (Hennebelle, p. 82). In a word, the best African filmmakers made their debut with Débrix at the Bureau du Cinéma, even though, today, directors such as Sembène have stopped asking for the Coopération's help and have accused its members of paternalism and imperialism. Sembène's position and that of other critics of the Coopération will be discussed later.

When Débrix died of a heart attack in 1978, the French production of African film, of which he was the architect, continued without a significant structural and conceptual change. In fact, France's decision in 1979 to put an end to African film production and to close down the editing laboratories at the Bureau du Cinéma was due less to Débrix's absence and more to the pressure on the Giscard government by some African political leaders who were worried about the influence of African films on their populations. Giving in to this pressure, the Giscard government gave orders to the administrators at the Coopération to freeze the aid to African film. Jacques Gerard, the man who took Débrix's place, was given the following explanation:

We're not here to decide what must be done and what mustn't. And we're not here to make decisions which always end up having political implications. In other words, we're not here to produce a film which, tomorrow, may bring us trouble.[9]

One of the films affected by the freezing of funds was *Finye* (1982), Cissé's prize-winning film. The Coopération had originally agreed to handle the postproduction cost of *Finye* in return for the rights to distribute it on a noncommercial basis. If all had gone as planned, *Finye* would have been completed in 1980. But the freezing of funds and work tools left Cissé unable to make progress on his film.

Finye is, in fact, a historical film that illustrates the many French policy changes toward African film production. It is a political film depicting the weakness of military regimes, student strikes, and African tradition versus modernity. The Giscard government could not accommodate such political films and materials and at the same time maintain friendly relations with African leaders who had been made unhappy by the films. Since the Coopération could not induce radical filmmakers such as Sembène and Cissé to make "escapist" films, it was ordered to suspend its aid to the whole Francophone film production.

Ironically enough, when the Mitterrand government came to power in 1980 and resumed aid to African film, *Finye* was the biggest recipient of this aid. The so-called "progressive" African directors became fashionable with the new socialist government in France. Furthermore, the new administrators at the Coopération began to criticize the old structures of African film production and to put forward new ideas for improving Franco-African cultural and economic relations.

African Cinema in the Mitterrand Era: The Coopération on Trial

According to the Mitterrand administration, their predecessors had not sufficiently addressed the issue of African film production. The argument was that the Giscardists did not attempt to develop an African film industry by building production and distribution facilities in Africa. They merely helped produce independent filmmakers whose films could not even be seen in their countries of origin. No effort was made to integrate African film production in the overall cultural, political, and economic development of the continent. Instead, few Africans were chosen and assimilated as filmmakers in the dominant French hegemony. Jean-Pierre Mounier, Mitterrand's technical adviser at the Coopération, described the old regime's contribution to African film as "le mal développement," characterized by a neocolonial mentality "to have a Francophone community, which is made of ex-colonized people, around France" (Gerard, pp. 18–21).

A new French policy of African film production was therefore necessary. This new policy, Mounier argued, must be globalist in order to include the economic aspects of development as well as the cultural. It was decided that the best way to help an African film industry was to pass France's financial and technical aid through an inter-African organization such as Organisation Commune Africaine et Mauritienne (OCAM), which regrouped all the Francophone countries in Africa (Gerard, p. 37). An inter-African film industry was deemed more realistic than a national one because it gave filmmakers a larger spectrum of cultural exposure and a better chance of recouping the production costs of the films. It was in this vein that the Coopération deemphasized its aid to independent directors and made more funds and equipment available to OCAM-sponsored film schools such as Institut Africain d'Education Cinématographique (INAFEC) in Ouagadougou. The Coopération also decided to support such branches of OCAM as Consortium Inter-Africain de Distribution Cinématographique (CIDC) and Consortium Inter-Africain de Production du Film (CIPROFILM). The role of OCAM will be discussed later.

In their reformist approach to African film, the administrators at the Coopération had also begun promoting films. The idea was to go beyond the old regime's policy of confining African films to academic circles, cinémathèques, and festivals, to exhibiting them in commercial French movie theaters and airing them on French television. This new decision could benefit both the filmmakers and the French people. It gave wider exposure to African directors, and it provided the French people with the opportunity to view Africa from an original perspective. It is interesting to notice that Cissé's film *Finye* was the first beneficiary of this promotion policy. Cissé was given ten million francs (about twenty thousand U.S. dollars) to advertise his film.[10] As a result, *Finye* was selected to compete in Cannes (1982), and it ran in French theaters for six months. Cissé's other film, *Baara* (1978), was aired on French television in a new program called *Cinéma sans visa*.[11]

After this historical overview, it is important to pause for a moment to evaluate the impact of France's aid on the development of African film. The point here is not to dispute the fact that the Coopération is the number one producer of African film. Clearly, for film historians, it is obvious, as Boughedir has said, that "Francophone African film was aided by France."[12] The purpose of this evaluation is to shed light on the political and economic contexts of such an aid.

Since the beginning of its involvement with African film, the Coopération had come under attack by film historians, filmmakers, and new
government officials. As it has been suggested above, the new socialist
administrators at the Coopération are the first to be critical of the
policies of their predecessors. They regret, for example, the aid that the
Coopération under Giscard gave directly to independent filmmakers.
Besides the fact that such aid could have provoked a political crisis
between France and some African countries, they argued that it did not
contribute to the formation of an African film industry. A sound French
policy should have been based on helping African governments and
inter-African organizations, such as OCAM, to create their own film
industry. Independent directors would then have to be recommended
by their government or the OCAM before France could help them. It is
in this light that some argue that the Coopération, from 1963 to 1979,
was less respectful to the independent status of the former colonies. By
extending its help directly to filmmakers to make films that might turn
out to be critical of the African governments, the Coopération was, in
the words of Jacques Gerard, "taking the risk of annoying the governments from which the filmmaker came" (Boughedir, p. 70).

The direct aid, which independent filmmakers have been enjoying at
the Coopération, has also been criticized by Frenchmen. Some argue
that the Francophone African focus is too narrow and unfair to other
deserving artists around the world. Thus, as Gerard Desplanques said,
"The time has come for the Coopération to think in terms of Third
World film, not just film in the ex-colonies."[13] Others believe that the
Coopération has aided African film too long. The pioneering days of
Rouch and Débrix are over. The Coopération cannot help every African
who comes with a script. After all, as Haffner put it, in France, too,
"there are directors who commit suicide because they cannot do their
work."[14]

The Coopération's aid has also been perceived as a French neo-
colonialist tool by some historians of African film. According to Bachy,
for example, the French production of African film is part of the
structure of an unchanged economic, political, and cultural dependency of the African states on France. Bachy argues that the French
have lured their ex-subjects with dreamlike opportunities which they
are led to believe are only available in Paris. Because these opportunities, such as filmmaking or the ownership of a refrigerator, for
example, have no economic basis in Africa, France is depended upon
for their maintenance. Bachy and other film critics have further explained that France's other method of maintaining its hegemony over
Francophone Africa is by ruthlessly punishing the African countries

who decide to break completely with France. Guinea-Konakry is one such warning. Since its independence in 1958, Guinea had tried to acquire an autonomous film industry, in the same way that it tried in other modern industrial fields. The country had equipped itself with laboratories in 35mm production. Ironically enough, unlike its neighbors, Mali, Senegal, and Ivory Coast, who go to France for help and as a result can boast of several features, Guinea has yet to produce anything beyond newsreels and documentaries. It is in this light that Bachy said that France had economically and culturally induced Guinea to "revert to the dark ages."[15]

There is another argument that France's aid to African films has made it easier for French distributors to maintain their monopoly on the African market. Critics such as Tahar Cheriaa and Férid Boughedir have denounced the monopoly of African theaters by European, Indian, and American films.[16] Since I am devoting chapter 7 to distribution, I am only discussing here the way that French African film production is perceived in the context of French film distribution in the Francophone areas.

Boughedir argues that whereas American films dominated in other areas of Africa, France has succeeded so far in maintaining the edge for the number of films seen in Francophone Africa. Boughedir saw France's aid to African filmmakers as an indirect way to protect the monopoly of French distributors. By aiding African directors, France kept them from reacting radically against the takeover of their market by foreigners. One must understand that the Coopération's aid is a guarantee that keeps the directors from worrying about a market where they can recoup the cost of their films. It is in this light that one sees the gist of Boughedir's paradoxical statement that "Francophone African film exists because of France and also does not exist because of France" (Boughedir, p. 31).

Francophone filmmakers themselves have complained about the conditions and the ways France has given its aid to African film. They have accused Débrix of imposing his own aesthetic views of Africa as a way of judging films. His open admiration for *Pousse Pousse* (1975) by Daniel Kamwa (Cameroon), for example, is judged by many as paternalistic and ethnocentric. *Pousse Pousse* is a comedy about the settlement of dowry in modern Cameroonian society. It is considered by many African directors as naive and iconoclastic toward African traditions and less critical toward the French cultural imperialism in Cameroon. The film is also edited loosely, which makes it unartistically repetitious. Débrix's preference for such a film over the films of Sembène, Pipa, and Mahama Traoré leads African directors to say that he despises African film and that he is opposed to the ideological and artistic maturity of its filmmakers.

Sembène goes beyond this criticism of Débrix as paternalist and ethnocentrist to attack the condition of existence of the entire French aid to African film. Sembène speaks from experience following the production of his film *Le Mandat* (1968) by the famous French Centre National du Cinéma (CNC). It must be pointed out that before Sembène, the CNC's aid was restricted to French nationals such as Godard and Truffaut of the New Wave. But André Malraux, the French minister of culture in 1968, granted special permission to Sembène to compete for the CNC's aid. Having won the aid, Sembène was required to take a French producer, Robert Nesle, who controlled the budget.

Sembène's experience with his producer was such that he decided, following the completion of *Le Mandat,* not to accept any aid from France in the future and to produce his films in Africa with African money. The first conflict Sembène had with Nesle concerned the choice of color for the film. Sembène wanted to shoot it in black and white because he was worried about the sensational effect a color film could bring to his story. He was also unsure about the way people would look in a color film under African skies. One time the production was also stopped because Sembène had refused to include sexual and erotic scenes in the film. He was forced to go to court to settle this matter.[17] It is in this sense that one understands Sembène when he said,

> Co-production with the West is often tainted with paternalism, and it is an economic dependency which, as such, gives the West the right to view Africa in a way that I cannot bear. Sometimes, one is also coerced into consenting to commercial concessions. In a word, Europeans often have a conception of Africa that is not ours.[18]

Another reason behind Sembène's decision to stop coproducing with the French is his dissatisfaction with the Coopération in the way it distributes African films. The Coopération being a nonprofit distributor, it attracts people of various ideological inclinations who want to use African films to reinforce their beliefs. Thus the same film can be used to illustrate integration and partition, tradition and feminism, revolt and feudalism. Sembène felt that this unrestricted distribution of his earlier films, which the Coopération owns, besides being exploitative, was counterproductive to and manipulative of his views. Since 1970, Sembène has managed to produce his films in Africa (Boughedir, pp. 31–32).

Even among African directors who still accept the technical and financial aid from the Coopération, there are those, like Cissé, who are not satisfied with the way it has molded African films into "sociological or anthropological documents." After the independence of most African countries, when anthropologists such as Rouch could no longer freely make films in Africa, the Coopération used films by Africans to fill the void. Thus, for the general public, African films, like the films of Rouch, are not usually considered entertaining; they are reserved for sociology classrooms, which Cissé refers to as "cultural ghettos." Cissé believes that this situation of African film is tied to the Coopération's contract, which gives it the right to distribute the films indiscriminately on a noncommercial basis for five years. Clearly this contract discourages businessmen from developing interest in the distribution of African film. Cissé argues that the situation can be repaired if the Coopération reduces its rights by distributing the films only in French embassies and cultural centers in Africa, while pushing for commercial distribution in Europe.[19]

One sees clearly with the above evaluation that the overriding statement against French aid is its neocolonialist aspect. There are two ways of identifying neocolonialism in French African film production. One way is through tracing the extent to which the French have tried to assimilate African filmmakers and films, thus making it difficult for them to stand on their own. The other is the Coopération's monopoly of the tools of work by centering them in Paris.

Assimilation is as important in French African film activities as it is in other Franco-African relations. It is based on the premise of selecting a few Africans at the top and giving them the same privileges as French men and women. Directing films is one such privilege. In this light one sees that even though the Laval decree was opposed to Africans filming in Africa, it was not opposed to Africans becoming directors of French mainstream films. For example, Vieyra and Le Groupe Africain du Cinéma were allowed to film Paris in *Afrique sur Seine* while they were denied the permission to make a film in Africa.

The structures of an assimilationist policy are also seen in the way the Coopération produces and distributes African films. By monopolizing the domain of African film production (financing, technical equipment, technicians), the Coopération conditions the directors to conform their scripts to acceptable French cinematographic standards. It is in this sense that controversial and anticolonialist scripts such as *La noire de* . . . are rejected. Those directors who had the Coopération as the producer of their films had French readers in mind while they wrote their scripts.

Just as it conditions, through production, the content of scripts, the Coopération can also determine, through distribution, the future of films. Since it cannot stop the production of anti-assimilationist and anticolonialist film such as *La noire de* . . . and *Emitai* (1972) by Sembène, *Soleil O* (1969) and *Les bicots nègres vos voisins* (1975) by Med Hondo, and *Nationalité: Immigré* (1974) by Sidney Sokhona, the Coopération controls their impact by buying the rights and distributing them. This is a clever way to absorb counterhegemonic products and even to assimilate them to the apparent concern of the Coopération, which is to promote African film. *La noire de* . . . is again a good example of this maneuver: rejected by the production sector, it was recuperated through the distribution sector.

Finally, the Coopération's concentration on the postproduction facilities in Paris and its failure to train Africans as editors, camera operators, sound engineers, and electricians convinced many critics of the Coopération's intention to keep African film dependent on France. Thus, while the Coopération made it possible for Sembène and Cissé to mature as film directors and to replace directors of the colonial era, such as Rouch, it made no effort to decolonize the tools of production in order for Sembène and Cissé to work autonomously in Africa.

The Mitterrand government's recent decision to help the OCAM build a film industry in Africa is certainly a hopeful sign that is watched with great interest by the FEPACI. The effort to train Africans in film technology at institutes such as the INAFEC is also praiseworthy. Meanwhile, until these actions materialize into production, distribution, and exhibition structures in Africa, African directors will need the Coopération's aid.

IV.

The Artist as the Leader of the Revolution

The History of the Fédération Panafricaine des Cinéastes

The history of the Fédération Panafricaine des Cinéastes (FEPACI) is crucial to an understanding of the development of African film production in general. However, it is in Francophone Africa that the political leverage of filmmakers has met with more success. The efforts of FEPACI in Francophone Africa contributed to the creation of national film centers in the different countries, to the setting up of an inter-African film distribution center (CIDIC), to production (CIPROFILM), and to the creation of the Ouagadougou festival as a way of promoting African films. This chapter is a study of the FEPACI with an emphasis on the role of Francophone filmmakers in the development of film in their countries.

African filmmakers are directly affected by the lack of national and international industries that include the structures of production, distribution, and exhibition. In the absence of such money-generating facilities, and because film distribution and exhibition are monopolized by foreign capitalists whose primary concern is to make a profit, Francophone directors are not only forced to depend on the French Ministry of Coopération and similar offices for the production of their films, but they also face problems of programming the films in movie theaters in their own countries and distributing them elsewhere. Such African classics as *La noire de . . . , Mandabi, Le retour de l'aven-*

turier, Concerto pour un exil, and *Cabascado* were never shown in the movie theaters in the countries of the artists who made them. African directors are also producers of their own films, and, as if that were not enough, they are forced, as in the earlier days of the invention of motion pictures, to carry their films from place to place for exhibition.

Since the mid-fifties, Francophone filmmakers, organized in national and international associations, have been fighting to change this situation, which Tahar Cheriaa calls "les écrans colonisés," and to set up new plans for the development of film industries in Africa. The strategy consists of denouncing the block-booking system of the foreign capitalists who prevent African films from being seen in Africa. The filmmakers also point out the negative influence on people of American, European, and Indian films that are unchallenged in Africa. Their advice to African governments is to nationalize film distribution, help fund African films by raising taxes on the import of foreign films and ticket sales, and encourage private investment in the production of African films.

Early Efforts to Create an African Cinema

Although the FEPACI is the most significant organization to have influenced governments and international associations in the development of African film, it is important to look first at the efforts of individual filmmakers and/or small organizations of filmmakers who paved the way for the FEPACI. In my chapter on France's contribution to the development of Francophone film, I described how Le Groupe Africain du Cinéma attempted to conceive of an African cinema even before African independence. In 1958 Vieyra, the leader of this small organization of filmmakers from Senegal and Dahomey (Benin), put forth the plans for a future African film industry for the Francophone African countries that were dependent on France (only Guinea-Konakry was independent at the time). However, he argued that the countries of the Communauté Francophone should get together to set up an international film center that would have its headquarters in Dakar (Senegal). This center was to serve for the production of educational, instructional, and feature films and was to be funded in the beginning by either the governments of the individual countries or by the central government of the Francophone community, or by both.[1]

After the independence of most African countries in the early sixties, the filmmakers still could not have access to production facilities and to the movie theaters for the projection of their films in their own countries. They consequently increased the political pressure on their governments to intervene and restructure the organization of film activities in a manner that would encourage African productions. Blaise Senghor, ex-member of Le Groupe Africain du Cinéma and director of *Le grand magal à Touba* (1962), criticized the situation by stating that although there were filmmakers in Africa who were authors of some films, there was no such thing as African cinema because the sectors of production, distribution, and exhibition were controlled by foreigners. Senghor believed that African countries, too, must create government-sponsored organizations such as the Office National du Film Canadien, which produces and distributes several short films on culture, education, and research, or the French Centre National de la Cinématographie (CNC), which controls film distribution and exhibition in France and disposes of funds to help produce French films. Similar organizations were necessary for the creation of an authentic African cinema that could be comparable to the New Wave and the French films of *Art et Essai,* all sponsored by the CNC. Senghor writes,

> . . . it is necessary that serious measures be taken to enable the countries to begin a politics of film production, distribution and exhibition that is real and that benefits all. The first measure from which all the rest follows is the creation of an autonomous administrative office, which is like the Centre National de la Cinématographie, and which covers all the issues concerning films.[2]

Timité Bassori, a filmmaker from Ivory Coast, also wrote in the early sixties to criticize the state of film activities in Africa. Bassori argued that African film could not grow when its future depended upon such organisms as the African ministries of information, which produced only newsreels; the Compagnie Africain Cinématographique et Commerciale (COMACICO); and the Société d'Exploitation Cinématographique Africaine (SECMA), which distributed foreign films and saw in the production of African films an interference with their profit making. (The COMACICO and the SECMA will be discussed at length in chapter 7.) African directors were forced to work as government employees in the making of newsreels at the ministries of information because the COMACICO and the SECMA were not interested in producing and/or distributing their films. Bassori argued that the imagination and the creativity of filmmakers were stifled at the ministries of information, which were little more than a photo service. Clearly, it was important that governments in Africa change the structure of the film industry. Bassori believed that such a change was all the more crucial because an authentic African cinema could be used to diffuse national culture and enhance national pride and to represent African culture on other continents.[3]

From the mid-sixties on, other filmmakers such as Sembène and Med Hondo became vocal in denouncing the monopolistic practices of the COMACICO and the SECMA and in applying pressure on their governments to restructure film activities. Between 1965 and 1967, national and international associations of filmmakers argued the case of African film at the Colloque de Gène (1965), the Premier Festival Mondial des Arts Nègres de Dakar (1966), and the Table-Ronde de Paris (1967). The filmmakers at each of these conferences and festivals gave advice to their governments on how to restructure the film market. An elaborate plan for change was submitted, for example, at the Festival Mondial des Arts Nègres in Dakar. The filmmakers recommended the creation of an inter-African film office that would gather and disseminate information about African cinema (film catalogs, statistics on numbers of exhibitions, inventories of the tools of production, and lists of film technicians in Africa).

The new office would propose legislation for the creation of national cinema that would be economically and culturally oriented. It would accommodate different departments on educational films, commercial films, and film of art and essay. There would be an effort, as much as possible, toward a complete transfer to Africa of the facilities of production and postproduction. The film market would be restructured so that a system could be put in place to account for the box-office revenues in each country and on the African level. The office would also reorganize the block-booking system that was used to discriminate against African films. In this vein the current programming system, which allowed theater owners to show two feature films, one after the other, would be changed to one film per sitting. The theater owners would be required to improve the conditions of the theaters, and more African films would be on the agenda.

Other recommendations of the filmmakers at the Festival Mondial des Arts Nègres included the creation of funds to sustain African film production, the building of cinémathèques and archives for the preservation of films, and the organization of festivals to promote African cinema and allow artists to exchange their views. Schools and institutes were also needed in Africa, where filmmakers, technicians, actors, and critics could be trained. The filmmakers believed that the funds for these proposals could come from taxes off the import, production, and exhibition of foreign films. Some additional funds could come from the ticket sales.[4]

The filmmakers' intervention at these conferences and festivals was significant because it underscored the need to control film activities, which in the eyes of the filmmakers constituted an industry for the development of Africa. The filmmakers' plan to restructure and to base film activities in Africa as an economic and cultural factor in the development of the continent gained support from many heads of states and specifically from Niger's president, Hamani Diori, who was then acting-president of the major economic grouping of Francophone Africans, the Organisation Commune Africaine et Mauritienne (OCAM).[5] Furthermore, the filmmakers used the conferences and festivals as platforms for pressuring African governments to stop compromising with the exploitative measures of the COMACICO and the SECMA. They also posed an ethical problem for the French government, which, on the one hand, was producing individual African filmmakers and organizing festivals to promote their films and, on the other hand, was not making an effort to stop the French-owned COMACICO and the SECMA.

The FEPACI and African Film

Clearly, the ground was prepared for an organization such as the FEPACI, which was created in July 1969 in Algiers. The governments were sympathetic to the idea of national cinema, the OCAM had demonstrated its intention of creating an inter-African film industry, and the monopoly of the film market by the COMACICO and the SECMA was weakening as countries such as Upper Volta and Mali made moves to nationalize distribution and exhibition in 1969. Filmmakers needed an organization such as the FEPACI in order to coordinate their efforts and be more effective. Because they were for the most part leftists and idealists who were committed to the notion of Pan-Africanism, the new members of the FEPACI believed their prophetic mission was to unite and to use film as a tool for the liberation of the colonized countries and as a step toward the total unity of Africa. It was in this sense that in its early days the FEPACI sought to be affiliated with its sister association, the Organization of African Unity (OAU).

In 1969, at the Festival Panafricain de la Culture in Algiers, African filmmakers gathered to create an inter-African organization. In 1970, during the third meeting of the festival, Journées Cinématographiques de Carthage (Tunisia), the filmmakers inaugurated the organization and called it La Fédération Panafricaine des Cinéastes. Clearly, the filmmakers in sub-Saharan Africa were benefiting from the experience of their counterparts in Algeria and Tunisia, who had already nationalized their film industries. By 1970, both Algeria and Tunisia had well-defined policies of production, distribution, and exhibition. The Office National pour le Commerce et l'Industrie Cinématographiques (ONCIC) in Algeria, and the Secrétariat aux Affaires Culturelles et à l'Information (SACI) in Tunisia were established for the restructuring of the film industry in favor of national cinema. The national film industry in Algeria had already produced such war epics as *L'aube des damnés* (1964) by Ahmed Rachedi, *Vent des aurès* (1966) by Mohamed Lakdhar-Hamina, and *La voix* (1968) by Slim Riad. In Tunisia, Journées Cinématographiques de Carthage was the first and only film festival devoted to Arab and African cinemas.

The FEPACI was designed to be an association of national filmmaker organizations. Unlike Le Groupe Africain du Cinéma, it was not for individuals who had no base in the national associations of their countries. Filmmakers were first encouraged to form national organizations and to affiliate them with the FEPACI. In this manner, in order for a filmmaker in Senegal, for example, to become a member of FEPACI, he must first become a member of L'Association Sénégalaise des Cinéastes. This was generally the rule except for cases in which the filmmakers were from an occupied country such as South Africa or from a colonized one such as Mozambique in 1970. Because it had become the association of associations, the FEPACI hoped to be more legitimate in the eyes of governments and other organizations. From its inception, therefore, the FEPACI was recognized by the OCAM, the OAU, and UNESCO, and it increased its membership to thirty-nine countries between 1970 and 1975.[6]

At the inaugural meeting in Carthage, the FEPACI set as its purpose to be committed to the political, cultural, and economic liberation of Africa, to fight the Franco-American monopoly of film distribution and exhibition in Africa, and to encourage the creation of national cinemas.[7] The commitment to the liberation of Africa meant for the filmmakers the creation of aesthetics of disalienation and colonization. Filmmakers were told to use semidocumentary forms to denounce colonialism where it existed and to use didactic fictional forms to denounce the alienation of countries that were politically independent but culturally and economically dependent on the West.

The second purpose of the FEPACI was to fight against the Franco-American monopoly of the film industry in Africa. This was supposed to be achieved by pressuring the governments to nationalize the sectors of distribution and exhibition. At this stage of the development of film in Africa, the filmmakers did not trust private businessmen, whom they suspected of collaborating with the French companies of COMACICO and SECMA and with the M.P.E.A.A. in the United States. The FEPACI could only work with governments to achieve the goal of breaking foreign monopolies and giving African films the chance to be seen in African theaters. However, the filmmakers could not trust the governments enough to ask them to nationalize the sector of production as well. They needed the freedom to express themselves in manners that were not always flattering to the governments. For this reason, they wanted to keep control over the small production houses, such as Film Domirev with Sembène and Soleil O films with Med Hondo. For economic reasons, they wanted the governments to take control of the distribution and exhibition so that they might have the chance to recoup the cost of their films (Boughedir, p. 63).

The last goal of the FEPACI's inaugural meeting, which was to create national cinemas, was to be achieved by raising the level of political consciousness of the filmmakers so that they might increase their lobbying power with their governments and ensure the emergence and maintenance of African cinemas. The filmmakers were also to persuade the governments to create more meeting places like the JJC and the Festival Panafricain de Ouagadougou (FESPACO) in 1969, which could permit them to meet regularly to exchange ideas and promote their films.

Between 1970 and 1975 the FEPACI achieved significant progress in the application of its inaugural resolutions. In Francophone Africa, national film industries were emerging. In 1970, Upper Volta reacted to the unfair monopoly of the COMACICO and SECMA and decided to nationalize its film distribution and exhibition by creating the Société Nationale d'Importation-Distribution (SONAVOCI). The same year, Mali followed suit with the creation of l'Office Cinématographique National du Mali (OCINAM). In 1974, Senegal and Benin got their own distribution houses, the Société Nationale Sénégalaise de Distribution, and the Office Beninois de Cinéma (OBECI). Senegal went as far as to create a Société National du Cinéma (SNC), which is famous for producing four feature films in 1974 alone.[8] Finally, in 1975, Madagascar nationalized the movie theaters and created the Office du Cinéma Malgache.

The French government, too, was forced to readjust its attitude toward the issue of African film development. Afraid that all the countries would nationalize their film import and therefore develop an anti-French attitude (Boughedir, p. 155), the government in France intervened with the COMACICO and SECMA, which forced it to adapt its colonial structures of film distribution to the present realities of Africa. In 1972, the COMACICO and SECMA were bought out by the French Union Général du Cinéma (UGC), and the Société de Participation Cinématographique Africaine (SOPACIA) was created to oversee film distribution in Africa (Boughedir, p. 156).

In 1975, the FEPACI met in Algiers again to discuss the future of African cinema. This meeting, which is now referred to as the Second FEPACI Congress of Algiers, was concerned with the role of film in the politico-economic and cultural development of Africa. The filmmakers decided that, given the need to raise the consciousness of the African masses and liberate them from the economic and ideological domination of the imperialist countries, they could not indulge themselves in manufacturing films of purely commercial value. They said that African filmmakers should unite with the progressive filmmakers in other countries and join the anti-imperialist fight. It was time to emphasize the instructional value of films. The filmmakers should question the images of Africa and the narrative structures received from the dominant cinema. The question for the FEPACI was how to insert film as an original fact in the process of liberation, how to put it at the service of life, ahead of "art for art's sake"—in other words, how to film African realities in ways that could not be absorbed by the dominant cinema. It was in this light that several filmmakers condemned *Le bracelet de bronze* (1974) by Tidiane Aw and *Pousse Pousse* (1975) by Daniel Kamwa for being overwhelmingly spectacular and less committed to demystifying neocolonialism. On the other hand, the films of Sembène, Med Hondo, and Mahama Traoré were praised for deemphasizing the sensational and commercial aspects and emphasizing the instructional values.

This Second FEPACI Congress also addressed the issue of censorship. The filmmakers argued that the governments had to let them work in freedom in order for them to contribute to the development of the countries in creative and critical manners.

> The State must play a promotional role in the edification of a cinema free of the shackles of censorship and other means of coercion that can affect the creative freedom of the filmmaker and repress the democratic and responsible exercise of this profession. The filmmaker's freedom of expression is, in fact, one of the indispensable conditions of his contribution to the development of the critical senses of the masses.[9]

After the Second FEPACI Congress in 1975, the filmmakers did not meet again until 1982 in Niamey (Niger), where they proposed what is known as "Le Manifeste de Niamey." This meeting was necessary for several reasons. Although FEPACI membership was growing and there were more films by Africans, there were no African industries of production, distribution, and exhibition. This was ironical because in 1979 the Francophone countries grouped around the OCAM had created the Consortium Interafricain de Distribution Cinématographique (CIDC) and the Centre Interafricain de Production de Films (CIPROFILM) to replace the Union Africaine de Cinéma (UAC), which was criticized for representing French neocolonial interest (Boughedir, p. 157). A meeting of the FEPACI was therefore necessary to remind the CIDC of its role in the promotion and distribution of African films. Another reason for the meeting was to reassess the role played by governments in film activities. The FEPACI had noticed that most African governments had doubled or tripled their taxes on the revenues of film distribution and exhibition. Some countries even took as much as half the cost of the ticket. Since these tax revenues were spent on activities that were outside the film industry, the FEPACI felt they obstructed the growth of national cinemas. The FEPACI also realized that in those countries where film activities were completely nationalized, the creativity of filmmakers was stifled by governments who only sponsored propaganda films. Finally, in countries such as Senegal and Ivory Coast, the governments, in a reversal of rules, cut the funds set up to encourage the creation of national cinemas.

A third reason that the FEPACI had to convene as soon as possible was the dissension, at the 1981 Ouagadougou Festival, of young filmmakers who called themselves Le Collectif l'Oeil Vert. The young filmmakers charged that the FEPACI did little to help the filmmakers other than to involve them in administrative red tape and visits from the officials of FEPACI in foreign countries.[10] It was generally agreed that the FEPACI had lost its dynamism after 1975. The young filmmakers, by creating Le Collectif l'Oeil Vert, had hoped to bring back this dynamism. Headed by Senegalese director Cheikh N'Gaido Bâ, Le Collectif l'Oeil Vert wanted to take "an immediate and empirical action" toward the solution of African film production. The filmmakers therefore decided to begin by locating one another's equipment and compiling a national inventory. They would also become less dependent on France and other European countries from whom they had been renting equipment. They called their strategy a cooperation "South-South," as opposed to the "North-South" cooperation that existed between the developed and developing countries (Boughedir, p. 65).

Even before the Niamey Congress in 1982, which reunited the FEPACI, the veteran of African cinema, Sembène, had said that the solution to the problems was not in the creation of a new organization, but in convening a meeting and discussing the issues.

Thus, whereas the 1975 Congress of Algiers emphasized the need for the filmmakers to put the instructional values of films ahead of their commercial values, the Niamey Congress was to emphasize the economics and the survival of the FEPACI itself. The Niamey Manifesto introduced new economic clauses in the development of African film that, as Boughedir put it, "contradicted the radical views of the 1975 FEPACI Congress."[11] The expression "Opérateur économique" was used, for example, to designate businessmen and private capitalists. While in the Second FEPACI Congress of Algiers, businessmen were seen as allies of the imperialist countries that were not to be trusted, the Niamey Manifesto described the "Opérateur économique" as necessary to the growth of African film and asked governments to introduce protectionist laws that could guarantee the investment of the "Opérateur économique" and thus encourage him/her to produce more films.

Another important measure in the Manifesto was to link film production with the four other major elements of film activities, namely the distribution, the exhibition, the means of production (equipment, laboratories, and studios), and the training of the technicians. Without the technicians and the means of production, films made by African directors will continue to depend on European technicians and postproduction facilities. Without an African distribution and exhibition industry, the filmmakers will not only have to depend on European governments and organizations for financial support, but once they have finished films, they will not have a market in Africa to show them.

A third proposal in the Manifesto was to go beyond the idea of national cinema in order to promote inter-African and/or regional cinemas. This idea, too, was economically motivated. The FEPACI knew that it was not possible for a filmmaker to recoup the cost of his/ her film in his/her country alone where the total number of theater tickets sold was less than the number of tickets sold in the Latin Quarter alone in Paris for a comparable time. In Africa, the population of most countries is under 15 million, and because of social and economic reasons, many people do not go to the movies. Clearly an inter-African movie industry offered better chances for filmmakers to recoup the cost of their films. In Francophone Africa, the CIDC is one such industry grouping fourteen countries (see note 5). In the perspective of increasing the chances for filmmakers to recoup the cost of their films, the FEPACI also asked African national television services to work with the filmmakers in coproducing and airing films.

The fourth proposal of the Niamey Manifesto concerned the necessity of implementing national control systems that could account for the number of theater tickets sold at the box offices in Africa. In Francophone Africa, for example, if the offices of the CIDC knew exactly the box-office revenues in each country at any given time, it would be easier to divide these revenues to the satisfaction of the filmmakers, the businessmen, and the government for tax purposes. The filmmakers would not trust the theater owners; they would have no other precise way to measure audiences' responses to their films. The implementation of a structure to control the box-office revenues would therefore help the growth of African film.

Finally, the Niamey Manifesto proposed a tax reform plan that would enable the African film industries such as the CIDC to be self-supporting. In this clause, the FEPACI argued that part of the money spent by African moviegoers, both in foreign and domestic films, should be invested in producing new films, refitting old movie theaters and constructing new ones, setting up film archives and cinémathèques, organizing festivals and other promotional activities, training film technicians, and acquiring new equipment. The governments were asked to reduce taxes as an incentive for theater owners to use the additional revenues to improve the conditions of the theaters and to construct new ones. On the other hand, it was proposed that governments begin using the remaining tax revenues in businesses relating to the development of film. It was in this sense that the FEPACI stated in the Niamey Manifesto that "the funds that go into producing African films, whether they are national, regional or inter-African films, should come from the twin sectors of distribution and exhibition, not from the government's budgets. It is only in this manner of film begetting film that a cinema industry is possible" (Boughedir, p. 172).

A Critique of FEPACI

After this panoramic look at the FEPACI, from its creation to the Niamey Manifesto, what can one say of the organization? The FEPACI is unique because it is a movement of the filmmakers of a whole continent, as opposed to such national cinematic movements as the Cinema Novo and the New Wave. The FEPACI is also unique because it is less a cinematic movement aimed at deconstructing traditional film narratives, as is the case with the New Wave, and more a politico-economic movement committed to the total liberation of Africa. As such, the FEPACI has more in common with its sister Pan-African movement, the Organization of African Unity, than with "purely" cinematic movements such as the New Wave and the Italian Neorealism. The success and the contradictions of the FEPACI should therefore be measured in terms of achievements as a liberationist movement that is committed to the independence and the unity of Africa.

As the above history of the organization shows, the FEPACI has achieved many of its goals. As a liberationist movement, it has led the African governments in breaking the monopoly of such foreign distribution companies as COMACICO and SECMA. It has influenced the governments to create national production centers and to take film seriously as a means of development. The efforts of the filmmakers led to the creation of the festivals of Ouagadougou (1969) and Mogadishu (Somalia, 1980). One can also say that in addition to the economic advantages, it is the spirit of Pan-Africanism that led the FEPACI in the Niamey Manifesto to go beyond national to regional and inter-African issues.

As a liberationist movement, the film directors of the FEPACI have also made several successful films that raise the consciousness of the audiences. Using documentary and didactic fictional forms to denounce neocolonialism and alienation, the filmmakers saw as their prophetic mission to employ film as "a weapon as well as a means of expression for the development of the awareness of class struggle."[12] In retrospect, one sees at least three types of cinema that developed out of this liberationist movement: the semidocumentary, the didactic-fictional, and film research. The semidocumentary depicts and denounces colonialism and/or settler rule and shows the progress of the forces of liberation. Typical examples of the semidocumentary form are the epics of the Algerian war, Sarah Maldoror's *Sambizanga* (1972), Haile Gerima's *Harvest, 3000 Years* (1974), the films by the Mozambican National Institute of Cinema such as *These Are the Weapons* (1979), and the films on apartheid in South Africa.

The second type of film, the didactic-fictional, opposes good and evil in Africa in a Manichaean manner. The films of this genre show the strong, usually from European origins, taking advantage of the weak, symbolized by Africa. Sometimes Islam and/or African governments replace the West as the oppressor in the films. The genre is more prevalent in Senegal, with Ousmane Sembène as its masterful practitioner. Another general trait of the films is a quest (mostly symbolic) to the West, characterizing alienation, and a return to the sources as a way of solving the problem. Typical examples of the form are the films of Sembène and Mahama Traoré, *Touki Bouki* (1973) by Djibril Diop Mambety, *Kodou* (1971) by Ababacar Samb-Makharam, *Soleil O* (1969) by Med Hondo, and *Le bracelet de bronze* (1974) by Tidiane Aw.

The third form, the film of research, is an outgrowth of the didactic-fictional form. Emphasizing less the Manichaeism of their predecessors, the filmmakers look for combinations of solutions to African problems. They depict social changes, breaks, and continuities in history and culture. They pose as challenges the ways in which tradition and modernity, educated and illiterate can be reconciled. Examples of this genre are the films by Souleymane Cissé, *Lettres paysannes* (1975) by Safi Faye, *Jom* (1981) by Ababacar Samb-Makharam, *Wend Kuuni* (1982) by Gaston Kaboré, the powerful documentary *Zo Kwe Zo* (1982) by Joseph Akouissonne, and *Djeli* (1981) by Lancine Kramo Fadiga.

It is important to notice here that all three genres are still being practiced in African cinema. Ideally, the first type coincides with the inaugural manifesto of the FEPACI, which postulates the need to unite and fight against colonialism and settler rule in South Africa. The second type, too, is symptomatic of the anti-neocolonialist and imperialist slogans of the Second FEPACI Congress, and the third type, including such popular films as *Djeli* and *Finye* (1982), seems to represent the Niamey Manifesto, which emphasizes film more as an industry and less as an anticapitalist weapon. The presence of all three genres at the same time indicates the historical situation of Africa as well as the ideological differences of the filmmakers.

As regards the contradictions of the FEPACI, they typically emanate from an insufficient analysis of the blending of political, economic, and artistic realities in Africa. As Cheriaa put it,

> In a place [Africa] where there hadn't been a structure and a tradition of national cinemas before, they [filmmakers] had believed that all that was needed, in addition to their own commitment to making films, was the support of the State, which they thought was determined to create national cinemas. Feeling very strongly about what they had to say and imagining themselves free to express it, they believed the states also were in a disposition to work with them. They did not doubt that a limit could be put on their freedom to act.[13]

The FEPACI, as a Pan-Africanist movement, worked to help individual countries gain control over the channels of distribution, exhibition, and sometimes even production. The FEPACI believed that it was making progress toward an autonomous film industry every time that a country nationalized its film activities. However, it soon became clear that the interest of the FEPACI could not always be reconciled with that of the countries it had helped. There were ideological contradictions that were determined by the fact of the African countries' economic and cultural dependence on the West. Thus, although politically it was prestigious for the governments to have national cinemas, economically they could not afford them without the consent of the Western countries. For political reasons, they exported independently made films by Sembène and Cissé (to cite only two), presenting them as national films, even though they had not been distributed nationally. For economic reasons, they collected taxes on film distribution and exhibition, and they used the tax revenues for other problems affecting the countries.

In those countries where the economic issues were temporarily overcome and national film production centers were created, the governments' politics of production were different from those of the FEPACI. Where the FEPACI was committed to making liberationist and Pan-Africanist films, the governments were interested in propaganda films. Where the FEPACI deemphasized the profit-making aspect of the films, the governments emphasized the need for nonpropaganda films to recoup at least their cost of production. The low box-office revenues of national films led to the closing in the mid-seventies of the government-sponsored production units in Ivory Coast and Senegal.

Clearly, these contradictions between the government's national interest and the FEPACI's radical liberationist interest are serious issues that kept setting back the progress of the movement. In Francophone Africa, for example, since the CIDC took over film distribution from the COMACICO and SECMA, many problems have surfaced that have prevented it from functioning full swing in the fourteen member countries. Some governments have failed to pay part of the tax revenues from the film market as membership fees to the CIDC. Some have frustrated the efforts of the CIDC to distribute African films by finding new customers in Switzerland, Société Commerciale de Films (SOCOFILM), which specialized in distributing American films.[14] Finally, some governments defended the right of theater owners who rejected African films on the grounds that the spectators preferred American and European films. The bottom line was, as Cheriaa put it, that there were African filmmakers and films, which he compared to heads, without facilities of production, distribution and exhibition, which he compared to bodies (Cheriaa, p. 8).

Another point of weakness in the FEPACI's endeavor to develop an African film industry is the overreliance of the organization on governments and foreign countries such as France for the production of the films. Thus, it is doubtful whether the filmmakers had thought as seriously about the means of production as they had about the need to nationalize the film market and to raise the consciousness of the audiences with African films. The needs to reflect more on the tools of production led to the creation of Le Collectif L'Oeil Vert in 1981.

The disillusionment of Le Collectif L'Oeil Vert in the superstructural ideology of the FEPACI helps to clarify the extent to which it had failed to integrate the means of production in the total liberation of African cinema. Thus, on the superstructural level, Francophone filmmakers have put a lot of pressure on their governments and on France to improve the conditions of production and distribution. It is also clear that the filmmakers are dynamic, pioneering, and inventive. To be sure of these superstructural qualities, it is enough to look at Sembène's original use of Wolof in *Le Mandat* (1968) and his attack on Islam in *Ceddo* (1976), Djibril Diop Mambety's editing style in *Touki Bouki,* Dikongue Pipa's camera angles and mise-en-scène in *Muna Mota* (1975), and Cissé's synthesis between tradition and modernity in *Baara* (1978) and *Finye.*

But on an infrastructural level, where the forces of production and the means of production are concerned, it is clear that the filmmakers have not done substantial research. The number of camera operators, electricians, sound-engineers, and editors is not increasing proportionally with that of directors. For the most part, after the directorial duties, French manpower is used to finish the films. A look at the tools of production also shows that the filmmakers usually accept equipment without thinking of their specific ends. For example, the 35mm cameras with color and fast film stock are used in spite of the high cost and relative unwieldiness. In this regard, Sembène's candid response to the crucial issues of 35mm versus 16mm is revealing:

> Now, as far as 16mm or 35mm is concerned, it varies according to the filmmaker. It is true that I have always worked in 35mm, but it was just chance that that happened because I have a 35mm camera. On the other hand, we have found a new method. The young people whom we have trained like 16mm color because it is much more mobile, the crew is smaller, and it can be blown up to 35mm.[15]

The young filmmakers Sembène is referring to are none other than Cheikh N'Gaido Bâ (Senegal), Sanou Kollo (Upper Volta), Lancine Kramo Fadiga (Ivory Coast), and many others who got together to create Le Collectif L'Oeil Vert. It is hard to understand why an astute man such as Sembène does not get rid of his 35mm for a 16mm that will cut costs by more than half of his long-awaited film, *Samori.*

The FEPACI is to be credited for the disintegration of such foreign monopolies as the COMACICO and SECMA, the creation of national cinemas, and such inter-African organizations as the festivals and the distribution and production units such as the CIDC and the CIPROFILM. Moreover, the FEPACI has contributed to world cinemas by creating a Pan-Africanist and liberationist cinema toward the total independence of Africa. It is therefore to be hoped that the young, such as Le Collectif L'Oeil Vert, will incorporate the tools of production as a realistic economic factor in film production. In colonial times, L. A. Notcutt, with his Bantu Cinema Experiment, invented an economically liberated cinema, although it was racist.[16] Rouch, too, made stylistic and economic breakthroughs with his 16mm camera in Africa. Finally, in Latin America, Solanas and Gettino give an important place to the 16mm or even much less expensive and practical cameras in their definition of Third Cinema, or alternative cinema. If they want to be liberated, African filmmakers must do more research into the tools of production.

V.

The Situation of National and International Film Production in Francophone Africa

The history of national film production in Francophone Africa began with the independence of the countries in the early sixties. The first equipment for film production and exhibition came as gifts from technologically advanced countries desirous of initiating economic and cultural ties with the newly independent countries. It was in this vein that the United States gave a self-contained movie van to the Republic of Togo as a means of congratulating them for becoming independent.[1] Guinea and Mali received equipment from such Eastern Bloc countries as Poland, the Soviet Union, and Yugoslavia. In 1966, West Germany offered Guinea laboratories and other equipment for 35mm production.[2]

This is not to imply that France played little part in the development of national film production in its former colonies. It simply indicates that national film production in Francophone Africa grew out of the need to produce indigenous newsreels, educational films, and propaganda. As an independence phenomenon, the history of production also began with the withdrawal of France from these countries in the late fifties and early sixties. Thus, with the advent of self-rule, all the countries became equipped with minimal production apparatus such as 16mm cameras, sound-pickers, electrical cords and lights, film stock, vans, and projectors. The filmmakers and technicians were usually from the countries that had donated the equipment, and the postproduction also took place in the donating countries.

In this chapter, I will show first the manner in which France reversed its colonial policy[3] and became active in her former colonies in setting up skeleton production structures for making newsreels, documentaries, and propaganda. I will then describe the structures of national cinema in those Francophone countries that have them. Finally, I will talk about the Consortium Inter-Africain de Production de Film (CIPROFILM) as an example of international production in Francophone Africa.

The African Newsreel Centers and the C.A.I.

The French African territories were introduced to film activities as early as 1905 when *L'arrivée d'un train en gare de la ciottat* and *L'arroseur arrose* by the Lumière Brothers were exhibited in Dakar (Senegal) by a French circus group and filmmakers. At the same time, film pioneer Georges Meliès shot short films in Dakar, two of which, *Le marche de Dakar* and *Le cake-walk des nègres du nouveau cirque,* can be seen at the Cinémathèque Française.[4] Since then, foreign distributors and producers developed film activities in Africa as a serious industry. The Africans, however, did not participate as conscious history makers in this development of film activities. They remained either as consumers of foreign films or as objects of stereotypical images for commercial and anthropological filmmakers. The situation was worse in Francophone Africa, where the Laval decree was set against the African participation in decisions concerning films (see chapter 3). As Rouch saw it, the French were far behind the British and the Belgians in involving their subjects in film activities. Citing Ghana, a former British colony, and Ivory Coast, a former French colony, two countries with comparable economies and populations, Rouch stated that it was a shame that, in 1957, next to Ghana's more than twenty powerwagons and 16mm projectors, Ivory Coast only had an old 16mm projector that was not even fit for films (Rouch, p. 395).

However, in 1958, in an effort to maintain its assimilationist policy and slow down the independence process in the colonies, the French government ordered the production of films intended for Africans. As is well known to African historians, 1958 was the year in which General de Gaulle himself traveled to Africa to seek the alliance of the Africans of the Communauté française for an upcoming referendum on whether the colonies should continue with France or break from her. Film, too, was supposed to play a propaganda role for the French government in 1958. It was in this vein that Pierre Fourré, a coordinator of film for the colonies, was asked to produce a series of films especially made for Africans. Accordingly, Fourré produced *Bonjour Paris, L'elevage du Mouton, Un petit port de pêche Français,* etc., films that praised the French civilization, know-how, and beauty. According to Rouch, these films intended for Africans were very simple, in an elementary French, and reminiscent of the British colonial films, such as *Mister British at Home,* which had been made ten years earlier and which had been intended to teach the Anglophone Africans the advantages of being British (Rouch, p. 399).

However, Fourré's experiment came a little too late. By September 1958, Guinea-Konakry became independent, and in 1960 the other Francophone countries gained their autonomy. It is obvious, therefore, that the French colonial production was not significant enough to leave a structural legacy of production that could be compared to the production structures left behind in Anglophone Africa and Zaire by the British and the Belgians. The French produced the films of the Fourré experiment in France and sent them to Africa for exhibition, unlike the British and the Belgians who had production facilities in their colonies.

It was not until the postindependence era, when, ironically, France was driven out of Africa, that the Francophone countries began to acquire some film production facilities, contributed by France and other countries. France's gift to its former colonies was serious enough to make the efforts of other technologically advanced countries seem trivial. The exception to this truth might be West Germany, which has demonstrated her commitment to the development of African film by building autonomous production facilities in 35mm in both Anglophone and Francophone Africa in the countries of Ghana and Guinea-Konakry.[5]

In the postindependence era of the early sixties, the Francophone countries were faced with the difficulty of diffusing information and explaining their political programs to their populations. The newspapers were of little help because fewer than one fifth of the citizens in any country could read. Therefore, along with radio, film was the best tool for reaching people. However, unlike the radio stations which all the new governments acquired, films were not within reach of the independent countries for two reasons: Francophone countries lacked production structures and the means to acquire them, and they also lacked film technicians and, in many instances, directors. It was under these conditions that any help was welcomed from the technologically advanced countries, be it donations of movie projectors or offers to film the independent celebration of a country.

France understood better than any other country the desperate situation of her former colonies. She offered them, accordingly, a plan to eliminate any competition from other industrialized countries. In 1961, the French government asked the four largest producers of filmed news in France, Les Actualités Françaises, Eclair-Journal, Gaumont-Actualités, and Pathé-Magazines, to subsidize a fifth one, the Consortium Audio-visuel International (C.A.I.), which would sign a contract with the former colonies to produce their newsreels, educational films, and documentaries. As the C.A.I. was created in Paris with postproduction facilities, partial production equipment was set up in the capitals of the Francophone African countries. In this manner, the newsreels were shot in the member countries in Africa, sent to the C.A.I. in Paris to be finished, and sent back to Africa for projection. The filmmakers and technicians were usually employees of Les Actualités Françaises and other such organizations that subsidized the C.A.I. Production was financed by the French government and the African countries. According to Débrix, these agreements were made on a commercial basis: "France pays half the cost of producing the filmed African news, and she gets in return half the revenues corresponding to her investment in the production. The system has worked for fifteen years (1961–1977) without a problem."[6]

As early as 1964, largely because of the C.A.I., all the Francophone countries had a production section attached to their ministries of information. As Rouch pointed out, these production sections included plans to make feature films and documentaries, even though their emphasis was to be "films d'actualité" (Rouch, p. 395). Some countries such as Niger, Ivory Coast, and Mali invited world-famous directors from Canada, France, and Holland to film documentaries and educational films for them. Rouch and Claude Jutra were invited on several occasions to make films in Niger. Rouch also made films for Mali and Ivory Coast. Jutra made Le Niger, jeune république (1960), a coproduction by Niger and the Office National Canadien du Film, to celebrate Niger's independence. Such Canadian masters of the documentary as Norman MacLaren, Michel Brault, and Jutra were also involved in making the first films of Moustapha Alassane from Niger. As early as 1961, Mali also created a Centre Malien de Cinéma for the "political education of the citizen and the worker" (Rouch, p. 396). The Malian government invited Joris Ivens to this center to make Demain à Nanguila, an educational film about the evolution of a young man and his country. This film is considered by Rouch as the best of its kind made by foreigners on Africa (Rouch, pp. 369–401).

However, before showing how some countries developed national film production, it is important to point out the limitations of the newsreel production centers of the ministries of information that led to the stagnation of the equipment and personnel in many countries. First of all, it is crucial to understand, as Rouch remarked, that the methodology of producing newsreels is different from that of producing regular films, although the newsreel production can provide the film technician with the training necessary for making films. The newsreel production operates on deadlines that require a division of labor and a sophisticated technological apparatus for shooting, editing, and recording. These exigencies of deadlines and specialized technology make the newsreel production seem mechanical, while the production of regular films involves individual decisions and creative acts. These differences led Rouch to argue that "because they did not understand the difference between the methods of producing newsreels and regular films, many African governments employed young and talented filmmakers in the ministries of information to make newsreels, thus driving these filmmakers to an impasse as far as artistic expression was concerned" (Rouch, p. 402).

A Francophone African filmmaker working for the ministry of information of his/her country was frustrated in other ways as well. Because he/she only had skeleton production facilities in Africa for the shooting of images, and the laboratories and editing tables were at the C.A.I. in Paris, his/her role was reduced to that of director of photography. To put it in Bassori's words, the filmmaker at the ministry of information was "doomed to covering official and political meetings. In this manner, he stagnates and stalls in a bureaucratic routine that is alarming."[7]

Another predicament of the filmmaker at the ministries of information was that foreign directors were hired to make documentaries and feature films in his/her place. The use of foreign directors was sometimes justified by the contracts of coproduction between Africa and the technologically advanced countries, which signed up their filmmakers and technicians as part of their end of the contract. In a coproduction between the C.A.I. and its member countries in Africa, for example, French directors and technicians of such sponsoring organizations as Les Actualités Françaises were used.

Another reason that foreign directors were employed by the ministries of information was the belief that they were the only experts in the fields. The ministries of information valorized them over their African counterparts and assured themselves that a documentary or a feature film made by these foreign experts would be an instant success. It is in this vein that a Frenchman, Claude Vermorel, made *Yao* (1968) for the Ivory Coast. As recently as 1982, the president of Gabon, Bernard Bongo, called Serge Gainsbourg, a controversial filmmaker in France, to make a film called *Équateur*. Gainsbourg was seen by many French people as a maker of pornographic films. Unaware of this aspect of Gainsbourg's art, Bongo gave him a huge budget (200 million French francs) to make *Équateur*, hoping that the film would be publicity for Gabon.[8]

Clearly, such aspects as the dependence of the African newsreel production on the C.A.I. in Paris, the differences between the production of newsreels and of features, and the resort to foreign directors for the making of documentaries and educational fictional films must be taken into account when one considers the reasons why national production did not grow naturally out of the newsreel production structure created by the C.A.I. in Francophone countries. Because they were reluctant to reexamine these issues, some countries considered film an expensive hobby that was best left in the hands of independent filmmakers with occasional government subsidies and/or tax relief, and they decided never to attempt to install national production facilities. With the advent of national television, other countries such as Ivory Coast, Gabon, and Congo placed film production as a subsidiary to television stations. A third group of Francophone countries such as Chad, Mauritania, Benin, etc., did nothing concrete to raise national film production above the level of the newsreels of the ministries of information. Only such countries as Guinea, Upper Volta, and Mali made efforts to create national structures of production. However, as will be seen later in this study, these national structures contain some of the same contradictions as mentioned in the newsreel production centers of the ministries of information.

Here I will focus on the different types of production that developed out of the newsreel facilities. Because of the lack of production tools, the financial means, and the limited number of qualified technicians, Francophone African countries employed complex strategies in order to gain access to the use of the seventh art. However, it is possible to trace the evolution of national cinemas along three lines in the former French colonies. First there is the line of the Francophone countries that practice laissez-faire or a liberal economic system. The majority of the former French colonies belong to this category. They often view nationalization of production as a repression of free enterprise. Because of this negative connotation of the concept of nationalization and the lack of autonomous facilities of production, some countries in this category have yet to go beyond the making of newsreels. However, because of the pressure on the governments by the FEPACI and local filmmakers, two types of state-sponsored production emerged in some of the so-called liberal countries. The first type, in Senegal, Niger, and Cameroon, was characterized by governments facilitating filmmaking with subsidies in one form or another. The other type, in Ivory Coast, Gabon, Niger, and Congo, consisted in the production and coproduction of occasional films by national television.

The third type of production that emerged in Francophone Africa is associated with Guinea, Mali, and Upper Volta, countries that had defied economic traditions inherited from France.[9] These countries attempted very early to nationalize production, distribution, and exhibition, as they made plans to create national cinemas. However, most of the plans did not materialize for reasons I hope to explain later. Because of the abortion of some of their plans (Guinea with facilities of production in 16mm and 35mm has produced fewer films than Ivory Coast and Senegal), it is hard to determine which politics of production is the right course for developing national cinemas. However, an in-depth look at the structure of each may help answer the question.

National Cinema in Senegal and Ivory Coast

When one looks first at those countries which did not have television facilities in the 1960s or a production structure of another kind to enable them to make films on the spot, but which managed to have national films, one notices the following facts about them: they depended on the technological support of France and they drew too much money from government funds. Senegal, Niger, and Cameroon, which are the best examples of this category, still do not have production structures. Yet they have more films than other Francophone countries, and their filmmakers are among the best known in Africa. As I showed in the chapter on France's contribution to African film production, the Coopération and the C.A.I. played important roles in producing the films from these countries, but the governments also had politics of production which, although it did not involve facilities of production, kept the filmmakers busy. For example, according to Mahama Traoré, president of the Association des Cinéastes Sénégalais, all the films made in Senegal between 1972 and 1983 were subsidized in one way or another by the government.[10] In Cameroon, the Fonds d'aide à l'industrie cinématographique, which was funded by tax revenues from film import and ticket sales, helped to produce some films.[11] Up until recently, when Niger acquired a television studio that coproduced some films, the Institut de Recherche en Sciences Humaines of the Ministry of Education, and the Centre Culturel Franco-Nigérien were the main coproducers of film in Niger (Boughedir, p. 77).

One could continue citing the different ways these countries, without national production equipment, managed to have record numbers of films financed for their filmmakers or for educational and documentary purposes. However, such a task would be repetitious and unnecessary in view of the fact that the reader would have a clearer sense of the situation if examined, for example, in only one country. Such an examination could focus on the lack of production structure that is common to all these countries and that determines them to turn to France for technological and/or financial assistance for the production of their films. Because Senegal leads the so-called liberal governments in the number of films she has financed, the history of how she acquired national films, which are produced in a different technological and artistic setting than the newsreels of the ministries of information, is appropriate for providing the reader with a clear view of the situation. It is hoped that the reader will be saved from the trouble of going through the endless surface differences in financing strategies in these countries where the politics of production is not supported by facilities of production.

Senegal was the first Francophone country to sign a newsreel production agreement with the C.A.I. According to Vieyra, who was head of Les Actualités Sénégalaises, the agreement was such that the C.A.I. provided Senegal with a cameraman/reporter who was in charge of filming the current events. The filmed events were sent to Paris to be developed and edited, along with other African and world events that were also provided by the C.A.I. Vieyra explained that the editing and the added commentaries were done according to the wishes of the Ministry of Information of Senegal. "The cost of production was split half and half between the C.A.I. and Senegal. The same agreement was later signed by Ivory Coast, Dahomey, Togo, Madagascar, Upper Volta, and Cameroon."[12]

At first the C.A.I. was making two newsreels a month for Les Actualités Sénégalaises. Vieyra said that, beginning in April 1962, the demand was increased to one newsreel a week. The total length of the film was 250 meters, of which 100 meters were devoted to Senegalese news (Vieyra, p. 184). However, even the one newsreel a week soon proved insufficient because it could not include all the activities that were deemed newsworthy by the different ministries. There was also a need for educational films and documentaries that could not be replaced by the newsreels. Finally, one must not forget that Senegal was the home of pioneers of African cinema, including Blaise Senghor and Vieyra, who were graduates of the French Institut des Hautes Etudes Cinématographiques (IDHEC) and who were anxious to make films in Africa, now that they were independent.[13]

Les Actualités Sénégalaises made plans, therefore, to create a Service de Cinéma that would be involved in producing and coproducing documentaries. Vieyra argued that the plans were first limited to documentaries because, after the newsreels, they were the least expensive (Vieyra, p. 186). Under the direction of Vieyra himself, several short films were financed by the Service de Cinéma. They were films on special topics that were ordered by different branches of the government. Vieyra directed *Une nation est née* (1961, 35mm color) on the anniversary of the independence and *Lamb* (1963, 35mm color) on wrestling, which is a popular sport in Senegal. Vieyra also made films, such as *Voyage présidentiel en Urss* (1962), that were presidential visits and more like newsreels than documentaries. Blaise Senghor also directed a short film, *Grand magal à Touba* (1962, 35mm color), on Islam, the most important religion in Senegal.

But until the late 1960s when Sembène came on the scene, Senegal did not give its own nationals the chance to direct features and/or major documentaries. It was in this sense that Les Actualités Sénégalaises hired Ives Ciampi, a Frenchman, to direct *Liberté I* (1960). A Franco-Senegalese production, the film was to explore the conflicts between tradition and modernity. According to Débrix, the filmmaker failed in this respect.[14] Another Frenchman, Jean-Claude Bonnardot, was also called to direct a major documentary, *Sénégal, ma pirogue* (1962). Just as Les Actualités Sénégalaises had to depend on the C.A.I. for the postproduction of its newsreels and on French directors for the making of features, the Service de Cinéma also depended on the French facilities of production and postproduction. When the Service de Cinéma was created to remedy the urgent need for documentaries and educational films, the project did not include buying production facilities, which, in the long run, would have saved Senegal a lot of money. Clearly, the Service de Cinéma was little more than a bank that financed films or tried to find financiers for them. In its role as a financier, the Service de Cinéma generously spent the money of the different ministries to produce film with 35mm cameras and other such expensive equipment from France. In its double role as a financier and an agent, it coproduced with the French Ministry of Coopération, through the Bureau de Cinéma and the C.A.I., the films of such Senegalese directors as Sembène, Babakar Samb, and Vieyra.

Clearly, the emergence of Senegalese cinema in the late sixties with Sembène and Mahama Traoré was due less to the availability of a structure provided by the Service de Cinéma and more to France's willingness to produce African films. Although I have explained in an earlier chapter some of the neocolonialist aspects of such a French venture, it is important to add here that because French equipment of production and postproduction was used by both Les Actualités Sénégalaises and the Service de Cinéma, it was clever of France to have created a system that systematically helped the production of African films and, at the same time, kept such countries as Senegal from having autonomous production facilities. Interestingly enough, some independent filmmakers adapted themselves to this creation and created their own production companies, without equipment of production, and went directly to the Coopération for help.[15] Thus, they were unwittingly postponing the day Senegal would be independent from France in matters of equipment.

However, in the early seventies, the Association des Cinéastes Sénégalais began to rethink the role of the Service de Cinéma and to put the pressure on their government to improve the conditions of production in Senegal. The filmmakers' action was determined by several factors. Directors such as Sembène had become disillusioned with foreign aid, which they had realized was "tainted with paternalism and neocolonialism" (see chapter 4). Because of the increase in the number of African directors, France also was beginning to find it difficult to produce all their films. Finally, the Pan-African Federation of Filmmakers had stepped up the pressure on African governments to liberate production, distribution, and exhibition of film in Africa (see the chapter on the FEPACI).

Bowing to the pressure, the government created, in 1973, a Société de Cinéma (SNC) within the Ministry of Culture. The purpose of the SNC was to encourage national production in fiction and documentary films. Filmmakers were requested to submit scripts on topics ranging from juvenile delinquency and urban problems to literacy campaigns. The best scripts were selected by a group of readers who were designated by the president of the SNC.[16] In this manner, six feature films were produced and/or coproduced by the SNC in 1974 (Vieyra, p. 207). They were *Xala* by Sembène, *Le bracelet de bronze* by Tidiane Aw, *Baks* by Momar Thiam, *Njangaan* by Mahama Traoré, *L'option* by Thierno Sow, and *Boram Xam Xam* by Maurice Dore, a French psychiatrist. Because of this unprecedented number of films produced by a national organization in one year, 1974 is considered the golden age of Senegalese cinema.

The SNC also worked with the Association des Cinéastes Sénégalais in ways that enabled young filmmakers to direct short films. According to Mahama Traoré, the SNC and the filmmakers' association agreed to give the newcomers the opportunity to express themselves by assigning them to the short film projects of the different ministries, instead of letting the ministries choose their own directors.[17] It was in this way that new and talented directors, including Moussa Bathily, Ben Diogaye Beye, and Cheikh N'Gaido Bâ, made their first films. Moussa Bathily, who had been the assistant of Ousmane Sembène, has since become the master of the documentary form with such prize-winning films as *Tiyabu biru* (The Circumcision) (1978) and *Le certificat d'indigence* (1981), a documentary on hospitals and the corruption of the medical profession in Dakar. Cheikh N'Gaido Bâ became the leader of Le Collectif l'Oeil Vert, an association of young African filmmakers who were defying the FEPACI and rethinking the structure of production of African films.[18]

However, like the preceding organizations in charge of Senegalese cinema, the SNC did not acquire the equipment of production as part of its politics of developing national production. The SNC merely took money from governmental budgets and gave it to filmmakers. With this money, the filmmakers bought film stocks from Paris, rented French cameras and other production equipment, if they didn't have them, and sometimes used French film technicians. The Paris studios were also used for film processing, editing, and sound-synchronizing.

Because only three films, *Xala, Le bracelet de bronze,* and *Njangaan,* were commercially successful for the films produced by the SNC, the project was phased out by 1976. The contents of *Xala* and *Njangaan* were also burdensome to the government and partly instrumental in shaping the decision to shut down the SNC. Several portions of both films were cut out before they were shown to Senegalese audiences.[19] *Njangaan* is an indictment of Islam, the main religion in Senegal; *Xala* depicts the impotence of political leaders.

Aside from the fact that the SNC ate the government's money and produced films that made the leaders uncomfortable, there was also a conflict with another governmental society, the Société d'Importation de Distribution et d'Exploitation Cinématographique (SIDEC). Where the SNC accused the SIDEC of not promoting and distributing its films, the SIDEC charged the SNC with interfering with distribution and exhibition and thus illegally appropriating SIDEC funds.[20] The conflicts could easily have been avoided had the government put together the two organizations under one ministry instead of having the SNC at the Ministry of Culture and the SIDEC at the Ministry of

Commerce in charge of distributing primarily foreign films. Had they been conceived together, the SIDEC would be distributing foreign films with a long-range plan of creating a subsidy from the tax revenues to buy equipment and to produce, promote, and distribute national films. In effect, the SIDEC could have been subsidizing the SNC. In Francophone countries that have liberal economic systems, only Cameroon, with the Fonds d'Aide à l'Industrie Cinématographique (FODIC), disposes of such a subsidy funded by tax revenues from film import and exhibition. However, the FODIC, too, had not managed to acquire the facilities of production in Cameroon. It is ironic that France, which is the model of the so-called liberal economic system that the Francophone countries had adopted, had her own Centre National Cinématographique (CNC), which subsidized the production and distribution of French films. Under the existing situation in Senegal, the SNC took the government money to produce films, and the SIDEC at the Ministry of Commerce took the tax revenue from distribution and exhibition and spent it elsewhere.

After the dissolution of the SNC, the government tried to contribute to national production by co-signing directors at banks. The Actualités Sénégalaises and the Service de Cinéma also resumed their activities as producers of short films. Furthermore, according to Traoré, there is a new production plan devised by the government and the filmmakers which, when unveiled, will have important consequences both in Senegal and the rest of Africa.[21] Perhaps this plan involves acquiring equipment of production and subsidies from distribution and exhibition to be used to help filmmakers. Meanwhile, production has dropped in Senegal. Some filmmakers are returning to the Coopération for assistance; others, such as Safi Faye and Bathily, are trying coproduction with Swedish and German television.

When one turns to the structure of production in other liberal countries such as Ivory Coast, Gabon, and Niger, one notices that they first depended on similar structures as Senegal and Cameroon, and when they acquired national television facilities, they used them to produce films. Unlike other Francophone countries who did not have television until the mid-seventies, both Ivory Coast and Gabon had television facilities as early as 1963. One year after the creation of Ivorian television, Timité Bassori made *Sur la dune de la solitude* (1964), a short TV film in 16mm that told the story of Mamy Water, a famous myth in West Africa about a siren. Since that time, the Société Ivorienne du Cinéma has been known for making its important films with the equipment and manpower of television. In Gabon, the films of Pierre-Marie Dong, *Carrefour humain* (1969) and *Sur le sentier du requiem* (1971), and those of Philippe Mory, *Les tam-tams se sont tus* (1972), to cite only these, were produced with national television facilities. Recently, Niger also had put television in charge of film production. Since then, it has produced *Kankamba* (1982) by Moustapha Alassane, *Si les cavaliers* (1982) by Mahamane Babake, *Le medecin de Gafire* (1983) by Moustafa Diop, and coproduced *Sarraounia, une reine africaine* (1986) by Med Hondo.

Television was gradually placed in charge of film production in these countries for several reasons. For economic reasons and because of the small number of technicians available in Africa, the countries employed filmmakers as cameramen and directors of news production at the television, and occasionally gave them the means to author films that were also used by television. By thus employing the filmmakers, the governments reduced the expenses that had been previously incurred by the national production centers, which had replaced the centers for producing newsreels. This was the case in Ivory Coast, where the Société Ivorienne du Cinéma was seen as a "budget-divore," eater-of-budget, and was dissolved to clear the way for the creation of a new society that would merge film and television.[22]

Another reason the television centers produced some films was the reluctance of the governments to acknowledge film production as a serious industry. Such an acknowledgment would entail a restructuring of the twin sectors of distribution and exhibition to allow the national films to recoup their costs of production. Consequently, the governments preferred to produce films through the television facilities and not worry about the problems of distribution and exhibition. This way they avoided creating autonomous national production centers, the survival of which would depend upon nationalizing distribution and exhibition. It was no accident, therefore, that after all the pressure exerted by the FEPACI on governments to nationalize distribution, exhibition, and production, Ivory Coast, Gabon, and Niger did not comply fully. Of course, other countries also were reluctant to comply with all the recommendations of the FEPACI, but because they didn't have television facilities, they dealt with the issues of national production in a different manner.

In order to give a clear idea of how television became important in film production, it is important to focus on the development of film production in one country as an example. Ivory Coast is a good choice because it not only leads the other countries of this category in the number of films produced by national television, but Ivory Coast also has had television since 1963. Furthermore, the history of production is more complex in Ivory Coast because it has had both a national production center and a television that produced and coproduced films for Ivorians and foreign directors. Clearly, an understanding of the reasons that led Ivory Coast to dissolve the film production center and put the television in charge of producing film will shed light on both the advantages and limitations of merging film and television.

Like Senegal, Ivory Coast enlarged her newsreel production facilities as early as 1960 to include a Service de Cinéma that made documentaries and educational shorts. The directors were from France, and the films were shot on order, ranging from such topics as presidential visits and independence celebrations to sport activities, economic instruction, hygiene, and ethnography.[23] The films were generally in 16mm and the postproduction was done by the C.A.I.

Soon after the creation of Service de Cinéma, however, it was dismantled in favor of a new production network that had more national ambitions, the Société Ivorienne du Cinéma (S.I.C.). As a matter of fact, a young Ivorian, Timité Bassori, had just returned home after earning a degree from the Institut des Hautes Etudes Cinématographiques in Paris. Bassori assumed the management of the S.I.C. and became one of the first Ivorians to direct films, write scripts, assist, and coproduce foreign directors. According to Belgian film historian Victor Bachy, the purpose of the S.I.C. was first to continue the production of newsreels, which it sold to different government branches, to commercial theaters, and to other countries. The second project of the S.I.C. included the production of shorts on education, information, and propaganda. The S.I.C. also planned to help produce features (Bachy, p. 20).

From 1962 to 1967, production at the S.I.C. was dominated by French directors. Only Bassori played a significant role when he wrote the script for *Croyances et survivances* (1965), directed by Yves Colmar, and made *Sixième sillon* (1966), a film celebrating the sixth anniversary of the independence (Bachy, p. 28). Bassori also assisted Christian-Jaque in directing *Le gentleman de Cocody,* a coproduction between the S.I.C. and France, starring the famous French actor Jean Marais.

In 1963, one year after the inauguration of the S.I.C., the Ivory Coast installed television facilities with laboratories and studios in 16mm. Consequently, the S.I.C. lost Bassori to television, where he became the undersecretary of programming. Bassori made three short documentaries (*Les forestiers, L'Abidjan-Niger,* and *Amedee Pierre*) for the television in 1963 before directing his first short fiction, *Sur la dune de la solitude.*

Television competed with the S.I.C. in other ways. In 1964, it produced a two-hour film, *Korogo,* directed by George Keita on the myth of "Queen Pocou," a legendary heroine who sacrificed her own son to appease the angry gods. The film was run several times on television, and, according to Vieyra, it is to date the most important television film made in Africa.[24]

According to Bachy, it wasn't until 1967 that the S.I.C. was able to assert itself. Then it was getting Ivorians to direct films that would have been directed before by French filmmakers. Bassori had returned to the S.I.C. because projects for features were under way (Bachy, p. 22). In fact, from 1967 to 1972, production at the S.I.C. was dominated by Bassori and another Ivorian director, Henri Duparc. Within this time, Bassori, working with 35mm equipment, directed several documentaries: *Kossu I, Kossu II*, on bridge construction; *Feux de brousse*, on brush fire; *Bondougou an 11, Odienne an 12*, and *Abidjan (perle de lagune)*, on national promotion. On his side, Duparc used 16mm film to make *Récolte du coton* (1, 2) on agriculture and *Profil ivorien, Achete ivorien, Tam-tam ivoire*, and *J'aie dix ans* on national promotion. The S.I.C. also produced features by Duparc, *Mouna ou le Rêve d'un artiste* (1969, 16mm) and *Abusan* (The Family) (1972, 16mm), and coproduced *La femme au couteau* (1969, 16mm) by Bassori.

The period 1967–1972, which Bachy called the *âge d'or* of Ivorian cinema, was also a period of continuity with France. *La femme au couteau* and other films of the S.I.C. were edited at the Bureau du Cinéma of the Coopération in Paris. Christian Lacoste, the French cameraman who shot the picture of *Borom Sarret* and *La Noire de . . .* by Sembène, was cameraman for *Abusan* and the short documentaries of Bassori before directing some shorts himself.[25] Finally, the C.A.I. continued until 1971 to handle the postproduction of newsreels and documentaries. In 1971, the C.A.I. put an end to the contract of coproduction with Ivory Coast (Bachy, p. 19), and the S.I.C. was free to go to other companies in France for postproduction.

Meanwhile, the television was introducing young talents as directors. In 1970, Gnoan M'Bala returned home after studying film production in Paris and Sweden. He went to work for the television instead of the S.I.C. because, in his own words, "Upon my return home, there weren't production facilities (at the S.I.C.)."[26] M'Bala proceeded to direct short fiction television films, which were well received in Ivory Coast and by international film critics and historians. He is one of the few African artists (Ferdinand Oyono in literature) who used comedy and satire in his art. His narratives revolve around such motifs as deception, mistaken identity, and the naiveté of people. In *La biche* (1971, 16mm), a black woman invites herself to a mixed couple's home where she passes for the cousin of the husband, who is black, and becomes his mistress without the wife, who is white, knowing it. *Amenié* (1972, 16mm) is about a peasant who moves to Abidjan and fools people by passing for a rich diplomat. The film is considered to be the author's best work (Hennebelle and Ruelle, p. 93; Bachy, p. 59).[27] M'Bala went on to make *Valisy* (1974, 16mm), *Le chapeau* (1976, 16mm), and *Ablakon* (1983), all of which were popular in Ivory Coast. The other young talent in television is N'dabain Vodio, who spent four years at the Gorki Institute of Cinema (V.G.I.K.) in Moscow. Less prolific than M'Bala, he directed two fiction films for television: *Le cri du Muezin* (1972, 16mm) and *Les collegiennes* (1976, 16mm).

Besides the fact that new talents like M'Bala preferred television to the S.I.C. and the C.A.I. was no longer coproducing the films of the S.I.C., there was a feeling of dissatisfaction with the organization at the ministry of information. The fiction films that the S.I.C. produced were not commercial enough to recoup the costs of production. Furthermore, as can be seen by the list of films directed by Bassori, the S.I.C. was developing 35mm to the detriment of 16mm. This factor increased the cost of production to a point that the Ivorians began to designate the S.I.C. as budget-divore.[28]

In 1975, Bassori became director of the S.I.C., replacing an administrator who was incompetent in matters relating to film production (Bachy, p. 22). According to Bachy, the new head of the S.I.C. directed about fifty newsreels and documentaries between 1975 and 1979. Bassori also produced a feature, *L'herbe sauvage* (1978) by Duparc, and coproduced with France and Germany *La victoire en chantant* (1975) by Jean-Jacques Annaud. The title of *La victoire en chantant* was later changed to *Noirs et blancs en couleur* (Black and White in Color), which won the Oscar for best foreign film in 1977 at the Academy Awards.

Bassori failed to save the S.I.C.'s reputation as a coherently managed profit-making enterprise. Although *L'herbe sauvage* ran for three months in Abidjan, the capital city, it was poorly received outside the country and by critics (Bachy, p. 57). As for *Noirs et blancs en couleur,* according to Bachy, despite the best foreign film award in Hollywood, it was a financial failure, as were all the other coproductions the S.I.C. did with foreigners (Bachy p. 22). In 1979, therefore, the minister of information put an end to the S.I.C., arguing that it made no significant contribution to the training of filmmakers and technicians, that it attracted little international exposure because of the quality of the films, and that it ignored commercial considerations and had become a financial burden to the government (Bachy, p. 50). A new governmental society was created to make film production a subsidiary to television

programming. The Centre de Production des Actualités Audio-visu-
elles et du Perfectionnement Permanent (CPAAPP) intended to make
the film needs of the different branches of the government coincide
with those of television. For this purpose, it could make documentaries, serials, and newsreels addressing the issues that the different branches of the government wanted filmed (Bachy, p. 24). It was
in this vein that the CPAAPP began employing such directors of the
S.I.C. as Bassori and Duparc, and those of the television as M'Bala,
Vodio, and Kobinan Adou. A recent catalog, *L'Audio-visuel en Côte
d'Ivoire: Annuaire 1984*, also cited the CPAAPP as having autonomous
facilities in 16mm, black-and-white production, and partial facilities in
35mm production.[29]

Clearly, the end of the S.I.C. and the incorporation of its directors in
the staff of the CPAAPP indicate that a liberal government like Ivory
Coast is in a weak position to promote national cinema. Conceived as
an industry, a national cinema cannot grow without a radical restructuring of the private sector that controls distribution and exhibition.
Distribution quotas would have to be fixed for foreign films in order to
leave room for national ones. Taxes would also have to be levied on
foreign film import and exhibition in order to subsidize the production
of national ones. Since Ivory Coast, like the other liberal countries, is
opposed to most of these measures, an easy way out is to keep the
filmmakers at bay by employing them at the CPAAPP and by occasionally assisting them with equipment and personnel in their independent
production.

The Ivorian directors had already learned to count less on the
government as a major producer and more on their independent resources. In 1981, a newcomer, Lancine Kramo Fadiga, revealed himself
with *Djeli* (16mm blown into 35mm), which won the best film award at
the festival of Ouagadougou. *Djeli* was financed and produced in a
three-year span during which Lancine used his personal funds and
those of his family and friends. He first had an agreement with the
S.I.C. to use the equipment and the technicians. After the S.I.C. was
dissolved, he renewed the same agreement with the CPAAPP and
finished the film (interview with M'Bala). Other independent directors,
proceeding in a similar manner as Lancine, produced their own films.
Jean-Louis Koula and Leo Kozoloa created their own production
house, Les Films de la Montagne, which specializes in advertising and
produced *Adja Tio* (1980, 16mm blown into 35mm), a feature on the
traditional forms of inheritance, directed by Koula, and *Petangin*
(1983, 35mm) on corruption, directed by Kozoloa.

According to M'Bala, it was not impossible for Ivorian directors to have a prolific independent production at the same time that they and the FEPACI were putting pressure on the government to nationalize distribution and exhibition in order to create subsidies for national production. M'Bala argued that Ivorian filmmakers were more fortunate than their counterparts in other Francophone areas because there were more production facilities in Ivory Coast. The branches of the government such as the Ministère de l'Education Nationale et de la Recherche Scientifique, the Ministère de l'Information where the CPAAPP was, and the Ministère des Affaires Culturelles disposed of cameras, tape recorders, laboratories in 16mm production, editing tables (the CPAAPP also had facilities in 35mm), and technicians. With the agreement of these agencies, the filmmakers could borrow both the technicians and the equipment. M'Bala added that the filmmakers could also gain financial support from private businessmen in return for inserting some of their products into the films. To give an example of the way independent directors/producers maneuver, M'Bala cited his most recent film, *Ablakon,* which he made by employing CPAAPP cameramen and equipment in return for some copies for television, the support from the private sector to be paid after the commercial distribution of the films, and the postproduction facilities of France in return for some copies that would be distributed on a noncommercial basis (interview with M'Bala). Finally, the success of *Djeli,* which both the S.I.C. and the CPAAPP helped to produce, led the minister of information to say that "the government has not turned its back on the filmmakers" (Bachy, p. 24).

National Cinema in Guinea and Burkina Faso

After this survey of production in the so-called liberal countries, it is important, for comparative purposes, to postpone the evaluation and look first at production in Guinea, Upper Volta, and Mali, where the governments had opted for nationalization. The radicalism of these countries came from the fact that they defied the French distribution and exhibition companies, COMACICO and SECMA, and attempted to set up their own production, distribution, and exhibition. Their originality lay in their belief that they must first control distribution and exhibition in order to nurture production. As early as 1958, the newly independent Guinea created Sily-Cinéma, a state organism, to control production, distribution, and exhibition. For fear that other African countries would follow Guinea's example, the COMACICO and SECMA reacted violently by refusing to provide the country with foreign films. Guinea overcame this obstacle temporarily by showing films from the Eastern Bloc. But in order to comply with the taste of a public that was accustomed to American and Western European films, Guinea had to make some concessions to COMACICO and SECMA. The compromise was mainly in the sector of exhibition where Guinea's twenty-eight movie theaters were divided between Sily-Cinéma and the foreign companies. The arrangement was such that the COMACICO and SECMA, by maintaining fourteen theaters, agreed to let Sily-Cinéma have access to their films. By allowing the foreign companies to maintain theaters in the country, Guinea also posed the condition that the profit from ticket sales be spent in the country. This historical move by Guinea, although not completely successful, is seen by film historians like Guy Hennebelle as an important gain in the decolonization of African cinema.[30]

In 1979, Upper Volta nationalized all six of its movie theaters, renewing the challenge Guinea had launched ten years before against the COMACICO and SECMA. The French companies reacted again by cutting the country's film supply for more than eight months.[31] As in the case with Guinea, a deal was finally arranged between Upper Volta and the two companies in which the COMACICO and SECMA kept their monopoly on distribution, and Upper Volta was allowed to keep the theaters (Vieyra, Hennebelle, and Bachy). The government subsequently created the Société Nationale Voltaïque du Cinéma (SONAVOCI) to manage the six theaters in favor of a national production.

Inspired by Upper Volta, Mali radicalized her action to take charge of distribution and exhibition. After 1962, the Office Cinématographique National du Mali (OCINAM) made plans to control the distribution and exhibition of foreign films and to produce and distribute national ones. Cautioned, however, by the way the COMACICO and SECMA had dealt with Guinea, Mali devised a less radical strategy that consisted of building theaters where there were none and progressively taking over those owned by the French companies. In 1970, after Upper Volta's coup, Mali put the OCINAM in charge of all twenty-four theaters, twelve of which were owned by the COMACICO and SECMA.[32]

It is important to notice that film occupied a primary position in these countries, unlike the secondary or marginal position it occupied in Francophone areas where the governments were reluctant to deal radically with the COMACICO and SECMA. The politics of production of the so-called radical countries went beyond attempts to nationalize distribution and exhibition to include plans to produce films on the spot. As early as 1960, Guinea had studios and laboratories in 16mm for the production of weekly newsreels. In 1966, West Germany offered to build in Konakry (the capital city) facilities in 35mm (see two notes above). Although the governments of Upper Volta and Mali had not yet acquired postproduction equipment, they had put aside funds to finance the production of national films.[33] The commitment of the government of Upper Volta to national and African cinema led the African filmmakers to choose one of the cities, Ouagadougou, as the site of a biannual African film festival. There is also in Ouagadougou the Institut Africain d'Education Cinématographique (INAFEC), the only institute of its kind where students from all over Africa were trained in film and television production. Among other facets of African cinema, Upper Volta is also the home of the CIDC, CIPROFILM, and the Société Africaine du Cinéma (CINAFRIC), the first private production and postproduction facility in Africa.

In order to give a better sense of the itinerary of production in the countries that did not hesitate to nationalize the industry of film, I will proceed in a different manner than I did with production in the so-called liberal countries. My reason for this different approach is determined by the fact that the history of production in Guinea is not similar to the one in Upper Volta in the same way that one can speak of the similarities of production between Senegal and Cameroon, Ivory Coast and Gabon, or Mali and Upper Volta. Therefore, while I can save the reader time by focusing on Upper Volta as a type representing Mali, I must deal with Guinea as a singular type.

The Guinean cinema began with the country's revolution against France in 1958.[34] According to Vieyra, the political courage of the Guinean leader, Sékou Touré, to break with France and set an example for other Francophone leaders who wanted to assume their own destiny led the country to have, in the early days of its independence, such national industries as a production center (Vieyra, p. 104). Unlike the other Francophone countries, which depended on the C.A.I. to make their newsreels, Guinea built, with the help of such Eastern Bloc countries as the Soviet Union, Yugoslavia, and Poland, facilities in 16mm black-and-white production. With these facilities in place, Guinea was able to produce one newsreel every week in the early 1960s (Vieyra, p. 105), while the other countries were going at the rate of one newsreel a month because of the time it took in Paris to develop and edit the film and add the soundtrack and/or commentary.[35]

Between 1960 and 1966, the Guinean production center also produced several short films documenting the revolution. Because the country did not yet have its own directors, such short films as *La révolution en marche* (16mm), *Au registre de l'histoire* (16mm), and *Croisìere de l'amitié* (16mm), were made by foreigners.

By 1966, important changes had taken place in the structure of Guinean cinema. The country now had more than six directors who took their training in the Soviet Union and the United States. The distribution and part of the exhibition were nationalized, and Sily-Cinéma was created with Bob Sow as head of the distribution and Mahamed Lamine Akin as head of production. It was also in 1966 that West Germany offered to build 35mm facilities. The future of Sily-Cinéma was guaranteed.

A look at films made by the Guineans between 1966 and 1970 will show that the majority of them were documentaries, educational films, and propaganda, as opposed to other countries where there were no structures of production and the filmmakers made mostly fiction films. Because the Guinean cinema was incorporated at its birth in the development of the country, film was assigned the function of disseminating the dominant hegemony of the government. Clearly, the Guinean filmmakers had little use for "fictional escapist" films. The documentary and education forms, to the contrary, were perfected by such Guinean directors as Costa Diagne (*Peau noire*, 1967, 16mm; *Huit et vingt*, 1967, 16mm; *Hier, aujourd'hui, demain*, 1968, 16mm), Mahamed Lamine Akin (*Le sergeant Bakary Woulen*, 1966, 35mm; *Mary Narken*, 1966, 35mm; *Dans la vie des peuples, il a des instants*, 1966, 16mm), Bary Sékou Omar (*Et vint la liberté*, 1966, 35mm), Gilbert Minot, Sékou Camara, and Moussa Kemoko Diakité. Diagne's film, *Hier, aujourd'hui, demain*, is narrated with masterful uses of ellipsis and allusion to the past, present, and future of Guinea. This led Guy Hennebelle to describe Diagne as "potentially one of the great African filmmakers of the future" (Hennebelle, p. 240). The film won the Joris Ivens prize in 1968 at the Leipzig festival.

In the early seventies, Diagne and Akin disappeared from the filmmaking scene,[36] but the documentary and educational tradition continued with newcomers like Minot and Diakité. Minot made *Le festival pan africain d'alger* (1968, 16mm) and several other shorts on presidential visits, political leaders (*Tolbert, General Gowon*, and *Amilcar Cabral*), environment, and sex education. Diakité made documentaries on agriculture (*Rizi-culture dans le bogate*, 1969), the funeral ceremonies of Kwame Nkrumah (1972), and education (*L'université à la campagne*, 1975). As Boughedir stated, Sily-Cinéma also produced several collective films in the seventies. There were theatrical plays on film (*La nuit s'illumine*, 1971; *El Hadj million*, 1972) that dealt with revolutionary subjects (Boughedir, p. 104). Finally, it is interesting to notice that Sily-Cinéma produced some didactic fictional films in the early seventies. Moussa Camara, who made *Ame perdu* in 1968, codirected *Un amour radical* (1972) and *Un grand père dans le vent* (1973) with Alpha Adama.

The second half of the seventies was also dominated by collective films. Individual directions included *Une autre vie* (1976) by Moussa Camara and documentaries on sports, *Hafia, Triple Champion* and *Le sport en Guinée* (1978), by Diakité.

Because of their didactic and nationalistic orientation, the productions of Sily-Cinéma of the sixties and the seventies were limited to Guinean theaters and to television, which was created in 1977. However, in the early eighties, Sily-Cinéma made international news through a coproduction with Morocco, *Amok* (1982), and a musical, *Naitou* (1982), directed by Diakité. *Amok* is a film on apartheid in South Africa and on the 1973 Soweto massacre. It is directed by Souhel Ben Barka (Morocco), and it stars Mariam Makeba, the famous singer from South Africa. Guinean technicians, using equipment from Sily-Cinéma, worked on the film. Dan Soko Camara, who assisted Ben Barka on *Amok,* directed *Ouloukoro* (1983). Diakité's *Naitou* is a musical about a young girl, Naitou, whose mother is assassinated by a jealous stepmother. The stepmother abuses Naitou and prevents her from taking part in the traditional initiation for all young girls. The stepmother is finally punished by an old lady who symbolizes justice. The film's originality lies in the fact that it is narrated through dance and music by the Ballet National de Guinée. Critics praised it for breaking language barriers in Africa (Boughedir, p. 74). *Naitou* won the UNESCO prize at the Ouagadougou festival in 1983.

Earlier in this survey, I said the Sily-Cinéma was part of the Guinean revolution and, as such, it was conceived as a national industry. As a state organism, Sily-Cinéma was supposed to be free from outside influence, as far as the means of production and the forces of production were concerned. I pointed out that in order to achieve this self-determination, Sily-Cinéma acquired facilities in 16mm, nationalized distribution and part of exhibition, and signed an agreement with West Germany to install 35mm facilities. It must now be pointed out that Sily-Cinéma failed in some respect. Despite the presence of the 16mm facilities, according to Minot, the rushes of Guinean production had to be sent out for laboratory work. Minot also pointed out that maintenance was lacking for the equipment.[37] It is also unfortunate that West Germany had not yet finished the installation of the 35mm equipment begun in 1966. Clearly, while this equipment was in storage rooms unused and growing rusty, Sily-Cinéma depended upon outside help for the 35mm production, too. The misuse of equipment is therefore a liability that may turn out too costly for Guinean cinema.

When one turns to Upper Volta, the other example of nationalized production, one notices at least two striking differences between its cinema and Sily-Cinéma. While Guinea nationalized distribution and part of exhibition and built production facilities, Upper Volta only nationalized the movie theaters and did not build production facilities, although such a plan was in the country's politics of national cinemas. The other difference between Sily-Cinéma and the SONAVOCI is that the former is completely owned by the state, while the state is a major shareholder and manager of SONAVOCI.[38] Thus, in Upper Volta there are independent filmmakers whose films the government produces or coproduces, while in Guinea, the emphasis is on collective cinema, or government films directed by the staff of Sily-Cinéma. As I pointed out earlier, in Upper Volta there is also a private production company, CINAFRIC, with equipment and studios in 16mm and 35mm, while in Guinea there is only the state organ of production. As for the nationalized Malian cinema, I believe that while it shares some common ground with the Guinean politics of production, it has more similarities with the cinema in Upper Volta.

When Upper Volta became independent in 1960, the new government planned to build both a television station and 16mm facilities in order to produce short didactic and educational films. In 1961, the ministry of information built studios that were supposed to become montage and sound-synchronizing rooms. However, because the C.A.I. was preparing in 1962 to sign a contract with most Francophone countries in order to handle part of the production and the postproduction of their newsreels and documentaries (Vieyra, p. 115 and Bachy, p. 19), Upper Volta did not get the necessary cooperation from France, which must have seen a duplication of the facilities of the C.A.I. in the construction of studios in Upper Volta. According to Vieyra, the project was thus abandoned at midpoint, leaving behind the acquired equipment to stagnate (Vieyra, p. 115). In 1963, however, France helped Upper Volta build a television station "which only works three hours a day, four days a week, airing programs provided by France. Only the news events are filmed in Upper Volta" (Bachy, p. 8).

Unlike Senegal and Ivory Coast, where national directors, trained in the late fifties and early sixties, took over the Service de Cinéma at independence, in Upper Volta there was no one trained to assume this duty. A French director, Serge Ricci, dominated the national production of newsreels, documentaries, and educational films from 1960 to the early 1970s. Working with a 16mm camera, Ricci made medium-length films on the independence movement (*Fiere volta de nos aieux,* 1961), economics (*Espoir d'une nation,* 1961; *Operation arachides,* 1962; and *Culture atelee et fertilisation,* 1964); health education (*Les grands marigots mangent les yeux,* 1964; *Comment nourrir mon enfant,* 1966), and from 1971 to 1972 three films on geography (Bachy, p. 22).

The first national filmmaker is Sékou Ouedraogo, who began as Ricci's cinematographer for a health education film, *L'usage du savon* (1967). In 1969 and 1970, Ouedraogo made two films documenting the regional fairs, *Foire regionales Voltaïques.* The most important event in the history of the development of the Voltaic cinema, however, was the nationalization of the theaters in 1970 and the creation of the SONAVOCI. In the beginning, the SONAVOCI was only an organization in charge of exhibition (Vieyra, p. 116). Nonetheless, its creation signaled a historic break between African cinema and the two French monopolist companies, COMACICO and SECMA, and the beginning of national politics of production subsidized by revenues from distribution and exhibition, a politics which had been proposed by the Federation of African Filmmakers. As the Voltaic minister of information saw it, the effect of the SONAVOCI went beyond the country and pushed other countries to admire Upper Volta and to reflect upon the future of their own cinema (quoted by Bachy, p. 14).

Within one year of the creation of the SONAVOCI, a Fonds de Développement du Cinéma Voltaïque was set up to promote national production. Such an initiative was encouraged by the financial success generated by the nationalization of the theaters. According to the minister, Upper Volta recorded "from the start, financial results which are very satisfactory. Aside from the fact that we control the revenues from the distribution market, we have created a Fonds de Développement du Cinéma Voltaïque which is completely subsidized by this market" (Bachy, p. 12).

Although the SONAVOCI did not invest right away in equipment, it financed the production of several shorts and feature-length films. In addition to financing the didactic films directed by Ricci between 1971 and 1973, in 1972 the Fonds du Développement du Cinéma Voltaïque financed *Le sang des parias,* which stands in history as the first national feature film directed by Djim Mamadou Kola. The period of the 1970s was also the time for the emergence of new Voltaic directors. In 1973, a health education film, *Histoire de la tuberculose,* was made by Hilaire Tiendrebeogo, rather than by Ricci, who had until then been the only director of such films for the government. In 1975, Augustin R. T. Taoko produced and directed the second feature film from Upper Volta, *M'Ba Raogo,* on the abuses of tradition (Bachy, p. 72). Other new directors included Réné-Bernard Yonly, whose feature, *Sur le chemin de la réconciliation* (1976), was produced by the government; Gaston Kaboré, Paul Zoumbara, Sanou Kollo, and Idrissa Ouedraogo.

In 1977, because of the increasing number of directors and the funds provided by SONAVOCI, Upper Volta created the Centre National du Cinéma (CNC) and set Gaston Kaboré at its head. According to Bachy, the function of the CNC was to continue the "production of 16mm educational and didactic films and the exhibition, with the means of cinema-on-wheels, of these films in the rural areas" (Bachy, p. 24). In addition to these duties, the CNC was to promote national cinema by aiding the production of short and feature films and documentaries. The CNC produced such short films as *Poko* (1978) by Idrissa Ouedraogo, *Yikyan* (1978) by Hamidou B. Ouedraogo, a Voltaic filmmaker living in Cannes (France), and *Beogho Naba* (1979) and *Les Dodos* (1980) by Kollo. Kaboré himself assumed the principal role of government filmmaker, which, as I pointed out earlier, had been taken by Ricci. Since its creation, the CNC has also produced two features, *Wend Kuuni* (35mm, 1982) by Kaboré and *Les Jours de tourments* (16mm, 1983) by Zoumbara. *Wend Kuuni* is set in precolonial Africa and deals with such issues as marriage and the concept of family, sex, and love. The manner in which the definition of these issues (themes) changes in the evolution of the narrative deconstructs the stereotypical view of precolonial Africa as a stagnating place or a primitive paradise of "y'en a bon banania." The film is internationally praised for its sensible treatment of children and for its cinematography (its use of long shots and long takes), editing style, and narrative use of the soundtrack.

Early in this survey of the politics of production in Upper Volta, I said that the government tried to build facilities of production but did not succeed. Even after the creation of the SONAVOCI, no state production facilities were put in place. The SONAVOCI, like the SNC in Senegal, depended upon French facilities for the production of the films it financed. It was only in 1981 that this pattern changed. A private businessman, Martial Ouedraogo, invested more than $300,000 in equipment (16mm and 35mm cameras, laboratories, editing tables, soundtrack facilities, props, etc.) and created the Société Africaine de Cinéma (CINAFRIC) (Bachy, pp. 61–69).[39] Although CINAFRIC was a private venture conceived to make a profit, Martial Ouedraogo's intention was to participate in the liberation of African cinema. In Upper Volta, the CNC could rent the equipment and technicians of

CINAFRIC and thus produce less expensive films on the spot. The same thing would be true for other African productions and foreigners filming in Africa. It was in this sense that Moustapha Ky, the administrative director of CINAFRIC, argued that "CINAFRIC is a business for the Voltaics and also for Africans since its benefits reach beyond national confines" (Bachy, p. 10). CINAFRIC is the only society of its kind in Africa; although some film critics called it the "Hollywood on the Volta," it is also clear that its goals of liberating African film from its technological dependence on the West coincide with the goals of African filmmakers and some governments.

According to Ky, the purpose of CINAFRIC was "first to produce films of all genres and lengths. It also collaborates with individuals and organizations to coproduce films. Finally, it rents equipment and studio space to people filming in Africa" (Bachy, p. 10). Since it opened its doors in 1981, CINAFRIC has produced two features, *Paweogo* (16mm, 1981) by Kollo and *Le courage des autres* (16mm, 1982) by Christian Richard, a French professor of film at the Institut Africain d'Education Cinématographique (Bachy, pp. 10–11). CINAFRIC had several projects in 1983, some of which included the signing of a contract with such African directors as Sembène to make a film for the company.[40] It is curious that French facilities were used in the early eighties to finish such CNC films as *Wend Kuuni* and *Jours de tourments*. CINAFRIC was available and its facilities could have been used to reduce the cost of production of these films.

A Critique of National Cinemas

However, before expounding on the contribution to inter-African cinema by CINAFRIC and other Ouagadougou-based institutes and organisms such as the INAFEC, CIPROFILM, and the FEPACI, it is important to evaluate the national productions just surveyed. The evaluation of some of the problems connected with national cinemas will make it clear that their solution can be found in international cinema. There are four main problems with the national production centers. First, in countries where the production facilities are lacking, the films require a considerable expenditure of governmental funds that should be spent on other priorities. Second, because distribution and exhibition are not organized in most countries, the governments and/or independents must assume all the expenses of production. Third, in countries with facilities of production, the equipment is not maintained in good condition or utilized at full capacity. Sometimes the project to build facilities is never completed and the equipment rusts. The fourth problem is that the government attempts to control the content of films, thus restricting the filmmaker's creativity. Clearly, the lack of production facilities is a serious problem concerning many areas of development in Africa. Its immediate consequence is to make Africa dependent on the technologically advanced countries. The cost of this dependency is so high that some developing countries have become selective about what is necessary to their survival and what is a secondary priority or luxury. Thus, instead of questioning dependency and planning systematically to rid themselves of it, they have normalized and/or fetishized it. It is in this vein that several Francophone countries considered film a luxury that they could not afford. In these countries, production is limited to newsreels and educational documentaries made for them by the C.A.I. on a contractual basis or by UNESCO and the like as a form of aid.

Even in those countries in which the filmmakers make it impossible for the governments to completely turn their backs on national cinema, the results are not encouraging. Both Senegal and Ivory Coast closed down their national production centers because they absorbed government budgets without being able to recoup their production costs. Aside from the fact that these national production centers depended on the C.A.I. and the Coopération to complete their films, they were not attentive to other means of production that could have significantly reduced the cost. Unfortunately, both Vieyra and Bassori, two important figures in Senegalese and Ivorian cinema, produced with 35mm facilities as soon as they had replaced the French directors. It is therefore fair to say that both the filmmakers and their governments failed to ground their politics of national production in an economically viable plan. While the filmmakers made the governments face their responsibilities to help national productions, they did not question the tools inherited from the C.A.I. for their high costs. As for the governments, they chose to remain blind to several factors that could have been beneficial in the long run. Because they depended on France in several areas of development, they continued to tie their film production to the C.A.I. They blamed African directors for making high-budget films that were not profitable. But, in Bachy's words,

> Can one really speak of the profitability of national film in a country where nothing is done to protect them? Where no legal disposition is taken to impose quotas on the import of foreign films? Where the exhibition of national films is only possible in one third of the theaters? Where there isn't an organization to sell them outside of the country?[41]

This leads to the problems of distribution and exhibition in Africa. It is important to point out that they should not be separated from the issues of national production. If well conceived, the distribution and exhibition of both foreign and national films can significantly contribute to production. By setting quotas on the number of foreign films that can be shown, the theater owners create additional space for national films. By using a percentage of tax revenues from distribution and exhibition to help produce films, the chances of production can be increased and the cost made less burdensome to the governments.

In order to encourage national production, a few countries have dealt, in one way or another, with these issues. Without nationalizing its theaters, Cameroon helps production by putting a certain percentage of the taxes on ticket sales in the funds of the FODIC, which subsidizes production. Ivory Coast encourages independent production by exempting national filmmakers from production and exhibition taxes. The SONAVOCI in Upper Volta and the OCINAM in Mali are national organizations that own theaters. The productions of the CNC in Upper Volta and the Centre National de Production Cinématographique (CNPC) in Mali are subsidized by a percentage from the revenues of the SONAVOCI and OCINAM.[42] In Guinea, Sily-Cinéma controls production, distribution, and part of the exhibition. The Guinean politics of production is spelled out by Minot, who states:

> From all the movies shown in a given country a certain percentage should go toward promoting production. The money that is collected will then be available for different filmmakers who have produced screenplays to produce their films. We're doing [this] in Guinea, but that is also because we control the production, the distribution, and most of the movie theaters. The government controls the national film enterprise [which] is responsible for importing all the films which are shown in Guinea. (Minot, p. 42)

When one turns now to look at the new production facilities that exist in Francophone Africa, the following facts become obvious: they still require foreign assistance because they are either incomplete or they don't have all the trained personnel necessary to run them. The equipment is often underutilized and not well maintained. They often duplicate equipment in 16mm and 35mm instead of specializing in one format and thoroughly exploiting its economic and aesthetic potentials.

The argument that the so-called autonomous production facilities are incomplete is true wherever one looks in Africa. In Guinea, the installation of 35mm facilities, begun in 1966 by the West Germans, is not yet in full service. Despite the resources of the television and the ministries in Ivory Coast, the 16mm facilities of Sily-Cinéma in Guinea, and the INAFEC in Upper Volta, "The situation right now in practically all African states . . . is that when you shoot your film, you have to send it to a European laboratory to have it processed" (Minot, p. 42). Despite the presence of the facilities, African films are also taken to Europe for editing and for the soundtrack. M'Bala from Ivory Coast argued that although he could have finished *Ablakon* in the country, he chose to mount the sound and edit the film in Europe because it was more convenient.[43] As I pointed out earlier, in Upper Volta the films of the CNC also were finished in France, not at the CINAFRIC's supposedly complete facilities.

I can make two types of inferences here: the facilities in Africa are either inadequate to work with, or the filmmakers and producers don't want to use them for reasons I don't understand at this moment. Meanwhile, the equipment deteriorates because it is not being fully used or properly maintained. As Minot concludes, "Getting it into top technical condition is difficult because of the weather conditions, humidity, heat, and so on. So when you have technical problems with your equipment it can be disastrous because then you have to send it back to be repaired" (Minot, p. 41).

Another problem with the so-called autonomous facilities is their failure to focus on one type of equipment and production. Unlike Hollywood, which privileged studio production over all others, and the different schools in France, which either specialized in 35mm production and never used 16mm, or vice-versa,[44] production companies in Africa, whether governmental or private, indiscriminately acquire equipment and facilities in all formats. Besides lacking character, this approach to production is wasteful. The equipment is duplicated and the technologically advanced countries that make them are increasingly required to repair the cameras or to render other services that are only available from them.

These countries could avoid duplicating equipment and thus economize on the cost of production. In Ivory Coast, for example, where television and several branches of the government own facilities, the government could regroup the equipment and qualified personnel in one or two places of production. If the government decided on two locations instead of one, the first one could consist of 16mm facilities that specialize in documentaries, educational, and research-oriented films. As has been shown in this study, the 16mm is also adequate for fictional films. In this case, the government must realize that the cost of producing 35mm films cannot be recouped on a national level alone.

No matter how successful the film might be, it must be distributed internationally in order to stand any chance of recouping its cost. The difficulties of recouping the cost of production with 35mm are clearly a good reason for these countries to work with the 16mm until they are able to fully develop inter-African productions. Thus, for Sily-Cinéma, it would have been better to deal with West Germany on improving the condition of the 16mm facilities and training Guinean technicians than to attempt to set up 35mm facilities.

Another way to avoid duplication of equipment is to allow CINAFRIC to play the role that the C.A.I. played in producing newsreels and documentaries. It was the C.A.I.'s merit to have proven that one production center could serve the film needs of all the Francophone countries. An African production facility such as CINAFRIC can serve the same function. What is more, it can do it without the neocolonial reasons that determined the C.A.I.'s actions, and it can do it cheaper because of the African setting. While the C.A.I. emphasized neocolonial dependencies vis-à-vis its African customers, organizations such as CINAFRIC will emphasize Africa's independence from France. The prospects of inter-African cinema will be discussed below in the section on CIPROFILM.

The final problem with the national production centers is their repression of counterhegemonic views or alternative hegemonies in the films they produce or coproduce. I have already mentioned that in Senegal the government used its right as producer to cut out parts it didn't like in *Xala* and *Njangaan*. In other countries, the governments, as producers, determine the content of the films. In Ivory Coast, the films (*Abusan, Amenie, Les collégiennes, L'herbe sauvage,* and *Djeli,* etc.) work with the government to combat migration from the village to the city, illiteracy, corruption, and the caste system. Before *Djeli,* the Ivorian cinema was criticized for being apolitical, that is, for not challenging the status quo.[45] In Upper Volta, the films are either set in the distant and safe past *(Wend Kuuni)* or else they concern nationalism *(Sur le chemin de la réconciliation).* As I have mentioned above, Sily-Cinéma only produced propaganda and documentaries about the progress of the Guinean revolution.

The criticism here is not against the government's attempt to make film participate in the development. On the contrary, a conception of film as a tool of development is revolutionary and praiseworthy. What is being criticized here is the governments' self-serving approach to the use of film. Because they repress opposing views, the filmmakers must always say the same things about the presidents, tradition and modernity, etc. If the filmmakers depict these subjects in a different manner, then they either go to jail, as Cissé did after his controversial film, *Den muso* (1978), or else the films are censored like many of Sembène's films in Senegal. The extreme case of repression is found in Guinea where the government did not even allow independent cinema to exist side by side with Sily-Cinéma.

Even though the governments have no experience in filmmaking, they must realize that directors are not mindless people who simply arrange convenient things in front of the camera. The African countries gain a better insight of themselves by considering the contribution of such talented directors as Sembène and Cissé as constructive criticism, instead of as antigovernment products. The governments should realize that it is easier to appropriate an opposing view and control its overflow than to repress it. They can take a lesson from France, which bought and distributed all the anticolonialist films of Sembène instead of trying to stop them. Recently, Mali also demonstrated the advantages of appropriating artists and their work. The government shocked many people by helping Cissé in the production and exhibition of *Baara* and *Finye,* two films on African trade unions and on the weakness of military regimes. As a result, the military regime in Mali is seen as respecting the freedom of expression.

To turn now to inter-African cinema, it is easy to see in it the answers to some of the problems posed by national facilities. The problem of depending on the postproduction facilities of Paris will be solved once the African countries of one cultural region, or the whole continent, regroup the main facilities of production in one country. Instead of being facilities that create needs for Africans in order to make them depend on European technology, the inter-African facility will emphasize an "inter-dependence"[46] of the countries upon one another. Such a strategy, besides reducing the cost of production, will also prevent the wasteful duplication of equipment. By regrouping the filmmakers and other technicians to work in one place, the strategy will provide them with the opportunity to exchange views and to formulate aesthetics that might characterize an African film school. The governments also will use the facilities for coproducing among themselves.

The idea of a regional or inter-African production, distribution, and exhibition is not new. As the chapter on the FEPACI shows, the filmmakers have been fighting since the early sixties for a unified and liberated African cinema. As recently as 1982 Le Collectif L'Oeil Vert, which is a radical faction of the FEPACI, declared that African directors were tired of depending on, and of being patronized by, the French and they "wanted to make coproduction on the African level and to put their strength together in order to have facilities of production."[47]

Although distribution and exhibition will be discussed in another chapter, it is important to point out that the CIDC, which took over the distribution of film in Francophone Africa after 1979, concluded in one of its studies that inter-African cinema is necessary because, considering the revenues from ticket sales, no individual country among the group is capable of sustaining a film industry.[48] In another study, the seminarians of the CIDC concluded:

> There cannot be a viable African cinema on the national level alone. There can only be on the regional and inter-African level. Therefore, any effort to organize and develop film on a national level must be done by counting on the help of a regional and inter-African cooperation and solidarity. Film industry, too, must be incorporated in the politics and the sets of economic development which are already in place regionally and internationally.[49]

The idea that an inter-African cinema is not new can also be seen through the efforts of the FESPACO and the INAFEC. Created after 1969, the Festival Panafricain du Cinéma à Ouagadougou (FESPACO) had as its purpose to contribute to the development of African cinema. Convinced that film constituted a cultural as well as a developmental tool, the government of Upper Volta created the FESPACO in order to facilitate the distribution of all African production and to raise the consciousness of people toward the issues and problems of African film.[50] The first year of the FESPACO only included films from the region (Mali, Senegal, Ivory Coast, Niger, Upper Volta). Since 1969, however, the FESPACO has become bigger and bigger. Today, with the Journées Cinématographique de Carthages (J.C.C.), it represents the most important occasions for African directors to screen their films. The success of the FESPACO has also inspired the creation of the third continental film festival, the Mogadiscio Pan-African Film Symposium (MOGPAFIS).

The Institut Africain d'Education Cinématographique (INAFEC) is another effort on regionalization and internationalization of African film. Created in 1976 in Ouagadougou with the help of UNESCO and the French Ministry of Coopération, INAFEC is a film and television school that trains African students to become film critics and journalists, sound engineers, electricians, camera operators, and editors.

The trend toward regionalization and internationalization of film, begun by the formation of the FEPACI, the creation of festivals, film institutes, and distribution, led to the creation in 1979 of the Consortium Interafricain de Production de Film (CIPROFILM). Based in Ouagadougou, CIPROFILM intends to produce educational and commercial films for the member countries of the distribution company,

CIDC. CIPROFILM will be funded primarily with revenues from the distribution of CIDC films and will become self-supporting. Plans include building production and postproduction facilities in 16mm and 35mm.[51]

However, unlike CINAFRIC, CIPROFILM has not yet built its facilities, and no film has been produced. The delay in the CIPROFILM project may be due to several factors. CIDC does not yet fully control the distribution market in Francophone Africa. It is also difficult for the countries in the region to break with France, on whom they have depended as long as they can remember. Finally, CIPROFILM's equipment will duplicate that of CINAFRIC and thus create competition in the same city. Ideally, CINAFRIC and CIPROFILM should work together. According to Bachy, there is an agreement between the two to divide the responsibilities. Since CINAFRIC has everything but film-processing laboratories, CIPROFILM will build these facilities (Bachy, p. 68).

There is no doubt that Francophone African cinema has come a long way. It has made progress in acquiring more equipment and in becoming less dependent upon France. There are more and more African names in the credits of African films as cinematographers, sound-pickers, editors, and producers. There are coproductions and plans being made for regional productions. Most countries now have production politics that cover distribution and exhibition and encourage national production. More importantly, young directors such as the group around Le Collectif L'Oeil Vert are inventorying the equipment of production in Africa in order to emphasize interdependence among Africans and to deemphasize dependence upon France. It is therefore possible to close this chapter with optimism. Ouagadougou is going to replace Paris as the center of production and postproduction of African film.

Ousmane Sembène (left) and Idrissa Ouedraogo (right). Photograph courtesy of Christine Delorme.

Moussa Kemoko Diakité.
Photograph courtesy of
Christine Delorme.

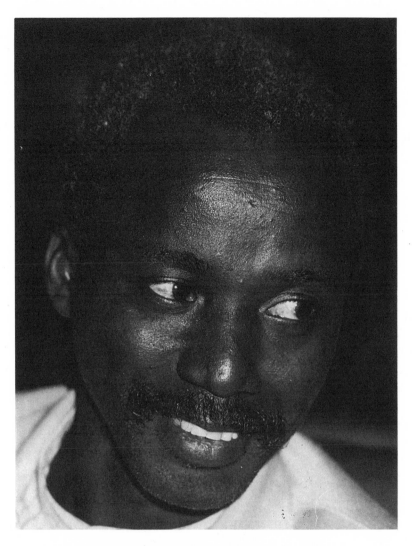
Souleymane Cissé. Photograph courtesy of Christine Delorme.

Gaston Kaboré. Photograph courtesy of Pamela Gentile.

Oumarou Ganda (right) in *L'exile* (1981). Photograph courtesy of Férid Boughedir.

Cheick Oumar Sissoko.
Photograph courtesy of
Pamela Gentile.

Left to right: Gaston Kaboré, Med Hondo, and Cheick Oumar Sissoko.
Photograph courtesy of Pamela Gentile.

VI.

Film Production in Lusophone Africa

Toward the Kuxa Kenema in Mozambique

My purpose in this chapter is to shed light on the progress of film production in Lusophone Africa. I will show that the background of national cinema in Angola, Guinea-Bissau, and Mozambique is in the documentaries and revolutionary films made for the liberation movements by such foreign directors as the Yugoslav Dragutin Popovic, the Guadeloupean Sarah Maldoror, and the African-American Robert Van Lierop. The rest of the chapter will be devoted to Mozambican cinema, not only because it is the most important in the area, but also because it embodies the experiences of such international directors as Ruy Guerra, Jean Rouch, and Jean-Luc Godard.

Unlike the British and the Belgians who set up facilities in the colonies to produce colonial films and to train their subjects to make such films,[1] the Portuguese limited production to monthly newsreels made for colonialist propaganda and pornographic films produced in the colonies by Portugal and South Africa.[2] They set up a limited infrastructure of production for the purpose of shooting the newsreels and the pornographic film, which they sent to Madrid or Johannesburg for the postproduction.[3] They were not interested in African cultures except to show their inferiority to European cultures. At the end of Portuguese colonialism, there were no production facilities or technicians that the independent states could inherit. Everything had to be built from scratch. To put it in Pedro Pimente's words, "In terms of production, we started from nothing. Not one Mozambican filmmaker

existed in 1975. We started training people and getting technology"
(Taylor, p. 30).

The films about such liberation movements as the P.A.I.G. in
Guinea-Bissau, the M.P.L.A. in Angola, and the FRELIMO in Mozambique are the first films in which the Lusophone Africans selected the
image, the ideology of the film's discourse, and the audience for whom
films were made. Although the filmmakers were foreigners, the films
were used as weapons against the oppressor. To use a terminology from
Solanas and Gettino in their theory and practice of Third Cinema, it
was with these "guerrilla" films[4] that Lusophone Africans first realized
the importance of cinema. Prior to these films, productions were objects of colonial representation.

The films were used in several ways by the liberation movements. The
documentaries exposed to the outside world the atrocities committed
by Portugal on the African people. They served a diplomatic purpose
by informing people "about what was going on" (Taylor, p. 30) and by
arguing for the right of African people to self-determination. In the
early days of its formation the FRELIMO, for example, invited filmmakers from Europe and the United States to film the revolution.
Vinceremos (1965), by the Yugoslav Dragutin Popovic, and *Viva
FRELIMO* (1969), by a team from Holland, are short documentaries
made clandestinely on the battlefront to show the progress of the
liberation struggle. *Viva FRELIMO* contains an interview with
Samora Machel, then leader of the movement and now former president of Mozambique. In Guinea-Bissau, the P.A.I.G. invited filmmakers from France, Italy, England, Cuba, Sweden, and Holland. In
1968, the British journalist Basil Davidson made a short documentary,
Terrorists Attack, on the Portuguese invasion of the headquarters of the
Freedom Fighters. In 1970, a French group made *No Pinch,* a 70mn
documentary on the people of Guinea-Bissau and their overwhelming
support of the P.A.I.G. program. Similar films were made in Angola in
the M.P.L.A.'s liberation struggle.

The films also served an instructional purpose. In this regard, the
liberation movements used films as a school to teach people about the
significance of the revolution and education and about the victories of
the liberation front. As stated above, the films contained interviews
with leaders who, aside from addressing the outside world, spoke to
their own people about rights, such as education, which were denied to
them by Portuguese colonialism and which the revolution provided
them. Before independence in Mozambique, when the FRELIMO had
its headquarters in Tanzania, a French group, Cinéthique, was asked to
explain "in a didactic manner the teaching methods of a FRELIMO

school in Tanzania" (Bachy, p. 41). The same year, a Swedish team, Lennart Malmer and Ingelo Romare, made *Dans notre Pays, les balles commencent à fleurir,* filmmakers from People's Republic of China made *Le peuple du Mozambique avance,* and African-American Robert Van Lierop directed *A luta continua,* all of which are short films in support of the revolution. Lierop described his films as a "media-treatment" of the liberation struggle which showed to the Mozambicans "how people in other parts of the country or in other parts of the world who have similar problems are dealing with those problems so that they can use those as models to try to change their lives."[5] Lierop's description of the function of his film is reminiscent of Solanas and Gettino's description of the effect of Third Cinema on people. They stated that this cinema created "with each showing, as in revolutionary military incursion, a liberated space, a decolonized territory. The showing can be turned into a kind of political event, which, according to Fanon, could be 'a liturgical act, a privileged occasion for human beings to hear and to be heard.' "[6]

Finally, the films served a cultural and entertainment purpose. To achieve this effect, the filmmakers had to transcend the documentary form, the mere recording and arranging of facts to be exposed. They had to make interventions that manipulated the events in order to achieve a greater aesthetic effect on the audiences. For example, the portion of the film spent telling the story of heroic moments was longer and more beautiful than usual in order to allow the viewer time for identification. The content of such heroic moments also included heroes/heroines and value systems that were supposed to have lasting effects. Sarah Maldoror did exactly this in her first feature, *Sambizanga* (1972). Based on the struggle of the M.P.L.A. in Angola, the film depicts a woman coming to a revolutionary consciousness. It also creates super-heroes who sacrifice their own lives for the liberation struggle. The aesthetic intention of the filmmaker was to create a positive role for women in the revolution and to essentialize the liberation struggle as the most important element in people's lives. *Sambizanga* has been criticized for being "too beautiful" and therefore less authentic to African realities.[7] Apparently, such criticism, while it is faithful to the constraints of socialist realism, remains blind to the need of the filmmaker to create idealized role models who are necessary for the new revolutionary state. Before *Sambizanga,* Maldoror made a short film on the liberation movement in Angola, *Monangambe* (1970), with the intent to teach and entertain. The film is about the visit of an Angolan woman to her husband, who has been jailed by the

Portuguese colonial authorities. The theme is emergent revolutionary Angolan culture, the sign system of which is different from that of the oppressor's culture.

Even before independence, film played an important role in the lives of Lusophone Africans. Unlike other African countries where film production was controlled by the colonial master, in the Portuguese colonies the guerilla movements were involved in the production of films, which they used as tools of liberation. Despite their limited resources, it was because they were aware of film as a potential tool of work and entertainment that the Lusophone countries in general and Mozambique in particular, soon after their independence in 1975, continued to use it as one of the key areas for development.

During its first year of independence, Angola produced several films on history, culture, and work. The filmmakers were from France and Brazil, but there were also some Angolans who received their training by assisting foreign filmmakers during the liberation struggle. They were Abrantes Menas, Antonio Ole, Luandino Vieira, a novelist and poet whose works were adapted by Maldoror (*Monangambe* and *Sambizanga*), and Ruy Duarte de Carvalho, who was born in Portugal but decided for Angolan citizenship. The films made in 1975 included *Angola, guerre du peuple,* a short film on the struggle of the M.P.L.A. by French director Bruno Muel, and *Geracao 50,* a documentary by de Carvalho on three Angolan poets (Agostino Neto, Angonio Jacinto, and Viriato da Cruz). But the most ambitious film project of that year was *Sou angolano trabalho come farca,* a series of eleven documentaries on workers. The films were made by Angolan directors (Ole, de Carvalho, et al.) with the help of Muel and the Collective Unicité from France.[8]

The Angolans also acquired television in 1975. However, they did not create facilities for film production. They continued to rely on European facilities as in the time of the liberation struggle. Unfortunately, Angolan production decreased after 1975, perhaps partly because filmmaking was only a secondary occupation of some Angolans who were trained during the revolution and partly because of the lack of production facilities. Now that Angola was independent, there was also the economic problem of recouping the cost of production of the films. In this regard, the country needed to nationalize distribution and exhibition, a task which so far has eluded many countries in the Third World where American, Indian, and Kung Fu films dominate the screens. In order to alleviate the problem, Angola joined Mozambique and other revolutionary countries in Africa in

1977 to create the Association Africaine de Coopération Cinématographique (AACC). Their purpose was to stop the foreign monopoly on distribution and exhibition by nationalizing the movie industry
and creating an inter-African distribution company that would use
films from African and other revolutionary countries. However, according to Pierre Haffner, AACC plans have not yet gone into effect.[9]
Meanwhile, in Angola, only two directors, Ole and de Carvalho, have
been working consistently. As filmmaker laureate of Angola, de Carvalho makes most of the documentaries needed by the country. In
1979–81 alone he directed *Presentz angolans/tempt mumuila,* which
included a series of ten films.[10] As for Ole, his important works include
Learn in Order to Serve Better (1976), *The Rhythm of N'Gola Ritmos*
(1977), *Pathways to the Stars* (1980), and *Mayombe,* which is un-
finished and co-directed with Guerra in Mozambique.

Guinea-Bissau had no significant postindependence production that
can be discussed in this study. In his book, *Le cinéma africain: Des
origines à 1973,* Paulin Vieyra mentioned some filmmakers for Guinea-
Bissau who were getting their training in the Soviet Union, Cuba, and
Senegal (see p. 114). Since independence, however, these filmmakers
must have turned to other activities. A dictionary established by Victor
Bachy on African filmmakers and their films did not include anyone
from Guinea-Bissau (Bachy, pp. 186–210).

In 1989, Flora Gomes entered history as the first director from
Guinea-Bissau. His feature film *Montu Nega* won several awards at
FESPACO. (See Chapter 10 on the place of *Montu Nega* in African
film.)

The extent to which postindependence film production slowed down
in all Lusophone countries except Mozambique, in spite of the
awareness in these countries of the persuasive potentials of film, may
also be blamed on the lack of leadership and politics of production. For
example, unlike Angola and Guinea-Bissau, Mozambique is especially
lucky to have at the head of the National Film Institute Ruy Guerra,
who was also a chef-de-file in the Brazilian Cinema Novo. As for the
politics of production, the Mozambicans also called upon such masters
as Rouch and Godard to research together which image, which production equipment, which producer would be right for a young country like Mozambique. This is not, however, to imply that everything
went smoothly for the Mozambicans, once they had brought together a
giant from Cinéma Vérité, one from the New Wave, and one from
Cinema Novo. In fact, there were conflicts and frustrations on the part
of filmmakers. However, the Mozambican film industry gained by the
presence of these three filmmakers.

The Clash between Guerra, Rouch, and Godard in Mozambique

Although at one point they coordinated their efforts, Guerra, Rouch, and Godard were in Mozambique for different reasons. Guerra was at the National Film Institute, Rouch was working on a Super 8 project with the department of communications at the University of Mozambique, and Godard and the French television production Sonimage had a two-year contract to study on video the television needs of the country before the arrival of television. Although Guerra and Rouch later disagreed on such issues as the way students were to be trained, the definition of mise-en-scène, the format of the equipment, and the intentions of the filmmaker, and although Rouch was forced to leave Mozambique because of these disagreements, it must be pointed out that both Rouch and Godard were invited to Mozambique by the government with the guidance of Guerra and the National Film Institute. As it will become clear with the history of each of the three projects and the evaluation that will follow, no matter what complications took place by bringing together filmmakers who were radically different in their conception of production, Mozambican cinema has become richer. Some critics compare it to Cuban cinema, while others simply see it as unique in Africa (Crowdus and Gupta, p. 29; Taylor, p. 30; Bachy, pp. 42–43).

The National Film Institute was created in November 1975, five months after Mozambique became independent. The speed with which the Institute was created shows that it was among Mozambique's top priorities. To put it in Pimente's words,

> . . . it was clear to our leaders that cinema could be very important for the new nation's development. That's why some months after Independence and in a moment when Mozambique was facing very difficult problems—for example, all the Portuguese were fleeing the country and for twelve million people there were only forty doctors—the government decided to found a film institute, just after it started a literacy campaign. (Taylor, p. 30)

In the beginning there were two reasons for creating the National Film Institute: "the decolonization of film distribution" and the production of national films and their distribution in Mozambique and outside the country (Taylor, p. 30). In the area of film distribution, the new leaders of Mozambique were concerned about the quality of films they received from America, Italy, Hong Kong, and India. These films, besides being a negative influence on the people, were also used to undermine the Mozambican economy. It was in this sense that Pimente argued that the distribution companies based in "Mozambique and South Africa used film to export currency in a classic situation of economic dependency" (Taylor, p. 30). The first priority of the Film Institute was to nationalize distribution, not only so that "the films distributed in Mozambique were in accord with political, cultural and human values" (Taylor, p. 30) of the country but also so that the revenues could be used to produce national films and to build new exhibition facilities in rural areas.[11]

In terms of production, in 1975 Mozambique had neither film-makers nor production facilities. The film need of the country was therefore filled by foreign directors like Robert Van Lierop from the United States and Fernando Silva, Celso Lucas, and Jose Celso-Correa from Brazil. There were also Cuban and leftist filmmakers from Europe. Silva made a documentary depicting the history of the struggle leading to independence, *Un año de independencia* (1975). In 1976, he directed *Mapi* on the attack of such Mozambican villages as Mapai by the Rhodesian army of Ian Smith. The film explains that the terrorist attacks were motivated by the support given by Mozambique to the liberation of Zimbabwe. In 1977, Lucas and Correa directed a 150mn documentary entitled *25,* on "all the stages of the liberation struggle led by FRELIMO from June 25, 1962, when the movement was founded, to June 25, 1964, the date of the first clash with the colonial regime, to April 25, 1974, when the colonial regime was defeated" (Hennebelle, p. 173). When the film was premiered in the United States, Lierop raised over $48,000, which he sent to Mozambique for the construction of a hospital (Crowdus and Gupta, p. 26).

While foreign directors were making the first films for Mozambique, the Film Institute was trying to acquire its own production facilities and to take the necessary steps so that Mozambican directors could replace foreigners. With the help of such foreign directors as Lierop and Haile Gerima, the Film Institute distributed its films to American universities and organizations in order to raise funds and buy equipment in 16mm and 35mm. The Institute also benefited from donations of equipment by friendly countries and institutions. By 1978 it had reached its goal of making films with Mozambican facilities of production. As Pimente put it, "Since 1978, we have had the basic technical facilities to pro-duce, in black and white, 16mm and 35mm films" (Taylor, p. 30). The Film Institute also succeeded in putting together a Mozambican team of filmmakers. Some were trained on the spot, like Camille de Sousa, Luis Simoa, and Goao Costa. Others, like Pimente, got their training in

Cuba and Paris, while still others, like Guerra, were veteran filmmakers who returned after years of exile.[12]

In 1978, Guerra became director of the Film Institute. Now that there was equipment, a seminationalized distribution that generated some revenues, and a qualified personnel, the Film Institute began the production of a monthly series called Kuxa Kenema, or "Birth of the Image."[13] According to Bachy, these series were different from the newsreels of the colonial era because "they analyzed, each, one subject in depth, instead of covering superficially several topics at the same time" (Bachy, p. 42). As the title of the series, Kuxa Kenema, indicated, the purpose was to create a new kind of cinema that could reflect reality in Mozambique; a cinema that was "a freedom tool," that made people ask "questions about themselves and the world, about all situations" (Taylor, p. 30). The creation of Kuxa Kenema also provided the Film Institute with firsthand experience of the way a film industry could develop in even the poorest of countries. According to Jacques d'Arthuys et al., the Film Institute, by nationalizing half of the distribution and exhibition, was able to raise funds in the big cities where the theaters were located and to produce Kuxa Kenema, which was shown in rural areas.[14] The Film Institute arranged special projection facilities such as cinema-on-wheels and church areas to show the films where people had never before seen motion pictures.

Clearly, many advantages could be derived from the experience of Kuxa Kenema. The films were used to diffuse the government's ideology in the rural areas, and a new cinema was being born as Kuxa Kenema, the villagers' first contact with film. As Pimente put it,

> For most of our people, cinema is a direct fruit of Independence. When we arrive in a very remote village and show a film, people will tell us, "This is a result of Independence because before Independence this village never saw a film." So most of our people have not been alienated by dominant imperialist cinema, and we can create a new audience which will use film other than to digest it to escape from daily problems. (Taylor, p. 30)

However, the scope of Kuxa Kenema was much too limited to fill all the needs of a national cinema. The films were documentaries, mostly on government propaganda and on South African and Rhodesian invasions of Mozambican villages. Among the ten films produced by Kuxa Kenema between 1978 and 1979, not one was a feature film. To compensate for this, the Film Institute developed additional projects that prioritized the production of features and educational films.

In 1978, the Institute of Film produced its second major historical documentary after the film 25. *Esta sao as armas* (These are the weapons) was also directed by a foreigner, Murilo Salles. By using footage from old newsreels, it reconstructs the successive situations in Mozambique during the Portuguese colonialism, the Liberation Struggle, and Independence. The film denounces the colonial regime for not educating the people and for keeping them at the margins of the technological benefits of the country. It praises the FRELIMO for having a literacy campaign even before Independence and thus helping people to maximize their productivity and to combat contagious diseases. The film also depicts the current problems of the country and the measures taken by the government to solve them. According to Bachy, *Estas sao as armas* was presented in 1978 at the Leipzig festival, where it received praise for being a good example, "confirming in a clear manner how film could be used to interpret past events (to denounce colonialism without hatred) and to direct future actions toward the transformation of the society" (Bachy, p. 43).

From 1975 to 1978, although Mozambican directors at the Institute of Film participated collectively in the production of the series Kuxa Kenema, they had not had the opportunity to direct a feature film. In 1979, however, Guerra made history by directing *Mueda: memoria e massacre* (Mueda: Memorial and Massacre), 35mm, B&W, the first feature by a Mozambican filmmaker. *Mueda* is a fictional account of the 1960 massacre of six hundred people by the Portuguese army in Mueda, a Mozambican village in the North, near the frontier of Tanzania. Filmed on location, *Mueda* is a mise-en-scène film that is effective because of the way in which the population of Mueda united to reclaim its freedom and the way it was slaughtered by the Portuguese army. The continuity in the diegesis is interrupted from time to time by eyewitness accounts by the survivors. Guerra also draws from his experience in Brazil as a director of Cinema Novo to capture the myth[15] associated with the massacre of Mueda. Knowing that the people of Mueda gather every year to commemorate the massacre, Guerra filmed their reenactment of the event, thus elevating it to the level of a popular myth that brings people together and reinforces their struggle for independence.

After *Mueda*, Guerra finished a short film on the first national festival of music and dance, *Unity in Feasts* (1980), which he had begun in 1978. The film brought together musicians and dancers from all over the country. In 1980, the Film Institute produced another film by a Mozambican director, Camille de Sousa. *The Offensive* is about the government's campaign against the misuse of its funds and the corruption of bureaucrats. Using the Cinéma Vérité style, the camera surprises people at work in different sectors of the government and gives an account of their productivity or nonproductivity.

After this survey of production by the Film Institute, I will now turn to the contribution of Rouch and Godard to Mozambican cinema. Rouch first visited Mozambique in 1977. An old friend, Jacques D'Arthuys, who had become the attaché culturel of France in Mozambique, invited Rouch and persuaded him to bring along his Super 8 camera. During the visit, he met with Guerra and other directors at the Film Institute. He employed some people at the Institute and made a short film, *Les chanteurs de l'usine de biere de Maputo,* about a beer factory's employees who "dance and sing about their life story in South Africa."[16] When Rouch returned to France, he finished the film and sent it back to Mozambique for Guerra and others to see. They liked the film and expressed their interest in seeing more.

In 1978, the negotiations between Rouch, D'Arthuys, and Guerra resulted in a major Super 8 project between France and Mozambique. France wanted to establish friendly relations with Mozambique, which was only three years old. France did not want to be called a neo-colonialist country in the same manner that it had been labeled in many Francophone countries. At the same time, it did not want to be too obvious with a country that was Marxist and that had close ties with the Soviet Union and other Eastern Bloc countries. France therefore decided that it would be better to limit involvement in Mozambique to a project like Super 8, which, after all, had not yet demonstrated economic potential. D'Arthuys implied as much when he said to Rouch, "They are ready at Foreign Affairs to give us plenty of money. It [Super 8] is almost the only area where France's aid will go. Therefore, we can do what we want" (Haffner, p. 20; quoted by Rouch, p. 21).

In order to understand Rouch's involvement in this project, one must realize that it had always been his dream to demystify the expensive production à la Hollywood with heavy equipment, large crews, elaborate mise-en-scènes, and armchair directors. It was in this vein that in the fifties and sixties he used 16mm instead of 35mm. Today, with the Super 8, he believes that there are even more possibilities for demystifying the so-called super-productions. He compares the Super 8 to a pen with which one writes. Thus, people who do not know how to write with a pen can use the Super 8 "to write letters." It was in this sense that Rouch used the term *carte postale,* or postcard, to refer to films made with Super 8. It was also in this sense that he said,

> The thing is that I have finally realized that it is not a dream to teach
> people to write with a camera. One may not make a Godard—let's not say
> a Godard, let's say a Hitchcock!—one may not make a Gance, but one can
> make people who know how to write with a camera, and write simple
> things. (Haffner, p. 25)

Rouch's dream led him to become president de la Cinémathèque and
director of research at the Centre National de Recherches Scientifiques
(CNRS), Université de Paris X Nanterre, where he and Jean-Pierre
Beauviala prepare students for advanced degrees in Super 8 production.[17] Before going to Mozambique, Rouch had also worked on a
Super 8 project in Boston with Richard Leacock.[18] It was, therefore, an
opportunity for him to take his project to Africa, where Super 8 was
regarded not as a toy to make family movies but as a tool for development.

As for the Mozambicans, the project seemed attractive because it
could be used to inform people about the literacy campaigns, the
proper use of agricultural equipment, health education, transportation,
and culture. Rouch and his crew agreed to go to the University of
Maputo communication department to produce films and to train
Mozambicans to work with Super 8. The French minister of cooperation provided $200,000 in funds, a laboratory complete with Kodak
equipment, ten editing tables, ten projectors, ten cameras, ten taping
devices, and six generators for production in rural areas. There were
four French instructors and Rouch; they had twenty students, whom
they divided into two teams.[19]

In four months the Super 8 group produced several short films.
According to Rouch, the work progressed like this:

> They shot in the morning, processed at twelve o'clock, looked at the film
> at one, did the editing between three and five. In the evening they returned
> to the marketplace, set the electrical facilities in place, and projected the
> film for the people they filmed in the morning. (Haffner, pp. 21–22)

The films were about wood choppers, markets, hospital employees
and patients, and government offices. The projection was used as a
means to inform people about their own professions or those of others.
For example, films of the hospital of Maputo were shown in the rural
areas, whereas the doctors in the city saw films about the rural hospitals. There were also films about patients interacting among themselves, which were shown to the doctors.

In the films of the first four months, twenty were retained, six of
which Rouch liked and wanted to keep. But since they only had

originals, which they were projecting for the people, the films were being used up. After all, Rouch himself had compared the Super 8 film to a postcard that one reads and throws away. Now that there were excellent "postcards," there arose the problem of saving them. Rouch tried to refilm them as they were projected on the screen. This method yielded, as one would expect, poor quality prints. Finally, the Super 8 group met with the video group of Godard, who worked on the other side of town. They decided to collaborate because Godard was also having difficulty with taking direct images on video. After recording the Super 8 films for Rouch, Godard's group realized that it was better to film with Super 8 first and to put it on video later.[20]

However, the French filmmakers were coming under heavy criticism by Guerra and the Film Institute. They argued that the video and the Super 8 were costly and counterproductive. Before going into the criticisms and the evaluation of the projects, it is important to survey the video project.

In 1978, at the same time the Film Institute created Kuxa Kenema and Rouch created the Super 8 project, Godard and his video production company, Sonimage, signed a two-year government contract to study the possibilities for television before its arrival in Mozambique. It is clear that the newly independent nation needed such a study just as much as it needed the Super 8 project and the Film Institute. In neighboring countries such as Zaire, the experience of television had helped make the people technologically and ideologically dependent upon the Western countries that had provided them with the equipment and the image. Mozambique welcomed Godard's study both as a means to avoid the traps and protect her independence and as a way to demonstrate the full potential of television to a young and underdeveloped country.

But in order to understand why Godard was interested in the study, one must look back, as Colin MacCabe suggested, at his old preoccupation with the relationship between television and movies, between television and video, and how their narratives address people. According to MacCabe, since 1964 Godard had been interested in working for television. Since 1968 he had made a series of programs for French television, and "all but one of the Dziga-Vertov films were financed by television."[21]

As a New Wave director, Godard wanted to discover new narrative forms by subverting the classical Hollywood narrative, and as a program director for Sonimage, he questioned the accepted forms of "direct address" used by conventional television (MacCabe, pp. 139–41). For him the use of direct address determined the form and content of conventional television and reduced every program to a stereotype. Thus, as MacCabe put it,

> It is, after all, a standard strategy of television documentary to consider the lives of 'ordinary people.' But such considerations are normally rigorously determined in advance. We will look at that couple because they are typical of the upper-middle income bracket, we will look at this adolescent in order to understand changing attitudes to violence. In every case the individual represents a type, understood in relation to an agreed image of society. (MacCabe, p. 145)

Godard wanted the viewer to participate in the production of images, instead of being a mere recipient of messages sent by the producer. Clearly, just as Rouch's chance to change the function of the Super 8 was offered to him on the road to Mozambique, Godard, too, was being offered an opportunity to create new television programming in a "virgin land." To put it in Godard's own words, he urged the Mozambicans "to take advantage of the audio-visual condition of the country and study television before it exists, before it floods . . . all the social corpus and geography of Mozambique" (Godard, p. 73).

In 1978, Godard, Anne-Marie Mieville, and the video equipment of Sonimage arrived in Mozambique. They worked with Carlos Gambo, who was in charge of television at the ministry of information. They set to work on five films, the first and last of which were narrated from the combined points of view of Godard (the producer) and Mieville (the commentator). The second, third, and fourth films were told from the point of view of the producer, a businessman, and the commentator, respectively. Godard believed that it was possible, after looking at these five films, to discover "how a society is formed and informed, and how it formed the independence of this information at the same time with the formation of the society's independence" (Godard, p. 77).

While in Mozambique, Godard also addressed such issues as the maintenance of the equipment, what image/sound to choose for the video, and whom to train. He was concerned about leaving the Mozambicans with something they could use themselves; he did not want the equipment to sit, unused, once he and Mieville left the country (Godard, pp. 81–116).

However, as I pointed out earlier, Godard, like Rouch, came under attack because of the high cost of his projects. Before the year was over, Godard's video project was canceled. Television arrived in Mozambique in 1979 without him realizing his dream.

After this survey, what can one say of the National Film Institute, the Super 8 and video projects, and the situation of film in Mozambique?

It is clear that the Film Institute succeeded in creating a national cinema, whereas other countries in Lusophone Africa achieved little. When one compares the national production in Mozambique to other countries in Africa, one realizes that in a short time it accomplished more than its counterparts. For example, the Film Institute had acquired basic facilities in 35mm and 16mm black-and-white production, whereas countries like Senegal and Kenya still depend upon U.S. and European technological facilities. Even though Guinea-Konakry and Ghana have better and more complete equipment of production than Mozambique, the Film Institute is able to produce more films. It is also interesting that the Film Institute has produced educational and documentary films as well as features, whereas Sily-Cinéma in Guinea-Konakry, which is comparable in many ways to the Film Institute, has not yet been able to produce even one significant feature film.[22] The Institute also trains people in filmmaking and, as a result, the staff has increased from six in 1975 to eighty today. It was in this sense that Pimente said, "Even after twenty years of independence, several African countries don't have a film institute. Since independence, we have made seventy documentaries and four feature films. It is our victory" (Taylor, p. 30).

Because of the accomplishment of the Institute, one may expect an evaluation to stop at the positive points mentioned above. However, it would be misleading to indicate that the Institute does not need criticism simply because it has accomplished more than its counterparts in Africa. There are, in fact, weak areas in the conception of the Institute, some of which were uncovered by the presence of Rouch and Godard. Rouch and his Super 8 group were specifically more critical of the Institute. Rouch believed that developing countries like Mozambique should be pragmatic and move fast if they wanted to catch up with the technologically advanced countries. For this reason, he thought that they should choose the most efficient, least cumbersome, and least expensive equipment. For example, if given a choice, they should take 16mm before the 35mm and choose Super 8 before 16mm and video. Rouch also thought that "the filmmakers from the developing countries should participate in the designing of the equipment they intended to use later" (Haffner, p. 26). Finally, for Rouch, a filmmaker was also a bricoleur; he should be able to patch things, to repair the equipment, and then learn to do without a missing part. Rouch criticized the Institute for lacking these capabilities. He pointed out that the Institute had taken three years to train filmmakers, when two months had been enough for the Super 8 group to train its students (Haffner, p. 24).[23] He also believed that the filmmakers at the Institute, like many other filmmakers in Africa, did not want to use the Super 8 because they were afraid it would make their work seem simple and would thus open production to others. It was in this sense that Rouch argued that his introduction of the Super 8 in Africa was a dangerous game, but a healthy one. While he was teaching everybody how to make film, he was also breaking the African filmmakers' monopoly of this form of knowledge. He said, "I play a very dangerous game because it is a struggle against the young corporation of cinema in developing countries" (Haffner, p. 26).

Godard, too, was concerned about the equipment in Mozambique. He believed that equipment and production should be chosen with the country's independence in mind. Thus, he saw a place like the Centre de Electronica, where the staff repaired cameras and videos, as more important than the Institute. He argued that "the audio-visual beginning in Mozambique should, therefore, be at the electronic center where maintenance would be provided and all the equipment gathered in one place. There would also be classes in theory and practice which could give everyone the opportunity to share in the experience of others" (Godard, p. 116).

Godard recognized that a young country like Mozambique faced many problems in creating her national cinema. But he trusted that Guerra, "a filmmaker who has directed several 'great' films for an international audience," could meet and overcome these problems. He said, "In Guerra's precise and fine movements, although full of an unrestrained energy, which are slowly released in order to take good measurements, one feels that here, in this side of the world, there is at best a chance to find an answer" (Godard, p. 117).

Clearly, what one learns from the presence of both Rouch and Godard in Mozambique is that for the Institute it is not enough to acquire equipment, to train filmmakers, and to make more films; to be independent, it must also question the tools of production. People must be trained to repair the equipment and, if necessary, to redesign it to meet the needs of Mozambique.

The Super 8 and video projects ended in 1979, and Rouch and Godard returned home, leaving the equipment behind. Rouch and the Super 8 group were the most criticized. They were automatically seen as neocolonialists because the label had already been applied to Rouch by some Francophone film critics and historians.[24] The Institute argued that the project was using Mozambicans as guinea pigs to test the Super 8 equipment, which they were marketing around the world (Haffner, p. 23). The Institute also accused Rouch of wasting film. A large sum of money was spent on production that Rouch himself called *carte postale*. The critics argued that a revolutionary country like Mozambique could not afford such a waste. Finally, Guerra said that Rouch's Cinéma Vérité style was too simpleminded and was detrimental to mise-en-scène. He pointed out that "when one makes a film in 16 or 35mm, it takes one some time to think about it. With the Super 8, however, this time of conception is cut out." Because Super 8 filmmakers did not take time out to think about the film, Guerra argued that they were "killing one of the fundamental rules of cinema, which is mise-en-scène."[25]

Godard was the best critic of his own video project in Mozambique. He admitted that it was better to film with the Super 8 first and to put the film on video later. This admission undermined his original idea that the video system provided more freedom and that it was more practical and less expensive (MacCabe, p. 134). On the ideological level, Godard also realized that they could not invent a new type of television in Mozambique because the area was occupied by a government and, as he had learned previously in France, within governments, creativity is not possible.[26]

Television broadcasts began in Mozambique in 1979, and the first films aired were those made by the Super 8 group. Although the projects had been frustrating to Rouch, Godard, and Guerra, they had not been a total loss. Furthermore, Mozambican cinema benefited, and will continue to benefit, from the experience.

VII.

Film Distribution and Exhibition in Francophone Africa

The French African territories were introduced to film activities as early as 1905, ten years after the invention of the Cinématographe, when *L'arrivée d'un train en gare de Ciotat* and *L'arroseur Arrosé* by the Lumière Brothers were exhibited by a circus group in Dakar (Senegal). Since then the distribution and exhibition of film in 35mm format expanded in the urban areas. In the rural sectors, where more than 80 percent of the population lived, there were no efforts to create projection sites or to create ambulant-cinema with 16mm projectors that were light and easy to carry around. In the Belgian Congo, for example, the missionaries used such ambulant-cinemas, and by 1955 they had "more than 500 film programs, with which they carried out more than 5000 shows a year in 350 sites in the Congo. They even crossed the frontiers and went in the neighboring countries as far as Togo."[1]

In Francophone Africa, distribution with the 16mm format was not developed along with the 35mm for at least two reasons. The companies that had a monopoly on distribution and exhibition preferred the cities where they could directly ship their films from Paris and make profits without many complications. Also, unlike the British and the Belgians who used film for educational, political and religious purposes in their colonies, the French were opposed to African involvement in film activities. It is also possible that the rural sectors, which were more traditional than the modern cities, were opposed to the penetration of film in the social and religious lives of people. Amadou

Hampaté Bâ, author of *L'etrange destin de Wangrin*, offers an example of resistance of rural Africans to the film medium. The first time a film was brought to Bandiangara, a small town in Mali, the district commissioner ordered the elders to summon everybody in the market place to see it. The town's Imam warned people that the film was another trick of the white man, who worshipped the devil. Only the elders showed up at the projection, explaining to the district commissioner that the others were too scared of cinema. The projection took place, but only one man defied the Imam's word and looked at the "Diabolic images"; all the rest closed their eyes during the show. One man was to explain later: "We attended the spectacle to show respect for the order established by the great commandant. But we closed our eyes and didn't see a thing, so our consciences were not disturbed."[2]

The distribution and exhibition of film in the metropolitan areas did not encounter similar resistance from the people. Built primarily for the entertainment of Europeans, the movie theaters were soon divided into rows of first-class seats for Europeans, second-class for the African elite, and third-class for the masses. Hampaté Bâ explains that cinema was a spectacle that attracted several people in the Europeanized African cities. He describes movie going in 1934 as an organized structure with cigarette, colanut, date, lemonade, and groundnut dealers in front of the theaters. When it was time to purchase tickets, Hampaté Bâ wrote, "The crowd rushes toward the window as if it is resurrection day. But everybody cannot get in at the same time. One must struggle to stay in line. One gets a first-, second-, or third-class ticket according to the amount one pays" (Rouch, pp. 1–9).

The Compagnie Africaine Cinématographique Industrielle et Commerciale and the Société d'Exploitation Cinématographique Africaine, known as COMACICO and SECMA, respectively, were two French companies that controlled distribution, exhibition, and film programming in Francophone Africa. They organized the market into three regions: the northern region comprising Senegal, Mauritania, Mali, and Guinea, with Dakar as its capital; the central region including the Ivory Coast, Togo, Benin, Upper Volta, and Niger, with Abidjan as the capital; and the southern region of Cameroon, Congo, Gabon, Chad, and the Central African Republic with its capital in Douala. From their central offices in Paris, COMACICO and SECMA sent copies of American, European, and Indian films to the capitals of the regions that determined the programs.

By 1960, there were 180 movie theaters equipped with 35mm projectors throughout the fourteen Francophone countries. According to Jean-René Débrix, eighty-five of these theaters belonged to

COMACICO and sixty-five to SECMA.[3] The remaining theaters were in the hands of private businessmen, usually from Lebanon and Syria. However, these theater owners also depended on COMACICO and SECMA for their supply of film. The movie theaters were either managed by COMACICO or SECMA, who hired employees to run them, or rented to individuals at 75 percent of the box-office receipts. In cases where the theaters were not theirs, COMACICO and SECMA contracted their films at 75 percent.

There were three types of movie theaters in Africa: the Salles de première vision, or the first-run theaters, situated in the capital cities and frequented by Europeans and the African elite. They handled one feature film, one or two shorts, and a newsreel at a sitting. The Salles mixtes, with first-, second-, and third-class seats, were located in the heavily populated areas of the cities. They held double features at every sitting. Finally, there were the Salles populaires, which screened two or three features at a sitting. The popular theaters were located in the Medinas or ghettoes. Débrix states, "In the first-run theaters films were shown for three days to one week before they were changed. In the mixed and popular theaters they were frequently changed after two days or daily by alternating them" (Débrix, p. 3). COMACICO and SECMA distributed 350 films every year. According to the records of the French government, 150–160 of the films were American, 90–100 were French, and 80–90 were Indian, Arab, and others (Débrix, p. 4). It is interesting to note that COMACICO and SECMA were distributing American films in Francophone Africa without distribution rights from the American Motion Picture Export Association (AMPEA). Prints of American films were sent to Africa from Paris during the colonial epoch and after independence, as if the new nations were still part of France. As I will show later in the study, AMPEA was not interested, at first, in Francophone Africa because, even though its films dominated the market, the African theaters were economically insignificant compared to other foreign markets. In the late sixties, however, the AMPEA became interested in Francophone Africa, if not for an economic reason, for political and strategic reasons.

The COMACICO and SECMA bought films in Paris for prices ranging between eight and twenty thousand French francs. In the early sixties the seat cost between one French franc and ten francs, from the popular theaters to the first-run theaters. The films generated between 200,000 and 400,000 francs each (Débrix, p. 4). With these structures in place, the profits soared for the COMACICO and SECMA as the number of spectators increased, and new theaters were built. By the time they went out of business in 1972, the number of theaters swelled to 250 and the two companies grossed an estimated 120 million French francs, or 24 million U.S. dollars, per year.[4]

The smooth operations of the COMACICO and SECMA were troubled first by the advent of independence in Francophone Africa. When Guinea-Konakry assumed self-rule, it nationalized its theaters and created Sily-Cinéma to control distribution and exhibition. The COMACICO and SECMA reacted by refusing to supply its films to Guinea. The theaters were closed for one year for lack of films. Then, Bob Sow, who was director of Sily-Cinéma, tried to find suppliers in the Soviet Bloc countries. The films acquired from the Socialist countries were not popular with the Guinean audiences, who, like audiences all over Africa, were used to adventure films, westerns, and gangster movies. Guinea returned to the negotiating table with the French monopolist companies. A compromise was reached by which the twenty-eight theaters were divided between Sily-Cinéma and the foreign companies. By allowing COMACICO and SECMA to control half of the theaters in the country, Guinea gained access to their films and posed the condition that the profit from the ticket sales would not leave the country. In 1962, Mali created the Office Cinématographique National du Mali (OCINAM) to control distribution and exhibition. However, cautioned by the way the COMACICO and SECMA dealt with Guinea, the Malians devised a less radical strategy that consisted of building their own theaters where there were none and taking over those owned by the French businessmen. At the end of 1969, Upper Volta (now Burkina Faso), reacting to an increase in ticket costs, nationalized film activities in the six theaters on its territory.

The COMACICO and SECMA reacted again by cutting film supply to the rebellious country. With only six theaters, the newly created Société Nationale Voltaïque du Cinéma (SONAVOCI) could not interest other foreign distributors in its market. Like Sily-Cinéma in Guinea, it was forced to work out a deal with the companies with the distribution monopoly. Upper Volta ended up with the ownership of the theaters, while the COMACICO and SECMA retained the monopoly of distribution. Even though Upper Volta had only six movie theaters in the entire country, it scored a moral victory against the foreign monopolist companies and collected enough revenue to improve the condition of its theaters, build new and modern projection sites, and create a national production center. Several African countries followed Upper Volta in creating national societies to supervise the film industry.

The operations of the COMACICO and SECMA were also criticized by the Federation of African Filmmakers. In the mid-sixties, after overcoming several difficulties to finance the production of their films, the first Francophone directors were shocked to find out that, because of the block booking practices of the two companies, they could not show their films in their own countries. Such early classics as *Black Girl* and *The Money Order* by Sembène, *Cabascado* by Oumarou Ganda, *Concerto pour un exil* by Désiré Ecaré, and *Le retour d'un aventurier* by Moustapha Alassane were seen for the first time in Paris while the monopolist companies prevented them from being screened commercially in Africa. Clearly, the COMACICO and SECMA preferred foreign films, which they bought at relatively derisory prices compared to African films, which had not yet recouped their cost of production. The filmmakers reacted by exerting pressure on their governments to nationalize distribution and film screening. This will not only provide choices in what films to screen, it will also promote national production. The filmmakers argued that distribution and exhibition constituted an important industry that could contribute to the economic and cultural development of the countries. COMACICO and SECMA delayed this development by dumping escapist films on the market and by not investing their monies in Africa. Once the industry was nationalized, part of the revenues from screening foreign and domestic films could be reinvested in the production of new films and in the construction of new movie theaters. In 1971, SECMA surrendered to the pressure and participated in the production of a feature, *Diegue bi* by Mahama Traoré. However, this only led to more polemics between the filmmakers and the monopolist companies because they could not agree on how to share the revenue from the box offices. In the late sixties, the French government, concerned that a nationalization of the film industry might bar French films from the screens, put pressure on COMACICO and SECMA to adjust their markets to the postindependence needs of the countries. It is important to point out that by 1970, the Francophone market was dominated by French and American films whereas American films dominated everywhere else in Africa and Europe. Mindful that the AMPEA might replace the French distributors after nationalization, the French government joined the Federation of African Filmmakers in their criticism of COMACICO and SECMA. However, the French Ministry of Coopération argued that nationalization, as much as it provided a moral victory, was not a practical solution in view of the small sizes of the markets in Africa. It was therefore suggested to the African governments that they needed "a system to control the box-office receipts in each theater and in each country, and a step-by-step africanization of the industry which permits the Francophone countries to rent together films for their theaters."[5]

Finally, two other factors contributed to the demise of COMACICO and SECMA in the late sixties and early seventies. While the AMPEA has had offices in Anglophone African capitals since the end of World War II and has supplied American films directly to the African intermediaries, there was no direct contact between the Francophone African countries and AMPEA until 1969. American films were rented in Paris by COMACICO and SECMA and sent to Francophone countries. But as Thomas Guback explained, after establishing themselves in Anglophone Africa, "American companies turned to French-speaking nations south of the Sahara, and AMPEA served as a precedent for strategy there. In September 1969, major American production-distribution companies created the West African Film Export Company Inc., but changed its name to AFRAM Films Inc. in December 1969."[6] AFRAM Films Inc. opened an office, first in Dakar, and distributed films from there. The arrival of AMPEA in Francophone Africa threatened the monopoly of COMACICO and SECMA and helped the birth of at least one new distributor in the area.

In 1972, AFRAM signed a contract with SOCOPRINT to distribute its films in Guinea and other Socialist African countries that had nationalized their industries. SOCOPRINT, a Swiss import/export company, created SOCOFILMS and began to compete for a share in the market. The role of SOCOFILMS will be discussed later in this study.

COMACICO and SECMA also had to contend with an increase in taxes on distribution and exhibition. Some countries turned to the film industry in the early seventies in order to cope with worldwide economic crises. The Ivory Coast retained up to 44 percent of the box-office receipts. In Guinea taxes were as high as 50 percent. The governments were also opposed to an increase in ticket prices, which COMACICO and SECMA argued was out of tune with the rate of inflation.

In 1972, COMACICO and SECMA were defeated in Francophone Africa, mainly because of the political pressure of the filmmakers, the trend of nationalization and the high tax rates on film-related activities, the criticism of the French government, which did not want to estrange its former colonies, the arrival of AFRAM in the region, and the emergence of new distributors such as SOCOFILMS.

The withdrawal of the two French monopolist companies led to complex maneuvers by governments and private businessmen to control the Francophone film industry. It is important to bear in mind that the task was easy for COMACICO and SECMA because they controlled both distribution and exhibition. With the present situation, however, a distributor has either to rent films to one country at a time or to organize the countries so that they can rent films together. Both choices were difficult in view of the poor condition of communication in Africa, the small sizes of the markets taken individually, and the different political systems. It was in this sense that different strategies were used by each of the parties vying for the monopoly of the market. Since 1969, the strategy of AFRAM has consisted in opening offices in the Francophone capitals and renting films to local theater owners, if they exist, or to international distributors who have some monopoly in the region. As Guback pointed out, Africa "constitutes a tiny economic market for American motion pictures, but that continent's political importance cannot be denied."[7] Clearly, therefore, aside from the fact that the American film industry is creating a future market in francophone Africa, the purpose of AFRAM is to ensure the American cultural presence with its films.

The French government, on the other end, created the Société de Participation Cinématographique Africaine (SOPACIA), a branch of the Union Général du Cinéma, to take over the stocks of COMACICO and SECMA. What the French government called a progressive Africanization of the film industry can be simply described as an attempt by SOPACIA to maintain the control of distribution, so as to ensure French presence on African screens, and to turn over the ownership and management of the theaters to Africans. SOPACIA used the same structures of COMACICO and SECMA with the only difference that it proceeded to sell the theaters to private businessmen in Africa. Some countries, including Guinea, Upper Volta, and Mali, had already nationalized their theaters. Others, such as Senegal, Benin, Congo-Brazzaville, nationalized theirs in order to stop SOPACIA from selling them to foreign businessmen. Yet in other countries, such as Gabon, Ivory Coast, Niger, and Cameroon, the theaters went to private businessmen.

Now that the COMACICO and SECMA were out of business, the Federation of African Filmmakers was working to make sure the issues of African film production and distribution would be handled by whoever replaced the monopolist companies. The aim of the federation was to have regional and international markets that could screen African films. The filmmakers wanted to put in place quota systems on the import of foreign films and create subsidies from taxes levied on box-office receipts in order to help finance African productions. The federation argued that as a first step, it was necessary to nationalize the industry as a means to avoid the control of the market by foreigners and the divestment of funds. There must be, to put it in Tahar Cheriaa's words, groupings and collective action on a regional level, everywhere that a linguistic and cultural unity permits (in the Maghreb or the Arab countries of North Africa, in French-speaking countries and in English-speaking countries). Founding large distribution companies on a regional basis will permit a complete and positive change in the above-mentioned monopoly of the market and consequently lead the film distribution system in Africa in a direction that is progressive and more compatible with African interest.[8]

In 1974, the French government, which stated its commitment to the Africanization of the industry, and the Francophone nations that were members of the Organisation Commune Africaine et Mauricienne (OCAM), created the Consortium Interafricain de Distribution Cinématographique (CIDC). The purpose of the CIDC was to facilitate the importation and distribution of film in its member countries. It also aimed to "emphasize the promotion of African films, and to reassure the directors that their features will not only be screened at home but also abroad. In a word, the CIDC will not only be concerned about providing African audiences with quality films, it will also make efforts to find outside markets for African films."[9]

Finally, the role of CIDC was to recommend lower tax rates to the member governments. The secretary of CIDC criticized the tendency in Africa to raise taxes while in other areas in the world they have been lowered as an incentive to growth in the industry. He stated that "the disproportionately high tax rates are at the root of the collapse of many inter-African industries such as CIDC. If nothing is done about it, more powerful foreign companies will, once again, take over the control of the market."[10]

The French government, by financially backing the creation of the CIDC, thought that it was the best compromise that could maintain French films on African screens. CIDC was supposed to take over both the structure and the stocks of the original organizations. It was then expected to open one office in Paris (CIDC-PARIS) and one in Ouagadougou (CIDC-AFRIQUE). The Paris office would supply the Ouagadougou office with several copies of acquired films which would then be distributed among the fourteen member countries.

Created in 1974, CIDC finally began operating in 1980, but without the monopoly that it needed to become a successful enterprise. In addition to the fact that it could not put out of business such distributors as AFRAM, SOCOFILMS, and SIDEC, it was trapped into supporting CIDC-PARIS with high salaries to the employees. CIDC was also criticized for not taking as its first priority the distribution of African films. By 1985 CIDC closed its Paris office and stopped all operations.

SOCOFILMS, one of the companies that CIDC could not compete with, was originally a Swiss textile company (SOCOPRINT) that specialized in import-export between Europe and the leftist African countries. When Guinea nationalized its theaters, SOCOPRINT created SOCOFILMS and began supplying the country with American and European films. When other Socialist African countries such as Upper Volta, Benin, and Congo-Brazzaville nationalized their theaters, SOCOFILMS became their supplier. With films mainly from AFRAM, SOCOFILMS undermined the monopoly of COMACICO and SECMA. When these companies went out of business, SOCOFILMS proceeded to replace them. It buys films in France from UGC and negotiates the distribution right in the fourteen countries so as to discourage any competition. As for American films, SOCOFILMS reached an agreement with AFRAM in 1980 to distribute them in Benin, Mali, Guinea, and Ivory Coast. AFRAM films are distributed in Senegal by SIDEC and in Cameroon by Joseph Kadji, a private businessman who owns twenty theaters. In other places in Francophone Africa, AFRAM rents films locally on the basis of a percentage of the box-office receipts. SOCOFILMS does not have the monopoly of the Francophone market because of AFRAM. And, not unlike COMACICO and SECMA, SOCOFILMS has no national roots in Africa. It takes advantage of the lack of direct business contact between Africa and the international companies of distribution in Europe. Thus SOCOFILMS is able to enrich itself as an intermediary between those who produce and distribute and those who exhibit the films. Like its predecessors, SOCOFILMS does not concern itself with either the production or the distribution of African films. It seems clear, therefore, that SOCOFILMS also may disappear as soon as the national and international societies in Africa consolidate themselves and create contacts with their European counterparts. Now that CIDC has come to a standstill, more attention will be paid to the operations of SOCOFILMS, and it will be pressed to prove how it is different from COMACICO and SECMA, which were considered neocolonialist and imperialist. This explains why the French ministry of foreign relations hesitates to publicly approve SOCOFILMS, despite the claim by the latter that it controls the Francophone market (see note 10).

The only other important company of distribution and exhibition in Francophone Africa is the Société internationale de distribution et d'exploitation cinématographique (SIDEC). The Africa Award (a reward to dynamic industries in the Third World by the International Review based in Madrid) went to SIDEC in 1985, indicating the importance it has taken in the eyes of the international business community. Aside from the fact that SIDEC regularly exhibits African films in Senegal, where it has a monopoly, it is also interested in coproducing with such directors as Souleymane Cissé of Mali.

SIDEC was created as a semiprivate company in 1973 by the Senegalese government and SOPACIA, a branch of the French Union Général du Cinéma, which had a 10 percent share. It is important to bear in mind that the same SOPACIA participated later in the creation of CIDC. However, it is obvious that, unlike CIDC, SIDEC has avoided many traps by restructuring what was left behind by COMACICO and SECMA. According to Yves Diagne, the agreement between SIDEC and SOPACIA was such that the French controlled all the transactions with their 10 percent share. SIDEC was forced to retain all the old employees of COMACICO and SECMA, and the route for film ordering was Paris as in the old days. According to Diagne, "No transaction could be signed with other countries without the approval of Paris, no matter how important the deal was to the successful functioning of SIDEC. Without the consent of Paris, no contract could be signed with a person of Senegalese origin or a foreigner."[11]

It was therefore necessary for SIDEC to make important decisions if it were to survive. In 1977, American films that had been kept off the market by SOPACIA returned and the old employees of the French companies were fired. This restructuring led to a rupture between the SOPACIA and the SIDEC, which has since become a national company.[12]

It is also necessary to point out here that, unlike CIDC, SIDEC has a relatively easier task. The film industry is better organized in Senegal than in any other country in Africa. Senegal is the only country where it is possible to check the number of admissions in the theaters per month. Because there is no system in place in the other countries to control the number of tickets sold at a time, the statistics on admissions are approximated. SIDEC has the monopoly of distribution and exhibition, and with eighty sites of projection and an average of 13 million spectators a year, it is able to survive modestly in Senegal alone. With a stock of five thousand films, an additional four hundred new films a year, and Dakar as the capital of the northern region, it was relatively easy for SIDEC to assume the role of international distributor first in Mali, Mauritania, and Guinea and later in the other regions. It is because of these economic factors that SIDEC is able today to employ five hundred people and generate an annual revenue of 8 billion French francs with a working budget of only 1.5 billion French francs. SIDEC now has customers in Niger, Ivory Coast, Gabon, and Cameroon.

Today fewer French films are shown in Senegal. Except for the blockbusters with popular actors like Belmondo, de Funes, and Delon, which SIDEC buys at high cost from SOCOFILMS, one rarely finds French films in Senegal. The reason for the scarcity of French films, as stated above, is that the major distributors like Unifrance Films and Gaumont, since SIDEC was nationalized, refuse to sell films directly to it and force it to deal with SOCOFILMS, an action which raises the cost of French films for SIDEC. The Senegalese have reacted by showing fewer French films and more American films, which now dominate the market.

An understanding of how SIDEC functions first as a national industry in charge of distribution, programming, and exhibition will provide a structural model to those countries that have not yet organized their film industries. SIDEC encourages both public and private development of film activities in Senegal.

It recommends tax rates to the government and subsidizes the Centre National de Production Cinématographique (CNPC) with part of the taxes levied from the distribution and exhibition of foreign films. It also uses some of the revenues to build new theaters and improve the condition of existing ones. Other national industries can benefit from this organization of SIDEC.

As an international distribution company, the SIDEC model may be preferable to that of the CIDC. It is first of all a national organization that is winning an international market because of its business skills, its dynamic leadership, and its good public relations. SIDEC had an economic and political basis to start with, whereas CIDC only had a political one. This is not to indicate that CIDC and the SIDEC were opposed ideologically; it is apparent that they both worked toward the development of African cinema. The success of SIDEC results from the fact that it operated on sound economic grounds. It teaches the developing African countries that similar regional distribution companies should be started in Abidjan and Douala, where the old structure of SECMA and COMACICO exists. The three capitals would be able to either buy films together or exchange them, and the African film industry would be in African hands.

Even though AFRAM (an affiliate of the American Motion Pictures Export Association) was a nonprofit organization, it had the merit of ensuring the American cultural presence in Africa. On the other hand, international film distributors such as AFRAM and similar companies in Bombay and Cairo began to trade with intermediaries other than COMACICO and SECMA in Francophone Africa.

In this manner new distributors were born as intermediaries between the major distribution companies and what remained of the structure of COMACICO and SECMA. The Senegalese government in Dakar, in an effort to block the sale of COMACICO and SECMA stocks in the northern region to private foreign businessmen, created the Société Internationale de Distribution et d'Exploitation Cinématographique (SIDEC). Once in possession of the stocks and the structure of COMACICO and SECMA in the North, SIDEC began to assume the role of an international distributor first in Mauritania and Mali, then in Guinea. Much like SIDEC in the northern region, SOCOFILMS, a Franco-Swiss distribution company, was trying to replace COMACICO/SECMA in the central and southern regions. In addition to these major new companies, smaller private distributors were sprouting everywhere. The situation was complicated by the fact that the former structures were replaced in Paris by the Société de Participation Cinématographique Africaine (SOPACIA)—a new branch of the Union Général de Cinéma (UGC), which oversees the interest of the French film industry.

Meanwhile, as SIDEC and SOCOFILMS compete for monopoly of the market in Francophone Africa, there are those who wonder about the market's economic and political significance. Some critics believe that the French government should not bother itself about the loss of the African market because less than 5 percent of the income generated by French films comes from Africa. Others believe that the French cultural interest provided by the showing of French films is more important than the economic factors presently involved.

In France the ministry of foreign relations is under pressure to ensure the French presence on the screens, now that CIDC is at a standstill. The ministry is hesitating between dealing with SIDEC, which is an African company but with a relatively small working budget, or SOCOFILMS, which is large but, not unlike COMACICO and SECMA, without national roots in Africa. While the AFRAM has installed offices in Dakar, Abidjan, and Douala to supply the national companies, SIDEC and SOCOFILMS, directly with American films, the French distribution companies such as Gaumont and Unifrance Films only deal with SOCOFILMS, arguing that the national distribution companies, including the SIDEC, are insignificant markets.

Today, there are more American films shown in Dakar than French films.

VIII.

The Present Situation of the Film Industry in Anglophone Africa

Recently, some Anglophone states have begun to encourage film production by nationalizing distribution and raising subsidies from the exhibition of foreign films to finance national productions through state-sponsored agencies. In Zimbabwe, for example, the government set up a production and training center with the help of the Federal Republic of Germany, which was also responsible for the National Film and Television Institute in Ghana and the Kenya Institute of Mass Communication. The production center in Zimbabwe has trained filmmakers and technicians who, so far, have made newsreels, documentaries, and short fiction films. In Tanzania, the Audio Visual Institute has been in existence since 1974, donated by the government of Denmark. It contains facilities for processing, printing, and mixing narrative and sound effects. The Institute trains filmmakers and technicians and produces educational, publicity, and documentary films. The Institute has participated in international film festivals in Mogadishu (Somalia) and Ouagadougou (Burkina Faso), presenting docudramas on the teaching of the *Ujamaa*. In 1985, a Tanzanian coproduction, *Arusi ya Mariamu* (The Wedding of Mariamu), directed by Nanga Yoma Ngoge and Ron Mulvihill (U.S.), was awarded the prize for the best short film at the Festival Panafricain du Cinéma de Ouagadougou (FESPACO). *Arusi ya Mariamu* is about the traditional science of healing and the conflict between tradition and modernity.

Like Tanzania, Kenya has just begun its interest in feature-film production. Two government branches, the Kenya Film Corporation (KFC) and the Kenya Institute of Mass Communication (KIMC), handle film activities. The KFC deals primarily with distribution, which it has monopolized since 1972. In Kenya, as in other Anglophone countries, U.S. films dominate the market, challenged only by Indian melodrama and Kung Fu movies. Since its creation, the KFC has distributed a few African films from Cameroon and Ghana, one of which, *Love Brewed in the African Pot* (1980, directed by Kwaw Ansah), is the third most popular film in the country, grossing 1,022,443 Kenyan shillings.[1] The KFC has also distributed American films in Tanzania, Somalia, Ethiopia, Zambia, and Uganda.

Other functions of the KFC involve the development of a mobile cinema system in the rural areas and video centers on the outskirts of Nairobi. According to Sharad Patel, "These films on wheels reach 500 semiurban and rural centers a month, attracting audiences of over 40,000 every evening. And thanks to advertising, not a single one of these moviegoers pays even a cent for this entertainment."[2] Therefore, the KFC limits its film production to videotaping urban products for advertisement in rural areas and for television commercials.

The KIMC, on the other hand, has facilities in 16mm production and laboratories where filmmakers train for the Kenyan television. So far the KIMC has produced tourist-attraction films (*Waters of Mombasa, Passport to Adventure, Immashoi of Massai,* directed by Sao Gamba), educational documentaries, and other information films. In 1985, Sao Gamba directed *Kolormask,* a didactic film about a Kenyan student who returns home with a white wife. The marriage is threatened by social and cultural differences between Kenya and England. Presented at the 1987 FESPACO, *Kolormask* was criticized for being too exotic in its emphasis on documenting African cultures. The real promise in Kenyan cinema may come from creative writers such as Ngugi Wa Thiong'o and Meja Mwangi, who are now turning to cinema as did Ousmane Sembène in Senegal and Wole Soyinka in Nigeria, for a more direct way of communicating with their audiences. Ngugi participated in the 1986 Edinburgh Film Festival, where he presented a short video about South Africa and discussed the film course he had taught in Sweden. As for Meja Mwangi, he was listed as assistant director in *Out of Africa* (1986), and his novel, *Carcass for Hounds,* was adapted into film by Ola Balogun.

The only countries in Anglophone Africa to have gone beyond the government productions to create an independent cinema are Ghana and Nigeria. Film production continues to progress in these countries despite the lack of strong support from their governments. In Ghana, independent directors like King Ampaw and Kwaw Ansah have replaced the old documentary tradition with feature films that blend comedy and melodrama and draw their themes from popular culture and the meeting between Western and African civilizations. In Nigeria, a Yoruba cinema has emerged since the early seventies to become an original expression of directors like Ola Balogun and Bankole Bello and popular Yoruba theater stars such as Chief Hubert Ogunde, Ade "Love" Folayan, and Moses Olaiya Adejumo.

The government branches that handle film industry in Ghana are the Ghana Film Industry Corporation (GFIC), the Ghana Broadcasting Corporation (GBC), and the National Film and Television Institute (NAFTI). Like similar government agencies in Kenya and Tanzania, the GFIC, the GBC, and the NAFTI manage the distribution, the censorship, training of technicians, and production of documentary and information films. The GFIC inherited the facilities of the Gold Coast Colonial Film Unit, which specialized in the documentary genre in the tradition of John Grierson. It is still possible to find in the archives of the GFIC pre-independence classics like *The Boy Kumasenu,* a film about the city life, as well as post-independence Nkrumah-era classics like *Tongo Hamile,* which is a screen adaptation of Shakespeare's *Hamlet.*

The GFIC has 16mm and 35mm production equipment with laboratory facilities. With GFIC alone, Ghana is better equipped than all of the other West African states, and it is capable of turning out more than 12 features a year. Ghanaian filmmakers trained at NAFTI and abroad find their first employment at GFIC and GBC. In this sense one can find the influence of GFIC's documentary style on such well-known Ghanaian directors as Sam Aryetey (*No Tears for Ananse,* 1968), Egbert Adjesu (*I Told You So,* 1970), Kwate Nee-Owoo (*You Hide Me,* 1971; *Struggle for Zimbabwe,* 1974; *Angela Davis,* 1976), King Ampaw (*They Call It Love,* 1972; *Kukurantumi,* 1983; *Juju,* 1986), and Kwaw Ansah (*Love Brewed in the African Pot,* 1980).

The GFIC manages distribution and censorship in such manner that national and Third World films are shown in the movie theaters in Ghana. It is pushing the government, for example, to put a quota on film import and to encourage film exchange between Third World countries. It is in this vein that "Cuba and Ghana have run seasons of each other's films and the Havana festival had a retrospective of African cinema in 1986."[3] The GFIC has had to deal with video piracy, too, because the shortage of foreign currency in Ghana makes the import of films expensive. Since 1982, video centers have opened everywhere in the big cities, and the most recent films are shown on video monitors in violation of the copyright and the cinematography laws in Ghana. More important, the pirated videos contribute to the economic crisis through the evasion of exhibition taxes and the uncensored showing of pornographic films that affect the patrons negatively.[4]

Unlike the case in Kenya and Tanzania, where film production is in the hands of the government, Ghanaian cinema is not limited to the productions of GFIC, GBC, and NAFTI. Ghana's best-known directors, King Ampaw and Kwaw Ansah, are independent directors who produce their films by raising funds locally and internationally. Ansah's latest film, *Heritage,* for example, is funded by the Social Security Bank, the Ghana Commercial Bank, the National Investment Bank, and the Cooperative Bank.[5] The relative freedom that the independent directors acquire in being their own producers enables them to make popular films that are not burdened by didactic and propagandistic precepts imposed by the government. This is not to say, however, that independent directors do not need governments and their agencies. On the contrary, both Ansah and Ampaw use the equipment and personnel of the GFIC and the facilities provided by such government departments as the army. Furthermore, filmmakers need the government to set quotas on film import and reduce entertainment tax for local films so that their films can compete with foreign products.

The significance of producing independently is seen in the fact that Ansah and Ampaw choose their films on an artistic and financial basis, not on the basis that the government wants this or that type of film made. It is the artistic freedom that enables them to go beyond the documentary tradition fostered by the GFIC and to look to popular culture as a source of fictional inspiration. As Jim Pines points out, their "films draw on local culture and experience" (Turner and Kumar, p. 93) and thus ensure a box-office return both in Ghana and in other African countries. The films of Ampaw and Ansah blend comedy and melodrama, ridiculing eccentric paternal figures and emphasizing the tragic clash between tradition and modernity. A look at the films reveals the contradiction between the values of the city and those of the village: they denounce acculturation and attempt to raise the consciousness of the characters in the end.

In *Love Brewed in the African Pot,* for example, Ansah draws upon elements from Ghanaian cultural experience to construct a narrative with the themes of repression and class difference. The story is about a love affair between Aba, educated in a posh Cape Coast school and trained as a dressmaker, and Joe Quanshah, a semiliterate auto mechanic (fitter) and son of a fisherman. Aba's father, Koffi Appiah, who is a civil servant, wants her to marry a lawyer, Bensah, instead of Joe.[6]

The film thematizes repression by putting into play two of the most effective dream sequences in African cinema.

The first dream shows Koffi Appiah's repressed origin returning to haunt him. Ansah positions the spectator in this dream sequence by describing the fishermen's tradition as a source of pride and authenticity, which has a deeper influence on Koffi Appiah's mind than the surface appearance of Western civilization among Ghanaian elites. The silent cinematic message satisfies the unconscious expectation of African audiences, the majority of whom come from traditions similar to those of the fishermen in the film. The violence with which Koffi Appiah is punished by his unconscious serves not only to vindicate the fishermen who are humiliated by him, and with whom the spectator identifies, but also to awaken the elites like Koffi Appiah who run away from tradition and mimic the West.

The other dream sequence concerns the return of Aba's worst repressed fears in the shape of a witch. Aba's desire to marry Joe, a "fitter" beneath her class, is in violation of class differences and of her father's interdiction of such a transgression. Aba overlooks these obstacles by simplifying and dismissing her father's Westernized ideas as irrational, grotesque, and superficial. On the other hand, she romanticizes the fishermen's tradition, which Joe represents, as strong, natural, music-loving, and authentic. However, when the forces of class difference turn Joe against her, she is no longer able to dismiss them as irrational and grotesque. In Aba's dream, her unconscious thematizes all the obstacles into the shape of a witch, dressed in a white dress. Aba succumbs to a powerful monster that, while awake, she dismisses as superficial and grotesque. Ansah has been criticized for failing to construct a more "realistic" face mask for the witch (Pfaff). What captivates the spectator, however, is less the realism of the form of the film than the content. In other words, the spectator accepts the dream because of its content, which is consistent with other rational elements that are presented in the story as obstacles to Joe marrying Aba. It is because the representation of the dream satisfied the collective psychic need of the spectator that *Love Brewed in the African Pot* beat record attendance in Kenya, Liberia, and Sierra Leone, where it was screened for three months (Pfaff). Ansah ensures the popularity of the film with African spectators by drawing from other popular experiences such as wedding ceremonies, wrestling matches, and musical performances.

The government of Nigeria manages the film industry through three agencies: the Film Unit, the Nigerian Film Corporation, and the National Film Distribution Company. The Film Unit, which was inherited from the colonial administration, produces educational documentaries and trains filmmakers for other government departments. As an office of the federal government, it functions to satisfy the country's need for documentaries in agriculture, health, and housing. Between 1979 and 1983, the Film Unit produced 25 documentaries, 65 newsreels, and 390 short information films. However, according to Françoise Balogun, who is the foremost authority on Nigerian film, the productions of the Film Unit do not reach a wide audience. "The Nigerian television is bombarded by foreign productions and it has no link with the Film Unit. Furthermore, there are no rules which require the theater owners to show a short documentary of the Film Unit before showing the feature films."[7]

The Nigerian Film Corporation (NFC) and the National Film Distribution Company (NFDC) are outgrowths of the 1972 Indigenization Act, which gave exclusive monopoly for distribution and exhibition of feature films to Nigerians with the capital and business contracts. The NFC was set up in 1979, but did not begin operating until 1982. According to Adamu Halilu, a filmmaker and former secretary of the NFC, its purpose was to promote production and to chart the course of the film industry complex. In view of the fact that films produced in Nigeria faced marketing difficulties, the NFC's role was to review distribution and to implement a quota system that would force theater owners to run one Nigerian film for every ten foreign films that they showed. The duties of the NFC also involved talking to merchant banks and businessmen on behalf of filmmakers and reviewing the entertainment tax with regard to Nigerian film.[8]

As for the NFDC, it has been in existence since 1981, replacing the American Motion Picture Export Association ten years after the Indigenization Act. Its functions include film importation, distribution, and exhibition. The NFDC own theaters around Lagos and shows some of its films in the National Theater, which is equipped with 16mm, 35mm, and 70mm projectors. The National Theater contains two projection rooms with 676 seats each, and the main hall with 5,000 seats. In 1982, forty-two films were shown there, including *Orun Mooru* and *Money Power* by Ola Balogun and *Love Brewed in the African Pot* by Ansah (F. Balogun, p. 25).

The NFDC also imports films for other national distribution agencies such as the Nigerian Motion Picture Corporation and the West African Pictures Corporation. All these companies show Nigerian films in their theaters; however, they charge more for them in order to make the same amount of profit they make for running less expensive foreign films that have already recouped their cost of production before reaching Nigeria. Nigerian filmmakers have pleaded with the government to reduce or completely eliminate the entertainment tax for local films so that they can compete with American and Kung Fu films, which flood the market. As Ola Balogun puts it, "The most that the government can do and should do is to help regulate film distribution and exhibition in such a way as would permit an individual Nigerian filmmaker to progress."[9]

The most important state participation in feature film production involves Adamu Halilu's *Shaihu Umar* (1976), which was totally financed by the government for the Nigerian entry in the 1977 FESTAC. The film, which tells the epic story of a Hausa religious leader, is based on a novel in Hausa by the first prime minister of Nigeria, Sir Abubakar Tafawa-Balewa. Even though *Shaihu Umar* is important because of its use of Hausa tradition and historiography and its glorification of Islam and the Hausa past, it risks letting the spectator down because of its length (140 minutes) and the repetitious scenes.

Independent production continues to progress in Nigeria, despite the difficulties mentioned above, because of the Indigenization Act, which enables the filmmakers to distribute their films and recoup the cost of production. Since 1972, for example, Ola Balogun has become the most prolific director in sub-Saharan Africa, producing at least one feature film a year. Balogun's films enjoy a big success in Nigeria, which lets him recoup his money each time and make new films. In 1978, he made *Black Goddess,* a film about Afro-Brazilians who returned to Nigeria after gaining freedom from slavery. It traces the roots of Babatunde, whose ancestor, Prince Oluyole, was captured in a tribal war and sent to Brazil as a slave two centuries ago. Babatunde travels from Lagos to Rio de Janeiro with the sculpture of the goddess Yemanja, which he hopes will be recognized by the part of the family that remained in Brazil. During a religious ceremony in Rio, Elisa, daughter of a priestess, reveals to Babatunde that what he is looking for is in the Bahia region. The mythico-poetic and historical aspects of *Black Goddess* are appealing to film critics. Even though the film did not meet the same success in Nigeria as the films based on popular Yoruba theater, it was internationally acclaimed, winning the award of the Office Catholique International du Cinéma. It also won an award for the best musical score at Carthage (1980) (F. Balogun, p. 66). In fact, Balogun's international reputation is no longer in doubt, with such features as *Cry Freedom* (1981), a film about liberation movements and based on the novel *Carcass for Hounds* by Meja Mwangi (Kenya), and *Money Power* (1982), which have more universal themes that would appeal to audiences beyond the frontiers of Nigeria.

Eddie Ugbomah comes after Balogun with more than eight feature films produced since 1976. Ugbomah's films are inspired by contemporary events and politics in Nigeria. His first feature, *The Rise and the Fall of Dr. Oyenusi* (1977), is based on a true story about a Lagos gangster in the seventies who was arrested and executed publicly. *The Mask* (1979) shows how a fictitious Nigerian president sent a secret agent to retrieve the famous mask of Queen Adesua of Benin, which was stolen by British colonizers and put in a London museum. The film, starring Ugbomah himself, uses the Manichaean aesthetics from James Bond films, thematizing the Nigerian hero as super clever and the British police as stupid. *Death of a Black President* (1983) is based on the events leading to the assassination of General Murtala Mohamed, who was head of state of Nigeria between 1975 and 1976.

More important, the Indigenization Act has attracted the stars of popular Yoruba theater to film. In 1976, Ola Balogun made *Ajani Ogun* with Ade "Love" Folayan, who is a star in the Yoruba popular theater. The film tells the story of a young man who has to fight an evil rich man to get his fiancée and his inheritance back. Long screen times are devoted to Ade Love in the title role, as he sings long romantic songs or fights with his opponents. Balogun directed the film with the help of Duro Lapido, who had a long experience directing his own plays for Nigerian television. The success of *Ajani Ogun* and the public's request for a sequel was such that Balogun and Ade Love teamed up again in 1977 to film *Ija Ominira* (Fight for Freedom), a popular story about a tyrannical king who was chased out of his kingdom. *Ija Ominira* is the first Nigerian film to have recouped its cost of production within one year (F. Balogun, p. 64).

The success of *Ajani Ogun* and *Ija Ominira* at the box office led other popular figures of the Yoruba theater, such as Chief Hubert Ogunde and Moses Olaiya Adejumo (alias Baba Sala), to seek out Balogun to adapt their plays to film. In 1979, Balogun and Chief Ogunde produced *Aiye,* based on a play written by Ogunde. *Aiye* is a story about a struggle between a traditional medicine man and an evil magician. The film is full of special effects that produce the sense of magic. The popularity of *Aiye* was also assured by the presence in the film of Chief Ogunde, whose name could bring loyal admirers of his theater to the movies. In 1982, another pioneer of Yoruba theater, Baba Sala, produced *Orun Mooru* with Balogun. Presented to the Pan-African Film Festival of Ouagadougou in 1987, *Orun Mooru* was one of the most popular films for the spectators in Burkina Faso. Baba Sala plays Lamidi, the hero, who decides to commit suicide after having been robbed by swindlers. As Lamidi undertakes his journey to the Kingdom of the Dead, he realizes that Death, Iku, is not ready for him.

Iku sends him to Ayo, the spirit of Joy. Ayo gives Lamidi two eggs without telling him that the first one contains wealth and the second, death. Ayo sends Lamidi back to earth, advising him to break the first egg immediately upon his return home and the second egg fifty years later. Following Ayo's recommendation, Lamidi breaks the first egg and becomes instantly wealthy. Led by greed, he thinks that he will become even richer by breaking the second egg. Yet, as Lamidi breaks it open, he finds himself confronted by Death (Pfaff). Other stars of popular theater have come to cinema as a result of the commercial success of *Ajani Ogun, Ija Ominira* and *Orun Mooru*. In 1982, Akinwauni Isola teamed with Bankole Bello, who assisted Balogun in the production of *Ajani Ogun,* to produce *Efunsetan Aniwaura*. Furthermore, Baba Sala, Ade Love, and Chief Ogunde have left Balogun to fly on their own wings as producers, directors, and actors of their own films. They believe that they owe their popularity at the movies less to the cinematic form that Balogun was giving to their films and more to their own performances as stars and the illusion of reality and magic provided by film.

After this brief survey of Yoruba theater on film, what kind of evaluation can one make of it? For her part, Françoise Balogun believes that Yoruba cinema is limited to Yoruba audiences because it stresses the inside aspects of Yoruba tradition, instead of the universal aspects. "Outside of the Yoruba country, the Yoruba cinema constitutes an exotic curiosity instead of an artistic expression" (F. Balogun, p. 87). She also states that Ola Balogun, her husband, is tired of directing "these fairy-tales" for Yoruba theater companies and is more inclined to direct films that communicate with the public at a deeper and more intellectual level (F. Balogun, p. 67).

Other critics believe, on the contrary, that the future of Nigerian cinema is in Yoruba popular theater. The question becomes, then, how to operate within the social conditions of cinema and popular theater in Nigeria and to create great works of art. In the words of Luky Isawode, "Today, there are countless numbers of actors, dramatists, playwrights, singers, martial artists, etc., in this country. What the Indians and Chinese did, Nigerians can also do."[10]

Wole Soyinka also thinks that the Yoruba popular theater can provide Nigeria with a new art form, as well as an economically viable industry for the producers and the businessmen. The stars of popular theater have, for years of production of their plays, already shaped the taste of audiences in Nigeria. The new Yoruba cinema can make this audience its own by carefully appropriating the elements of popular theater (stars, magic, dance, and music) that appeal to the spectators and mixing them with that which cinema offers (photography, close-ups, and illusion of reality and magic produced by editing and putting together images). For Soyinka, what filmmakers need in Nigeria is an "intermutual interrelation" between theater and cinema, keeping in mind all the time that the two media are not exactly the same.[11]

Soyinka believes that the Yoruba cinema is economically viable because it does not resort to the aesthetic precepts that are molded by Western cinema and that are expensive to produce in an African film. The least expensive cameras, 16mm and Super 8, can be used in the production of Yoruba cinema without a loss of quality. Because the Yoruba theater comes to cinema already equipped with its own actors, costumes, stories, and props, all the filmmaker has to do is to put the theater in a cinematic time. It is in this sense that Soyinka states his preference for Cinéma Vérité as a model for Yoruba cinema. This cinema is not only relevant to the social conditions of Nigeria because it reflects stories and spectacles based on everyday life and on the collective myths, but it also provides an aesthetic and economic alternative to the Western superproduction. For Soyinka, the Yoruba cinema can manipulate the technology provided by film to evolve a new art form for the masses, as opposed to an elitist art form open only to the intellectual (Theater and the emergence, p. 1010).

Soyinka's interest in the interrelation between theater and film is not, however, limited to these written statements. In 1971, Ossie Davis adapted his play *Kongi's Harvest* on film in which the role of Kongi, a totalitarian leader, was played by Soyinka himself. The Nobel Prize-winning playwright has since denounced the film version of *Kongi's Harvest* as unfaithful to the script he wrote for the screen adaptation (Theater and the emergence, p. 97). In 1984, Soyinka directed his first feature film, *Blues for a Prodigal.*

Considering the success of Yoruba cinema in Nigeria and the fact that the best Yoruba films like *Orun Mooru* are also popular in other African countries, it may be that the filmmakers in other parts of Africa should seed a more popular form of cinema looking at existing popular spectacles like theater, wrestling matches, song, and dance. Both Nigerian and Ghanaian cinema can learn from the mistakes and innovations of the Francophone cinema that preceded them and that is world famous, with such directors as Ousmane Sembène and Souleymane Cissé. The movement toward popular culture constitutes a step toward giving African cinema its own identity.

It is obvious from this survey that there were enough resources in Anglophone Africa to enable the emergence of a regional and international film industry. Since the early 1970s, film distribution has been nationalized in such countries as Tanzania, Kenya, Nigeria, Ghana, and Ethiopia. The Indigenization Act has enabled private Nigerians with the business contracts to take control of film distribution and exhibition. Not only does this create new jobs for Nigerians, but it also stimulates the economy because the revenues from distribution and exhibition remain in the country instead of being evacuated to banks in London, Bombay, or New York, which was the case when foreigners controlled the industry. A regional system of film distribution can also come from the nationalization of the industry. The cost of foreign films can be reduced by acquiring films through a cooperative constituted by different countries in a region. It was in this sense that Kenya used to distribute films in the seventies to Zambia, Ethiopia, and Uganda. Such a regional distribution network has been in existence in Francophone Africa since 1973, even though it has yet to fight foreign distribution for control of the market.

Distribution is also the key to national film production. Because of import quotas, France and Germany, Europe's two most important film producers, have survived the bombardment of their film market by the U.S. Motion Picture Export Association of America (MPEAA). Similarly, a quota on the import of foreign films in Anglophone Africa can liberate more screen space for African and Third World films. For example, audiences in Anglophone Africa should be given the opportunity to see the independent Afro-American and black British cinemas. Like France and West Germany, Anglophone countries in Africa can also raise taxes on the distribution of foreign films to subsidize national film production. At the same time, the governments can lower entertainment taxes for national films to make it easier for them to compete with the imported films.

Like film distribution, film production can also be regionalized in Anglophone Africa. So far, coproduction of films has yet to take place between Africa and the West. The landscape and the people in Africa are often used as a backdrop for stories about Westerners: *King Solomon's Mines* shot in Zimbabwe, *Out of Africa* in Kenya, *Dogs of War* in Ghana, etc. With the number of filmmakers available in Africa today, it is ironic that some Anglophone African countries call upon Westerners to direct documentaries and educational films intended for Africans. Coproductions are desirable, but, if possible, they should be between African nations. There are many reasons why I assert this principle. First, by using Africans, the producers will spend less. Second, the film, by its double or triple nationality, increases the chances that it will recoup its cost among an African audience. Coproduction among Africans may also put to full use the equipment in such countries as Ghana, Kenya, and Zimbabwe, where all the production facilities exist but feature films are rare. Most important, aesthetical films run far less risk of misinterpreting African cultures and reifying African people when made by African directors. Ghana has opened the way for such coproduction on the African level. In 1980, Ola Balogun shot *Cry Freedom* in Ghana with the cooperation of NAFTI. More recently John Akomfrah of the Black Audio Film Collective and director of *Handsworth Songs* (winner of the first Paul Robeson Prize at FESPACO) has turned to Ghana for the location as well as subject of his second film. Haile Gerima also is looking to Ghana for a possible location for his next film.

IX.

African Cinema and Festivals

FESPACO

When it first took place in 1969, only five African and two European countries participated in the Festival Panafricain du Cinéma de Ouagadougou (FESPACO). By 1985 it had become the biggest cultural event in Africa, with thirty-three countries competing for the now prestigious Etalon de 'Yennenga award and several other prizes such as the ones conferred by the Organization of African Unity, UNESCO, the Institut Culturel Africain (ICA), the Agence de Coopération Culturelle et Technique (ACCT), the Organisation Catholique Internationale du Cinéma et de l'Audio-visuel (OCI), and the European Economic Community. The Ninth FESPACO (23 February–2 March 1985) brought to Ouagadougou, Burkina Faso, more than five hundred guests: film-makers, journalists, and critics from Africa, Europe, and America. An unprecedented half-million people participated in the events.

While such newspapers and specialized magazines as *El-Joudjahid* (Algeria), *Le Monde* (France), and *Cahiers du Cinéma* have regularly covered the festival since 1969, FESPACO 1985, which was attended for the first time by newcomers such as the *Los Angeles Times* and the independent British TV network, Channel 4, marked a clear improvement over the preceding ones. It was also at FESPACO 1985 that the OAU award was inaugurated. The purpose of this chapter is to explain the success of the FESPACO in becoming the most important and culturally unifying event in Africa, despite the ideological contradictions and linguistic differences between some African countries.

FESPACO had to overcome several obstacles and undergo several transformations before becoming the international event that it now is. Begun in 1969 as La Semaine du Cinéma Africain, it was only at its third meeting in 1972 that the Ouagadougou film events took the name FESPACO and introduced competition between films for awards. The 1969 Semaine du Cinéma Africain was organized by Burkina Faso (then Upper Volta) and the French Ministry of Coopération, which was the biggest producer of African films. Five African countries (Senegal, Mali, Upper Volta, Cameroon, and Niger) and two European countries (France and Netherlands) were represented by filmmakers and their films. On the African side, *Borom Sarret* (1964) and *La noire de . . .* (1966) by Ousmane Sembène, *Et la neige n'etait plus* (1964), *Le retour de l'aventurier* (1964), and *Aoure* (1966) by Moustapha Alassane, and *Cabascado* (1964) by Oumarou Ganda were shown. On the European side, Jean Rouch showed *Jaguar* (1966), *Moro Naba* (1957), and *Bataille sur le grand fleuve* (1950), and Joris Ivens showed *Demain à nanguila* (1963). In total, twenty-five films were exhibited on a noncompetitive basis.

This first Semaine du Cinéma Africain (1–15 February 1969) had many structural elements and rules that are still maintained by the FESPACO. It had a local committee of Voltaics in charge of the organization. The committee was assisted by subcommittees for the reception, housing, information, programming, and entertainment. The French cultural attaché in Ouagadougou participated in the organization and the Ministry of Coopération in Paris supplied most of the films and contributed funds for the festival. The Semaine du Cinéma Africain had as its objective "to make people discover and to promote African film which for the most part was ignored. The purpose of this encounter was therefore to show that there exists an African cinema, which was made in Africa, by Africans, on African subjects."[1] Some ten thousand people saw the films, and this encouraged the organizers to have a Semaine du Cinéma every year.

The second Semaine du Cinéma (1–15 February 1970) was more successful on all levels. Nine African countries (Algeria, Tunisia, Ivory Coast, Mali, Guinea, Ghana, Niger, Senegal, Upper Volta) and the French government participated in the events. Thirty-seven films were exhibited, including *Mandabi* (*The Money Order*, 1968) and *La noire de . . . (Black Girl)* by Ousmane Sembène, *Dianka-bi* (1969) by Mahama Johnson Traoré, *La femme au couteau* (1968) by Timité Bassori, *L'aube des damnes* (1965) by Ahmed Rachedi, and *La voix* (1968) by Slim Riad. The number of spectators also jumped to twenty thousand, making the Semaine du Cinéma a major international event both in the eyes of filmmakers and the governments. The second Semaine du Cinéma was special and innovative for at least two reasons. It took place just after the government in Upper Volta had defied the foreign monopolists and nationalized its film industry.[2] The second Semaine du Cinéma also included Maghreb countries (Algeria and Tunisia) and an Anglophone country (Ghana), showing that the festival had pan-African visions and that it was not limited by a parochial Francophone outlook.

The nationalization of film distribution and production in Upper Volta and the success of the two Semaines du Cinéma convinced other governments of the existence of an African cinema and of its economic, political, and cultural importance. During the Semaines du Cinéma, filmmakers and journalists not only exchanged notes and criticism, they also explained to government officials the importance of de-colonizing their movie theaters. The nationalization in Upper Volta marked the beginning of similar actions by Mali the same year and later by other countries. Upper Volta's symbolic action against the foreign distributors and the exposure the two Semaines du Cinéma provided for African films also encouraged the filmmakers of the continent (La Fédération Panafricaine des Cinéastes—FEPACI) to unite with the Voltaic government and change the Semaines du Cinéma into a continental festival that could engage African films in competition and make awards. The second phase of the Ouagadougou film events began with qualitative and quantitative innovations and with a new name: the Festival panafricain du cinéma de Ouagadougou (FESPACO).

There was no festival in 1971 because of the Voltaic government and because the African filmmakers were still at work laying down the conditions of eligibility for the films that were to compete for awards. They had to contact African governments and international organizations for their sponsorship of the events, improve the structure of organization left behind by the Semaine du Cinéma, and make provisions that were necessary for an international event such as FESPACO. It was only after these conditions were met that FESPACO took place in March 1972.

The preamble of FESPACO was similar to that of Semaine du Cinéma. The main objective was "to facilitate the dissemination of African films so as to allow contacts and confrontations of ideas between the filmmakers. The aim was also to contribute to the development of cinema as a means of expression, education, and a means to raise consciousness."[3] According to the rules, the competition is open only to African films. Each African country is allowed to enter two films by two different directors. The films must be proposed "by the competent authorities of the said country, and in the absence of such authorities they are selected by the delegates attending the Festival" (9ème . . . . , p. 25). At the last instance, a film accepted in the official contest has met the following criteria: it is directed by an African, it is less than three years old, it is entering FESPACO for the first time, and it is in a 16mm or 35mm format. Finally, Article 13 of the rules said that "the official jury of the FESPACO is an international one which is made up of a chairman and ten members at the most, including two Burkinabê (formerly Voltaics) (9ème . . . , p. 25).

The first prize, Etalon de 'Yennenga, of the 1972 FESPACO went to Oumarou Ganda (Niger) for his feature film, *Le wazzou polygame* (1971). The second prize went to Moussa Kemoko Diakité (Guinea) for *Hydre dyama* (1970), a documentary codirected with a non-African, Gerhard Jeutz. Other winners included Ahmed Rachedi (Algeria) for *L'opium et le baton* (1970) and Kwami Mambu Zinga (Zaire) for the best short film, *Moseka* (1972).

The 1972 FESPACO (known as the third FESPACO even though it is technically the first one) set the tone for the ones that followed. More and more African countries took part in the events. The audience grew from 100,000 in 1972 to 500,000 in 1985. More awards were offered (from six in 1972 to twenty in 1985), and FESPACO began to enjoy the same reputation as other international film festivals. According to Filippe Sawadogo, general secretary of FESPACO, the objective of each FESPACO is to be better than the preceeding one and the "ultimate aim is to be perfect" (9ème . . . , p. 48).

Since 1972, only two decisions affected the progress and regularity of FESPACO. The first was made during the fourth FESPACO (1973), to alternate FESPACO with the Journées Cinématographiques de Carthage (JCC), which was the major festival site for African and Arab films. Because the FESPACO had become so important, and because the filmmakers at FESPACO in Upper Volta were for the most part the same as those at the JCC in Tunisia, there was concern that the same film would dominate both festivals. In order to reduce the number of films shown at both festivals, the filmmakers proposed a plan to the governments to alternate FESPACO and JCC. It was in this sense that the two festivals became biannual, with FESPACO taking place in odd years and JCC in even ones.

The other major irregularity in the FESPACO followed a frontier dispute in 1975 between Mali and Upper Volta. In that year the festival, which was now biannual, did not take place. It was in 1976, three years after the fourth FESPACO (1973), that the fifth FESPACO took place.

Fortunately, the only effect the irregularities had on FESPACO was the delay in time. Although this alternation with the JCC forces fans who cannot afford to go to Carthage to wait two years for the Ouagadougou events, it also has contributed constructively to FES-PACO.

The quality of the films selected has improved over the years; the organizing committee has more time to promote the festival and invite film historians and scholars from the different corners of the world. The two years it takes to put a FESPACO together has also contributed to an increase in the number of international organizations that fund the festival. Because of the alternation of FESPACO and JCC, they do not have to compete for funds at the same time from such organizations that fund the festival as the Agence de Coopération Culturelle et Technique or UNESCO. Finally, there are economic advantages for the spectators. They have more time with the biannual festival to save for the ticket to Ouagadougou, unlike the annual one, which seems always to come too soon. As for the irregularity caused by the conflict between Mali and Upper Volta, it was soon forgotten after the fifth FESPACO (1976). The best proof of this is the fact that a Malian director, Souleymane Cissé, has since broken all records by twice winning the Etalon de 'Yennenga, at the sixth FESPACO with *Baara* (1979) and at the eighth FESPACO with *Finye* (1983).

After this historical overview, it is important to pause for a moment to evaluate FESPACO and its impact on African culture. I have already indicated the success with which FESPACO has developed since 1969 and the innovation of each FESPACO over the preceding one. I would like now to focus on the ninth FESPACO (1985) in order to illustrate some of these innovations. The most obvious difference between FES-PACO 1985 and the preceding ones was in theme: "Cinéme et Libéra-tion des Peuples." For the first time FESPACO had a theme and the festival reflected it in several ways. The theme of freedom was denoted by signs like "Libérez les écrans africains," "FESPACO '85, Arme de la Libération des Peuples," "FESPACO '85, Hommage aux Peuples en Lutte," which were everywhere, on posters in front of movies theaters and hotels, on banners, flyers, newspaper headlines, radio and televi-sion. The theme of freedom was also seen in the selection of films that were shown on a noncompetitive basis. There was a special retrospec-tive on Algerian war epics and on Latin and Central American Third Cinema films.[4] There were also anti-apartheid films.

Another feature of FESPACO 1985 was a colloquium on African literature and film. African writers such as Mongo Beti and Kitia Touré, filmmakers Ousmane Sembène and Haile Gerima, critics, historians, and many others were brought together to discuss the possibilities of adapting African literature into film. There were also films adapted from oral literature: *Toula* (1972) by Moustapha Alassane, *Wend Kuuni* (1982) by Gaston Kaboré, and those adapted from written literature such as *L'aventure ambigue* (1984) by Jacques Champreux and *Petanqui* (1984) by Yeo Kazoloa from the novel *Quinze ans, ça suffit* by Ousmane Amadou.

The purpose of the colloquium was to make accessible to the public at large the rich body of African literature which is so far only available to a small elite who know how to read and write. As Algerian critic Azzedine Mabrouki put it, "Because film is the only cultural product which is capable of reaching the largest number of audiences (television has not yet made its impact on Africans), it can be used to mediate between the written works and the African audiences."[5] In other words, the filmmakers must familiarize themselves with African literature and learn narrative techniques and rhetorical devices from it. This will not only make the film more coherent historically and ideologically, it will also contribute to the poetics of African cinema.

Most of the discussion centered around the notions of representations, verisimilitudes, and faithfulness to the original text. Champreux's adaptation of the *Ambiguous Adventure* by Cheick Hamidou Kane was criticized, for example, for not being true to the characters and the decor of the book. It was argued that the dignified air with which the Djalobés group is portrayed in the book, and for which it is known in West Africa, is missing in the film. Champreux is also said to have overemphasized the Senghorism or the symbiosis between cultures. For Champreux, this marriage between cultures is necessary, and those who cannot adapt to it become insane and dangerous like the fool in the film. Critics said that in the book, Kane had deliberately left the issue ambiguous. Others argued that the strong point of the film was to have clearly explained to people the Senghorism that is in an elliptical Cartesian dialectic in the book.

The different criticism leveled at the film *Ambiguous Adventure* led Haile Gerima, an Ethiopian residing in the United States and director of *Harvest, 3000 Years* (1975), to say that it was not always a good idea to adapt into film African literature that is written in the former colonial languages. Arguing from personal experience, Gerima said that in order for him to film a script written in English, he must translate it first into Amharic, his mother tongue. During the translation process, several cultural subtleties may be lost. Another objection to the adaptation of African literature in English, French, or Portuguese is that the choice of the colonial language has already removed and

FESPACO 1985, scene from Ouagadougou entitled *Battle of the Rails*. Photograph courtesy of Christine Delorme.

deterritorialized the literature from its cultural setting. For all these reasons, Gerima believes that the oral literature is a richer and more authentic source of inspiration for African film.

Another important addition to FESPACO 1985 was the strong representation of Afro-American filmmakers, distributors, promoters, critics, and historians. There were special screenings of films from the Diaspora such as *Burning an Illusion* by Menelik Shabazz (Barbados), *Rue case nègres* by Euzhan Palcy (Martinique), *Passing Through* by Larry Clark (U.S.), *Losing Ground* by Kathleen Collins (U.S.), etc. The Afro-American filmmakers and historians gave a seminar at the Institut Africain d'Education Cinématographique de Ouagadougou (IN-AFEC), Africa's only international film school, on the issues of distribution, coproduction and student/scholar exchange. They discussed several ways they could work together and help one another. Drawing on his own experience in producing *Passing Through,* Larry Clark showed how African directors can cut the cost of producing their films, help each other with camera work, editing, and even acting, and not have to depend on expensive Hollywood studios or unionized cameramen and actors.

Gerima, who was at FESPACO 1985 both as a filmmaker and as the North American distributor of the Comité Africain des Cinéastes (CAC), signed distribution contracts with several filmmakers. There was the question of letting filmmakers from the Diaspora participate in the official competition of FESPACO in the future. Short of agreeing to this, the African filmmakers decided to study the issue and promised, at any rate, to open the future festivals more to their brothers and sisters from the Diaspora. Prix du Public (a new prize at FESPACO), which was open to all the films shown at FESPACO 1985, was awarded to *Rue case nègres* by Euzhan Palcy.

To turn now to the cultural significance of the festival, I would again like to focus on FESPACO 1985. In Third World countries, film is particularly important because, as a cultural vehicle, it can also communicate social and political issues. Film instructs and entertains by means that are not available in other representative arts. In Ouagadougou, the unique quality of film is understood by everyone. Every FESPACO is an opportunity for filmmakers to cover new issues and problems that are turned into cultural events for the festivalgoers to see. At FESPACO 1985, for example, Angolan director Ruy Duarte de Carvalho dramatized famine in a film called *Nelisita* (1984). The film tells the story of two families caught in the mythical "great famine." The narrative, which is drawn from two folktales of eastern Angola, beautifully depicts the hero, Nelisita, as he fights different evil spirits and

survives the famine. Although the story has a once-upon-a-time aura to
it, this is not an escapist film. De Carvalho intertwines the myth of
folktales and the reality of famine in Africa today in an effective
manner. Thus, what would have been a purely cathartic and escapist
film in a consumer-oriented Western cinema, has here been given a
historical and cultural dimension. By mixing the myth with current
events, the film teaches the viewer how to survive famine. The film won
second prize at FESPACO 1985, giving de Carvalho (a Portuguese by
birth, an Angolan by citizenship), who has been making documentaries in Angola since 1975, his first international recognition as a
director.

Paul Zoumbara from Burkina Faso is another director at FESPACO
1985 who succeeded with *Jours de tourments* (1983) in broadening
the concept of culture beyond entertainment. The film is about a young
peasant, Pierre, who wants to change an arid patch of land into a
garden. He forms a farmers' union with his peers in the village in order
to dig wells and fight the drought. His ambitions of self-reliance
threaten the merchant of the village who sells millet and rice. The film
can also be "read" as a love story between Pierre and his fiancée, Sali.
Pierre does not want to marry Sali until he is able to support a family.
In *Jours de tourments*, Zoumbara broadens the concept of culture to
lay claim on such social and political issues as agriculture for self-
reliance, workers' unions, and migration to urban areas. For a revolutionary country like Burkina Faso where Sankara's regime is teaching
people about freedom and self-reliance, films such as *Jours de tourments* are the best tools of instruction.

At FESPACO 1985, seeing Zoumbara's film with a Burkinabê audience was an unforgettable event. The film is in Dioula (also known as
Bambara and Madinka), a language widely understood in West Africa.
The Burkinabê spectator identifies with Pierre, the hero of the film,
laughs with him or at the misfortune of his enemies, and sometimes
even shouts at the screen in order to warn him against imminent
danger. Seeing *Jours de tourments* with the Burkinabê is an experience
comparable to seeing Superman with Americans, with the difference
that one is revolutionary and the other is escapist. FESPACO awarded
Zoumbara the Oumarou Ganda Prize, which goes to the first feature
film of a director whose creative efforts are particularly noteworthy.
Other highlights of FESPACO 1985 were *Histoire d'une rencontre*
(1984) by Brahim Tsaki (Algeria), a love story between two young
people who are deaf and dumb and from different social backgrounds.
Tsaki displays a remarkable talent by narrating the story through
gestures. *Histoire d'une rencontre* won the Etalon de 'Yennenga. The

best short film was awarded to *Arusi ya Mariamu (The Wedding of Mariamu)*, codirected by Ron Mulvihill (United States) and Nanga Yoma Ngoge (Tanzania). The film is about the traditional science of healing, and it effectively depicts the conflict between tradition and modernity in a developing country.

The importance of film as a cultural and political act is also understood by African governments and international organizations. FESPACO is not only a platform for the dissemination of a pan-African spirit, but also a place to assert national identities. The international media is watching, and for each film that wins an award, it is a victory for the country of origin of the director. Furthermore, FESPACO is used as a platform to make political statements of international values. In front of television cameras and microphones, filmmakers and government representatives denounce the apartheid regime in South Africa. At FESPACO 1985, for example, Thomas Sankara, the head of state of Burkina Faso, gave a press conference not only to address film issues, but also to explain the domestic and foreign policy of the country. The delegate from the Organization of African Unity said in his address to the press that FESPACO was the reflection of the most complete dialogue between African cultures. He believed that "every event of the FESPACO is a victorious moment for the OAU."[6] It was in this sense, he continued, that the OAU had decided to create a prize, the "Unity Awards," to promote African cinema.

It remains to assess the contradictions of FESPACO. The question of languages is at the heart of these contradictions. Some filmmakers and critics have accused FESPACO of having a Francophone bias because the festival has so far been dominated by French-speaking countries and their films. The fact that most of the filmmakers, from the beginning of FESPACO to the present, have been aided by the French Ministry of Coopération has led some observers to point to a French neocolonialism in African cinema.

It is necessary, however, to look at the question of languages alongside the spirit of pan-Africanism that exists at every FESPACO. It is true that France participated in the founding of the Semaine du Cinéma Africain in order to promote films that were produced by the Ministry of Coopération. Furthermore, it is clear that Francophone countries lead other African countries in production (excepting Egypt and the Maghreb) because of the production and postproduction facilities France has made available to them since their independence. Dependence on French facilities has until recently prevented the Francophone countries from building their own facilities of production and postproduction. But it seems to me that the strength of FESPACO has been gradually to dismantle French hegemony in Ouagadougou and to replace it with a pan-African hegemony. Because of the persistent criticism of the Francophone bias by such African directors as Lionel Ngakane and Gerima, FESPACO now provides earphones for non-French speakers, selects jury members from Anglophone, Lusophone, and Arabophone countries, and writes most of its programs in French and English. While it is true that the prestigious Etalon de 'Yennenga has so far only gone to Arab and Francophone countries, at FESPACO 1985 Anglophone and Lusophone countries such as Ghana, Nigeria, Tanzania, and Angola won awards ranging from the Best Cinematography and the Critics Award (Ghana), Best Actress (Nigeria), Best Short Film, and the OAU Award (Tanzania) to the Award of the Seventh Art (Angola).

Another contradiction in FESPACO that, in my opinion, will also be solved with time concerns the Africanity of a film. In other words, is any film presented by an African government eligible for the official competition? At FESPACO 1981, Souleymane Cissé tried to stop *A banna* (It's finished) (1980) sent by Mali, arguing that the film was directed by a woman from Czechoslovakia instead of by the proposed author, Kalifa Dienta. The FESPACO overruled Cissé's objection without further investigation because it did not want to antagonize Mali. In the past, films co-directed by Africans and non-Africans had won awards at FESPACO. Some obvious examples are *Hydre dyama* (Third FESPACO) by Moussa Kemoko Diakité (Guinea) and Gerhard Jeutz and *The Wedding of Mariamu* (Ninth FESPACO) by Nanga Yoma Ngoge (Tanzania) and Ron Mulvihill. Some Afro-Americans present at FESPACO 1985 tried to stop *The Wedding of Mariamu* from participating in the competition, arguing that the film was presented in the United States as only being directed by Mulvihill. The objection came particularly from Pearl Bowser, who was a member of the jury and a film distributor in North America. It was overruled without further investigation. On the other hand, FESPACO also has to decide on the Africanity of films that are produced by African countries and directed by non-Africans, and vice versa. Such was the problem with *Le courage des autres* (1982) produced by CINAFRIC (a private production company in Burkina Faso) and directed by Christian Richard (France). The film was prevented from participating in FESPACO 1983. Filmmakers from the Diaspora want also to have their films included in the official competition. FESPACO has yet to accept them, but there is no doubt in Ouagadougou that their argument is a good one in view of the fact that their films promote African culture and they are suppressed in the West.

Only time and the prospect of a developed industry will solve these complex issues. Meanwhile, since the purpose of FESPACO is to encourage African production, the collaboration of governments and non-African directors is necessary in order to allow FESPACO to measure the efforts of those who have not had access to the camera until recently.

FESPACO has succeeded in interesting all the African countries in film production. Ouagadougou is now the place to score pan-African as well as national victories. Even though critics and historians of African cinema agree that the quality of the films at FESPACO 1985 was slightly below that of FESPACO 1983, no one was disappointed. There were so many cultural and intellectual activities going on in Ouagadougou that it will take more than the films in competition to evaluate FESPACO 1985—and for that matter any FESPACO.

X.

African Cinema Today

The eleventh Pan-African Film Festival of Ouagadougou (FESPACO '89) demonstrates how diversified African films are today. Next to *Yeelen* (Souleymane Cissé, 1987), and *Yaaba* (Idrissa Ouedraogo, 1989), which put into play the theme of the return to the sources, an Africa without the presence of outsiders, there are *Camp de Thiaroye* (Ousmane Sembène and Thierno Sow, 1988) and *Mortu Nega* (Flora Gomes, 1988), which make the colonial question their main subject. *Finzan* (Cheick Oumar Sissoko, 1989), *Bal poussière* (Henri Duparc, 1988), and *Bouka* (Roger Gnoan M'Bala, 1988) are social realist narratives that deal with questions of modernity and tradition.

This thematic diversification produces a typology of narratives that compete for the spectator's attention. Each one of the narrative movements—the return to the sources, the historical confrontation between Africa and Europe, and the social realist—presents an image of Africa that makes a claim to be fuller and more faithful to reality than the others. At FESPACO '89 many people interpreted the diversified styles of films as a sign of maturity in African cinema. Others, pointing to *Yeelen* and *Yaaba,* argued that it marked the end of *"mégotage"* (filmmaking on shoestrings that reflects the "miserable" African condition of life)[1] and the end of an era that privileged polemical and loosely constructed contents at the expense of cinematic forms. And others expressed concern that some filmmakers have used this opportunity to turn their backs on politics and on a serious questioning of the oppression of women and the marginalized. This argument also put forth that filmmakers, by emphasizing beautiful images over serious content analysis, had surrendered to European notions of what African cinema ought to be.[2]

Clearly there are many African images, and it seems trivial to expect filmmakers of different generations, different countries, and different ideological tendencies to see the same Africa everywhere. It is therefore not my intention to sort out which modes of representation are right and which are wrong. It seems to be more fruitful to trace the evolution of these new African cinemas from FESPACO '87 to FESPACO '89 and to attempt to evaluate each narrative movement in the context of its own modes of production.

Social Realist Narratives

First let's examine the narrative of the movement I call the social realist tendency, which defines itself by thematizing current sociocultural issues. The films in this category draw on contemporary experiences, and they oppose tradition to modernity, oral to written, agrarian and customary communities to urban and industrialized systems, and subsistence economies to highly productive economies. The filmmakers often use a traditional position to criticize and link certain forms of modernity to neocolonialism and cultural imperialism. From a modernist point of view, they also debunk the attempt to romanticize traditional values as pure and original. The heroes are women, children, and other marginalized groups that are pushed into the shadows by the elites of tradition and modernity.

The social realist tendency, which uses melodrama, satire, and comedy, communicates more with African spectators than the two succeeding movements, which, as I will show, require more from the spectator because of their involvement in history and philosophy. The social realist movement draws from existing popular forms such as song and dance, the oral tradition (both literary and rumors), and popular theater (Yoruba theater in Nigeria and the Koteba in Mali and Ivory Coast). Such popular music stars as Salif Keita, Papa Wemba, and Alpha Blondy have appeared in the social realist films. Ousmane Sembène is known for this type of cinema from his ground-breaking *Le mandat* (The Money Order) (1968) to *Xala* (1974), both of which describe the plight of the marginalized in the postindependence era. Souleymane Cissé also made his reputation at FESPACO by winning two Grand Prix with *Baara* (1978) and *Finye* (1982), both of which are social realist films. There are other notable directors of the movement, such as Moustapha Alassane with *F.V.V.A.—Femmes, villa, voiture,*

argent (1972), which parodies the postcolonial bourgeoisie; Mahama
Johnson Traoré with *Njangaan* (1974), which deals with the role of
Islam and Koranic schools in contemporary Africa; Daniel Kamwa
with *Pousse Pousse* (1975), about the problem of dowry; Ben Diogaye
Beye with *Sey Seyeti (A Man, Some Women)* (1980), about polygamy;
and Lancine Kramo Fadiga with *Djeli* (1981), which examines marriage between people of different castes.

At FESPACO '87, the social realist movement affirmed its domi-
nance with films such as *La vie est belle* (Ngangura Mweze and Benoit
Lamy, 1986), *Nyamanton* (Cheick Oumar Sissoko, 1986), *Visages de
femmes (Faces of Women)* (Désiré Ecaré, 1985), and *Desebagato ou le
dernier salaire* (Sanou K. Emmanuel, 1986), all of which are anchored
in one popular form or another. Similarly, FESPACO '89 was the site of
a social realist cinema that seemed to have won the hearts of the
spectators. Duparc's *Bal poussière*, a social comedy about polygamy
with subplots of literacy, money as a sign of corruption, and tradition
as a burden, was the most discussed film in Ouagadougou. The spectators also rushed to see *Les guerisseurs* (Sijiri Bakaba, 1988), the
main attraction of which involves performances by Salif Keita, Alpha
Blondy, Nayanka Bell, and Georges Tai Benson, stars of popular music
and television; *Saaraba* (Amadou Saalum Seck, 1988), *Kolormask* (Sao
Gamba, 1986), and *Testament* (John Akomfrah, 1988), all dealing in a
different manner with the question of returning home after years of
exile in Europe; *Bouka,* which looks like with a modern eye at such
traditional issues as inheritance of wives, polygamy, and fetishism; *Zan
Boko* (Gaston Kaboré, 1988), about the expansion of cities, which
forces some villagers to abandon their land and, therefore, lose their
identity; and Sissoko's *Finzan*, much awaited at FESPACO '89 because
of the director's reputation with *Nyamanton*.[3]

Let's now examine some examples of the social realist movement as a
way of showing the manner in which its films position the spectator. In
1987, *La vie est belle* and other social realist films broke the intellec-
tualist tradition of African cinema and adopted populist themes that
are dear to the working class and the unemployed. The aim of the
filmmakers was to transform the polemics against the elite into jokes
made at the expense of the elite and to make films that appeal to the
African masses because they can identify with the characters in them.
To capture the masses' desire on film, the filmmakers have drawn from
popular musicians, the latest fashions, and the new ways of talking in
the capital cities. *La vie est belle,* for instance, tells the story of a village
musician, Kourou (Papa Wemba), who loses his audience to the radio,
which plays popular music. He decides to go to the big city, Kinshasa,

to sing and play an electric guitar. In the city, Kourou works as a shoeshine boy, a dishwasher, and a messenger before realizing his dream as a musician. The film also deals with the themes of polygamy, witchcraft, businesswomen in Kinshasa, Kourou's love affair with Kabibi (Bibi Krubwa), and the lifestyle of the nouveaux riches.

The first reason why *La vie est belle* attracts African spectators is the setting of the story in Kinshasa, regarded as the capital of African music with more than two hundred bands. It is also a city of high fashion, of ambiance, where the latest steps in dance are created, and of contradiction, where the rich and poor, the modern and traditional live side by side. Kinshasa, as reflected on the screen, mirrors what many African masses desire when they leave the villages for the pursuit of their dreams in the cities. Kourou's experiences demonstrate that the spectator can entrust the city with the power to transform his/her village looks into glamour and to provide him/her with more leisure time. The title *La vie est belle (Life is Rosy)* indicates that even the poor are happy in the heated nights of Kinshasa, the modern city with magical powers to make one forget one's problems.

But this popular myth of Kinshasa is not without criticism in the film. Kinshasa is also the city where appearance (the way people dress and speak) counts more than substance. Kourou puts on a suit and passes for the director of a big company; Amoro (Tumba Ayila), the dwarf who goes around laughing and saying that "life is rosy," is in reality a lonely and unhappy person. The elite, such as Nvouandu (KanKu Kasongo), flaunt their Mercedes cars and show no sympathy for the poor. It is also in the same Kinshasa where the charlatan witch doctors control the lives of the rich and poor, the educated and the illiterate, the Christian and the Moslem. Finally, the experience of Mamou (Landu Nzunzimbu), a clever businesswoman in the film, shows that Kinshasa's modernity does not include the end of polygamy for women.

The other reason that *La vie est belle* appeals to African spectators concerns the casting of Papa Wemba as Kourou. Popular music stars such as Franco, Tabu Ley, Salif Keita, and Papa Wemba have an enormous influence on lifestyle in Africa. Papa Wemba, known as the number one "Sapeur"[4] in Zaire, has many fans who imitate the way he talks and dresses. In *La vie est belle*, it is Papa Wemba as Kourou who imitates the ordinary man. Identification works both ways: the spectator identifying with the image of his/her desire, and Papa Wemba (Kourou) identifying with the working class in his roles as shoeshine boy, dishwasher, messenger, and the poor man whose girlfriend has been stolen by a rich man. The leitmotif Jourou repeats in his songs is "travaillez, prenez de la peine, c'est le fonds qui manque les moins" (Work hard, what we need most of all is good will). By popularizing this verse from the poetry of La Fontaine, Kourou implies that work alone can provide the solution to people's problems.

In fact, Kourou also mentions in his songs the famous "Article 15," which means *débrouillez-vous* (help yourself) for people who can no longer depend on the government for jobs, education, and health care in Zaire. Perhaps spectators used to the social realist films of Sembène and Cissé are disappointed that the film neither criticizes the system that oppresses the working class nor makes any effort to make it realize its condition as an exploited group. This is reinforced by the leitmotif which seems to empower the working class's image of itself as heroic and which prevents it from reacting against the incompetence of the African governments to make things better. But the invaluable lesson that *La vie est belle* teaches us is that the social realist movement can use popular forms as a vehicle for messages and images. The resort to popular forms is also a way to create an African audience for the films.

The social realist cinema also positions the spectator by addressing the issues of women's liberation in contemporary African society. The films show that while African men have accepted progress in certain areas of modernism, they are regressive when it comes to giving up male privileges. The filmmakers often thematize these issues by constructing social comedies involving a man with more women than he can satisfy sexually (*Finye, Xala,* and *Bal poussière*); by watching a man make a fool of himself by clinging to old-fashioned patriarchal means of treating women as objects (*Visages de femmes, Finzan,* and *Bouka*); and by giving the woman "the right to speak out, and the right to be heard—whether this right was won or granted, exercised spontaneously or in organized ways"[5] (*Nyamanton, Visages de femmes,* and *Finzan*).

Much of the popularity of *Bal poussière* in Ouagadougou derives from its positioning of the spectator to laugh at the excesses of polygamy. The protagonist, Demi-Dieu (Bamba Bakary), is the richest man in town, so he can buy anything he wants, including a sixth wife, Binta (Hanny Tchelley). But Binta, the modern woman, introduces concepts into his household that not only compromise Demi-Dieu's traditional image but also push the other wives to ask him for more sexual relations. The consequences are terrible for Demi-Dieu: "Each one of his wives made him swallow dishes with aphrodisiac ingredients in order to have him all to herself, and the pleasure of the 'happy husband' soon turned into exhaustion."[6] *Bal poussière* is simultaneously entertaining and didactic. It entertains by making the spectators identify with Binta as she makes fun of a regressive, polygamous man. Binta's actions are to women spectators like the revenge of women on polygamous men. The men laugh because they think they are superior to Demi-Dieu and that they will never fall into the same trap. The instruction the spectator unconsciously appropriates from *Bal poussière* concerns the impractical aspects of polygamy. The spectator feels that he is wiser than Demi-Dieu and, unlike him, prefers love with one woman to sex with several. Toward the end of the film, Binta is reunited with the man she loves.

Sissoko's *Finzan* also takes advantage of the spectator's willingness to laugh at characters who are morally, intellectually, or physically lower than himself/herself. The film tells the story of Nanyuma, who was married at fifteen against her will. *Finzan* begins with the death of Nanyuma's husband and the traditional custom of inheritance of wives by the brothers of the deceased. Bala, who already has two wives, wants to take Nanyuma as his third. Nanyuma defies the village customs and runs away to the big city. But she finds that when it comes to sexism, men in the city are no different from those in the village. The spectator is first sutured into this tragicomedy by the way in which Bala is constituted as a regressive, phallocentric character. For spectators in West Africa, Bala's role is recognizable from the traditional Koteba theater: he is a buffoon whose trademarks embody cowardice, jealousy, and greed. In folktales, the hyena often occupies the same role. Furthermore, the name Bala signifies stupidity, crudeness, and greed in Bambara (the language spoken in the film). The acting of Bala (played by Oumar Namory Keita, an actor from the Koteba in Mali) is exaggerated in the film to underscore its link with theater. Bala cannot sleep until he gets Nanyuma (Diarrah Sanogo), who keeps rejecting him. He disrupts everything in the village to talk about her, including a meeting between the village chief and the district commissioner. In one scene, he is seen singing praise songs to himself, describing how lucky he is to inherit Nanyuma; in another scene he is crying as he accuses the whole village of cheating him out of his rights.

On the serious side, the film thematizes the problems of excision and polygamy, and it posits women's emancipation as the condition of progress. Sissoko models Nanyuma after women characters such as Sogolon in *L'épopée de Soundiata* (Djibril Tamsir Niane, 1965), Kani in *Sous l'orange* (Seydou Badian, 1957), and Salimata in *Les soleils des indépendances* (Ahmadou Kourouma, 1969). Like Sogolon and Salimata, she is forced to marry men against her will and is forced to surrender by men holding knives. Like Kani, she seizes her right to speak and be heard. The film follows the African feminist discourse

Borom Sarret (1963), directed by Ousmane Sembène. Photograph courtesy of Férid Boughedir.

Touki Bouki (1973), directed by Djibril Diop Mambety. Photograph courtesy of Christine Delorme.

The Money Order (1968), directed by Ousmane Sembène. Photograph courtesy of Christine Delorme.

Wend Kuuni (1981), directed by Gaston Kaboré. Photograph courtesy of Christine Delorme.

La vie est belle (1986), directed by Ngangura Mweze and Benoit L'Amy. Photograph courtesy of *California Newsreel*.

Camp at Thiaroye (1989), directed by Ousmane Sembène and Thierno Sow. Photograph courtesy of Christine Delorme.

Finzan (1989), directed by Cheick Oumar Sissoko. Photograph courtesy of *California Newsreel*.

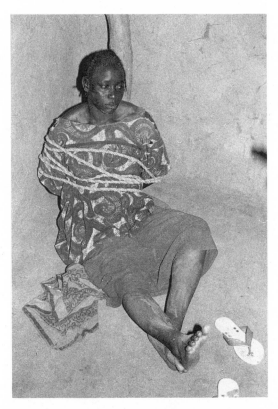

Finzan. Photograph courtesy of *California Newsreel*.

Saaraba, directed by Amadou Seck. Photograph courtesy of *California Newsreel*.

Zan Boko, directed by Gaston Kaboré. Photograph courtesy of *California Newsreel.*

that links social and economic progress with women's liberation. As Fatou Sow states, "The marginalization of women has contributed to the failure of many development projects."[7] *Finzan* positions the spectator to identify with this point of view and to accept women as equal partners in the development of Africa.

Colonial Confrontation

The second cinematic movement in Africa concerns films of historical confrontation that put into conflict Africans and their European colonizers. These films have so far generated more controversy. The majority of African spectators view them with a sense of pride and satisfaction with a history finally written from an African point of view. Some European spectators, on the other hand, characterize them as polemical, poorly constructed, and belonging to the 1960s rhetoric of violence. Between 1987 and 1989, both the French and the British used the above adjectives to shun *Sarraounia* (Med Hondo, 1987), *Heritage Africa* (Kwaw Ansah, 1988), and *Camp de Thiaroye.* Yet these films were among the most popular at FESPACO '87 and FESPACO '89. The festival's international jury awarded the 1987 Grand Prix to *Sarraounia* and the 1989 prize to *Heritage Africa.* With regard to *Sarraounia* and *Camp de Thiaroye,* it is remarkable that the French government has deviated from its commitment to the production and promotion of African cinema; neither film was selected for the Cannes Film Festival. Commenting on the popular reception of *Sarraounia* in Ouagadougou, Serge Daney states that this "anticolonialist fresco, with a nice production budget, remains the falsely rebelled dinosaur that was sulked by us in Paris."[8]

These films position the spectators to identify with the African people's resistance against European colonialism and imperialistic drives. The stories are about colonial encounters, and they often pit African heroes and heroines against European villains. They are conditioned by the desire to show African heroism where European history only mentioned the actions of the conquerors, resistance where the colonial version of history silenced oppositional voices, and the role of women in the armed struggle. For the filmmaker, such historical narratives are justified by the need to bring out of the shadows the role played by the African people in shaping their own history. It is also the case that they want to film a liberation struggle to keep it forever in people's minds.

The historical narratives certainly remind the viewer of such war epics as *Chroniques des années de braise* (Mohamed Lakhdar-Hamina, 1975) and *L'opium et le baton* (Ahmed Rachedi, 1970), which are based on the struggle of the Algerian National Liberation Front (FNL). But the precursors of the genre in sub-Saharan Africa are *Emitai* (Ousmane Sembène, 1971), which deals with the Diola people's refusal to surrender their rice to the French Army during World War II, and *Sambizanga* (Sarah Maldoror, 1972), which is based on the struggle of the Popular Liberation Movement of Angola (MPLA). Furthermore, unlike the Algerian war epics that deal exclusively with the FNL, the sub-Saharan historical narratives, while they are centered on the encounter between Africans and their foreign invaders, are not limited to contemporary wars of independence and resistance. As *Ceddo* (Ousmane Sembène, 1976) and *Sarraounia* show, they also include the representation of resistance to colonialism in the nineteenth century. All these films depict women coming to a revolutionary consciousness; they also create idealized heroes for the spectators to model themselves after. While they are similar to all war movies with their heroes and villains, they are unique in that they push the war itself into the background and examine African cultures and their incorporation in the characters' quest for freedom. In other words, they valorize African cultures in order to emphasize the dehumanizing effect of colonization, which is intent on destroying them. Oral literature, religious rituals, the African systems of thought, and the performance of griots are invoked and transformed in the service of liberation struggles.

To illustrate my point, I will next examine the way in which the historical encounters are narrativized in specific films. *Sarraounia* centers on the historical encounter in the nineteenth century between the French colonial troops and the Aznas of Niger. Based on the novel by Abdoulaye Mamani from Niger, the film depicts Sarraounia, a proud and skillful warrior and queen of the Aznas, in conflict with Captain Voulet of the French colonial forces. Sarraounia's entourage includes advisors, warriors, a lover, and a griot who sings her praise and describes her actions in war. She is an expert sorceress and a judicious queen who crushes her enemies and remains loyal to her friends. Sarraounia's goal is to keep her kingdom independent from both European colonialism and the Moslem conquest that is threatening from the East. The narrative reveals her strategies in war as she ambushes the colonial army or retreats when the situation calls for it. She is also a good orator who can use words to rally her men in the most difficult moments and deploy slogans against slavery and shame to tease them into fighting. Men and women from neighboring kingdoms join Sarraounia after their own armies have surrendered to the French and their people have been massacred. Sarraounia also has a love life that is momentarily complicated by her determination to be equal to men.

Sarraounia, like other films about the historical encounters between Europe and Africa, thematizes the role of women in precolonial Africa, the existence of a dynamic African culture, and the importance of resistance against foreign invaders. Filmed in CinemaScope, *Sarraounia* gives aesthetic pleasure by showing an African woman taking the hero position of Western films and becoming larger than life. In one scene, Sarraounia is shown in confrontation with her lover, who is also one of the best warriors in the army. Sarraounia challenges his advice to lead the attack in one way and not the way she wants. She takes that as an opportunity to remind him that she is the queen in charge of the army. In another scene, she is shown in the middle of her army, which has just retreated from the reach of cannon fire; it seems futile to go on fighting such an unequal battle, and her army is losing heart. It is then that the queen stands up and fills the screen with her height as she speaks to her people about the importance of resistance, the shame of slavery, and the need to fight for autonomy. It adds to the aesthetic of the film to see this scene and many others with African spectators in Ouagadougou or Dakar. They applaud Sarraounia for speaking for them. The scene re-creates for them other resistance scenes from the past, such as the one led by Samory Touré, and in the present, such as the liberation struggles in Southern Africa. Toward the end, Sarraounia is also immortalized by the song of the griot. As she is shown walking ahead of long lines of her people, the griot states that Sarraounia has taught the African people that death is preferable to shame and that the struggle will continue until everyone is free.

In other scenes, the spectator is told about Sarraounia's power and prestige by other characters in the story. Some Moslems hate her because she refuses to submit to their faith; others admire her because she defies the French. The film depicts Captain Voulet as possessed with the idea of conquering Sarraounia. He is therefore characterized as an evil man who regresses into irrationality as Sarraounia eludes him from battle to battle. Casting Sarraounia in a larger-than-life role is important because it shows that African women were active in the war against colonialism and that they are capable of leading the present struggle against imperialism, neocolonialism, and apartheid. In *Sarraounia*, Med Hondo goes beyond paying lip service to African women's liberation to a radical conception of African women as larger than life, like male heroes such as Samory Touré, Shaka, and Soundiata Keita.

While *Sarraounia* is concerned with resistance to colonization, Flora Gomes's *Mortu Nega*, winner of the prestigious Oumarou Ganda Prize at FESPACO '89, deals with the liberation struggle in Guinea-Bissau. The film is set between 1973 and 1977 and depicts Guinea-Bissau during and after the war. The story centers around the lives of Diminga (Bia Gomes) and her husband, Sako (Tunu Eugenio Almada). It opens with Diminga getting ready to join Sako at the war front. As she goes from battle zone to battle zone, the camera reveals Guinea-Bissau in a state of ruin and desolation. The only hope in the middle of this despair comes from rumors that the liberation struggle will soon triumph. Diminga's arrival at the camp where her husband is stationed coincides with the news of the assassination of Amilcar Cabral. This leaves Diminga and her husband only a few minutes to talk to each other before he has to resume fighting to finish off the enemy. The war ends, but Sako has to remain with the army for a few more months. He asks Diminga to return home and wait for him there. On her way home, she discovers a new country that is learning to live in peace. Sako comes home, and now they have to cope with new problems such as the drought and development issues. The struggle must therefore continue, even though the war has ended. Everything seems to be at a standstill around Diminga; Sako is sick, and his sickness seems to symbolize the country's morale. It is then that Diminga and other women organize a funeral ceremony in order to question the gods and themselves about the significance of death to the living. The next morning, the magic seems to have worked, the sky looks like it is going to rain, and there is a smile on Diminga's face.

Mortu nega works on one level as a love story. The title means "the negation of death," life in defiance of death. Thus, Diminga's love for Sako is paralleled in the film by the people's love for their country and their determination to defy death to free it from the Portuguese colonizers. The love affair with the country is shown in the way in which the camera fluidly lingers on every corner of the landscape through which Diminga traverses, as if it were the most precious place. This affection for the landscape is also linked to the theme of the liberation struggle, which engages the soldiers in zones occupied by the enemy. The soldiers are happy every time they hear on the radio or through rumor that an area has been liberated. After the war, people's love for the country is also seen by the way they treat it like a new baby in need of care. The film takes us to hospitals and offices during Sako's illness, in order to criticize the complacency of people who forget that independence means continuing the war on other fronts as well: illiteracy, drought, and corruption. It is in this sense that *Mortu nega,* also considered by the people of Guinea-Bissau as a film of hope, breaks with the tradition of films that celebrate the liberation struggle and makes a movement toward self-criticism.

On another level, *Mortu nega* is a film about women's roles in the liberation struggle. Like the main character in *Sambizanga*, who leaves her village in search of her husband in the city and in the process gains consciousness of the liberation struggle, Diminga also learns the importance of solidarity with the freedom fighters through her journey to join Sako. She knows that there has to be complete trust between men and women if their hiding places are to remain secret from the enemy. The wounded, for example, are left behind with women, and most of the messages are transmitted by them. The story unfolds from Diminga's point of view. It is through her eyes that the postindependence bureaucratic stagnation and the complacency of the officials are revealed. She criticizes Sako's war comrades, who are now important personalities in the government and promoting their own self-interest while people are suffering from famine, illiteracy, and lack of health care. Finally, in the most magical moment in the film, she organizes a funeral ritual with the other women to question the gods, notably *Djon Gago,* who represents life and death, about the meaning of independence now that the enemy is gone. Normally the funeral dance is performed in West Africa by men, with women singing and clapping their hands or acting as spectators. In the film, however, Flora Gomes draws on Cabral's notion of national culture, which transforms traditional rituals into revolutionary praxis, to bring women out of the shadow. After performing the funeral dance, Diminga and the other women come, one by one, to demand the right to a better life, given all the lives that have been sacrificed for independence. The close-up shots of Diminga, as she asks the gods to bring rain and prosperity, make her look defiant and radiant with power. The magic of the scene is such that it leaves no doubt that the gods will comply with Diminga's request. At FESPACO '89, Bia Gomes won honorable mention for her portrayal of Diminga.

Camp de Thiaroye is another film about the historical confrontation between Europe and Africa that was popular at FESPACO '89. Set in 1944 during World War II, the film is about African infantrymen in the French army who were called *"les tirailleurs senegalais."* These were enlisted men from the colonies throughout Francophone Africa who, after fighting the war against the Germans and Italians in Europe and Africa, were massacred in Thiaroye, near Dakar, by orders of high officials in the French army. The viewer learns through flashbacks, personal narratives, and dream sequences that the war experience has provided the African enlisted men with a different way of looking at white men. After seeing the German occupation of France, which is close to their own experience as colonized subjects, and after fighting ferociously to free France, they no longer see themselves as second-class citizens. While stationed at Thiaroye, the soldiers begin to ask for such rights as compensation for their wartime efforts, equal salary with French soldiers, and equal treatment for all soldiers. These historical events lead to the bombing of Thiaroye at the end of the film.

Even though based on real events, *Camp de Thiaroye* is a carefully crafted story that uses conventional narrative devices such as suspense, allusion to other historical events, and local sounds to create the impression of reality. The film won the Jury Special Award at the Venice Film Festival for its masterly use of these cinematic techniques. The suspense in *Camp de Thiaroye* concerns the fate of the soldiers. From historical knowledge, the spectator already knows that they will be massacred; the question is when and how they will die in the story. It is here that Sembène's long experience as a storyteller pays off. He succeeds in making the audience forget temporarily that the characters will die at the end by making them identify with the historical, cultural, and social development of the characters. The soldiers' memories of their villages, or marriage and death, and the cultural differences between the Bambara and the Bantu are depicted in order to anchor the characters as average human beings with a specific history and culture. The use of sound is important here because it accentuates the spectator's relation to the characters.

On one level, the use of broken French by the soldiers provides a comic flavor to the film. This kind of French, first common among veterans of World War II and now in use in such capital cities as Abidjan, makes the spectators laugh with a sense of recognition every time the speakers inflect the Parisian syntax in order to express an African idea. The spectators laugh at the soldiers' speech because of its transgressive nature. Students in Francophone Africa are taught to use *Francite* (a term coined by Léopold Sédar Senghor to mean the use of French logic in expressing oneself) as the means of address. Respect for French grammar is necessary in such a climate of assimilation. Clearly these rules, which reinforce the conditions of speaking French in Dakar, Bamako, and Ouagadougou, also restrict the number of speakers. By letting the soldiers violate the grammar of *Francite, Camp de Thiaroye* takes the French language away from the elite and gives it to the people. As he did with *Le Mandat* (1968), where the actors speak Wolof for the first time in an African film, Sembène sets the tune in *Camp de Thiaroye* with the use of an Africanized French. The result is a popular film with actors who play their roles with ease and express themselves with clarity. Sembène commits this taboo against *Francite* more to valorize the Africanized French, as English has been in Anglophone countries, and less to indicate that Africans are incapable of speaking the Parisian French. In fact, spectators at FESPACO '89 applauded the African sergeant (Ibrahima Sane), who is shown in one scene to possess a better command of both French and English than the French captain.

Camp de Thiaroye also appeals to audiences in Africa because of the allusions it makes to the Black Diaspora and the similarities it draws between the condition of the African soldiers in Thiaroye and the Nazis' treatment of Jews in the concentration camps. The Diaspora narrative has for its theme the encounter in Dakar between a black American soldier and the African sergeant. First they fight, the American accusing the African of stealing a U.S. army uniform. The conflict is resolved later, as the narrative emphasizes what the two men have in common and what they can contribute to each other's lives. The African enlisted men, for example, are impressed to see a black soldier treated equally with white soldiers in the U.S. army, and they wonder why they are not treated the same way in the French army. The black American, on the other hand, is impressed by the sergeant's knowledge of jazz, black American literature, and culture. The allusions to the concentration camps are narrated from the point of view of a mute enlisted man (Sijiri Bakabe), who keeps having flashbacks to his experience in Germany to draw an analogy between the suffering of people at Thiaroye and that of Jews at the hands of the Nazis. Toward the end, when the tanks are coming under the French general to destroy Thiaroye, the mute enlisted man wakes everybody up, screaming and gesturing that the Bosch are coming. But his comrades think he is hallucinating as usual, until it is too late to flee.

Kwaw Ansah's *Heritage Africa* is the last film to date about the historical confrontation between Africa and Europe. Like *Camp de Thiaroye*, it uses the classic Hollywood narrative to convey its message. The film is full of flashbacks, dream sequences, and all the elements that are necessary to turn the denouement into a climactic moment of resolution and illumination. The story revolves around the life of Kwesi Atta Bosomefi (Kofi Bucknor), whose elevation to the post of district commissioner in the colonial administration causes him to repress his African identity. Kwesi's tragedy begins in school, where he changes his name to Quincy Arthur Bosomfield and where he is forced to deny or reject part of his culture for every British value he learns. He is later shown hiding his mother from his friends because he is embarrassed by her village ways, whipping his son for participating in a traditional dance, and giving away a "50-year-old bronze Kuduo casket, the priceless and sacred container of the spirit of his entire lineage,"[9] to the colonial governor, Guggiswood (Peter Whitbread).

Unlike the films discussed above which are representations of historical encounters based on real events, *Heritage Africa* puts into play the psychological history of encounters between Africa and Europe. In other words, Kwaw Ansah is interested in the history of the repressed identity and the ways in which the repressed returns with a vengeance. In *Love Brewed in the African Pot* (1980), Ansah criticized a particular breed of Ghanaian elites (judges, lawyers, and accountants) for rejecting their origins.[10] In *Heritage Africa* he describes how the structures of alienation led the elites to push their African identity into the background. The elites' practice of denying the contribution of African traditions in their socioeconomic development is put into question in one scene that drew tears from the spectators in FESPACO '89. Kwesi's mother (Alexandra Dua) comes from the village to pay him a visit. She arrives at his home while he is entertaining his city colleagues. He meets her at the door and pushes her behind the house, where he gives her a stool and tells her to wait until his friends leave. She sits down and, while waiting for him, falls asleep. This scene is empowered by its use of irony. The spectator knows that Kwesi is ashamed of his mother and wants to make her pass as one of the servants, while she sees him as the worthy son from the village who will carry on the family tradition. She thinks that the ancestral casket will be safe with him, but no sooner does he receive it than he delivers it to the colonial governor.

The narrative of *Heritage Africa* equates Kwesi's betrayal of his mother to the betrayal of "Mother Africa." As Françoise Kaboré puts it, "The mother represents the symbol of love and protection (in Africa). Perhaps this is why Kwesi's betrayal of the mother country for the colonial power turns against him. The mother country is the incarnation of tradition and nationalism."[11] Thus, in a series of encounters with Kwame Adroma (Tommy Ebow Ansah), the freedom fighter, Kwesi sides with the colonizers' point of view.

The Return to the Source

To turn now to the films dealing with the theme of returning to the source, it is first important to put such a movement into perspective. Souleymane Cissé, whose film *Yeelen* is considered the best example in the genre, argues that he had to look for a different style after making *Baara* and *Finye,* which were overtly political and didactic. As he himself put it, "There was also tension building around me because of my previous films, and it was clear that if I wanted to stay in my country and enjoy a degree of freedom of expression, I had to lighten things a bit, or to make a different type of cinema."[12]

There are at least three reasons why filmmakers turn to this genre: (1) to be less overt with the political message in order to avoid censorship, (2) to search for precolonial African traditions that can contribute to the solution of contemporary problems, and (3) to search for a new film language. An underlying desire behind the making of these types of films is to prove the existence of a dynamic African history and culture before the European colonization. Gaston Kaboré's *Wend Kuuni* (1982), for example, shows the Mossi Empire in its splendor with trading centers. The film also shows that African women did not wait for the arrival of Europeans to start fighting for their rights.[13] In *L'exile* (1980), Oumarou Ganda describes the sanctity of the given word and the regime of truth in precolonial Africa.[14] All of these films define their style by reexamining ancient African traditions, their modes of existence, and their magic.

Unlike the films about historical confrontation that are conventional on the level of form, these films are characterized by the way the director looks at tradition. It is a look that is intent on positing religion where anthropologists only see idolatry, history where they see primitivism, and humanism where they see savage acts. The films are characterized by long takes with natural sounds. Unlike conventional film language, which uses close-ups to dramatize a narrative moment, the close-ups in these films serve to inscribe the beauty of the characters and their tradition. Pointing to their aesthetic appeal, some filmmakers and critics have acclaimed the return to the source movement as the end of "miserabilism" in African cinema and the beginning of a cinema with perfect images, perfect sound, and perfect editing.[15] Others, on the contrary, have criticized the films for being nostalgic and exotic in their representation of Africa. They argue that the return to the source films are influenced by the vision of the European anthropologists, which they seem to put into question. In her excellent review of FESPACO '89, Thérèse-Marie Deffontaines describes Idrissa Ouedraogo's *Yaaba* as a "simple village story. A postcard which is magnificently photographed. Every shot is an aesthetic success. *Yaaba* provides the spectator with an idyllic image of an Africa which is devoid of every material contingency."[16]

Let's now look at some of the themes in *Yeelen* and *Yaaba* as a way of illustrating the return to the source films. In *Yeelen,* Cissé thematizes the classic conflict between the old and the new by pitting Soma Diarra (Niamanto Sanogo), a member of the feared Bambara secret society, the *Komo,* against his son, Ninankoro (Issiaka Kane), who must use the wing of the *Kore* (a secret tablet that to the Bambara embodies the many levels of knowledge) to destroy the *Komo.* *Yeelen*'s structure is influenced by the oral tradition of the Mande population of West Africa, which includes the Bambara. Like that tradition's classics, *L'epopée de Soundiata, La dispersion des Kusa,* and *Kambili, Yeelen* depicts a stagnating and oppressive system (the *Komo* cult) as unacceptable, and calls for a new, prosperous era. Heroes in these narratives undergo a voyage of initiation where they acquire the knowledge and weapons necessary for important social transformation.

Thus in *Yeelen,* Ninankoro sojourns in Fuladougou (the land of the Fulah) where he learns to fight and, most important, he finds a wife who will bear a son who symbolizes the future. A crucial difference between *Yeelen* and its predecessors in the oral tradition is in Cissé's conception of the hero. Whereas Soundiata, Maren Jagu, and Kambili represent the future as well as the present in their narratives, Ninankoro is part of the present only in *Yeelen;* his son is the future. Thus it is the son, not Ninankoro, who is named Nankama (destined for), a title also used in the praise songs of Soundiata and Kambili.

Yeelen is also concerned with the manner in which the camera looks at Africans and their customs. Bambara dialectics are revealed through vital oppositions, such as the pestle of *Komo* and the wing of *Kore,* milk and water, father and son, life and death, etc. Cissé also shows the manner in which the Bambara manipulate time. In the film, the *Komo* leaders have the power to freeze time in order to make the origin and the end coincide. All Cissé's films end as they begin, but in *Yeelen* we are provided with a detailed description of time in Mande societies. The *Komo* ritual, for example, is filmed from beginning to end in long takes with minimal editing. The uninterrupted shots remind the viewer of Sembène's filming of the long sequence in the King's court in *Ceddo.* Cissé's camera, used more in an attempt to describe the "right image" than to reveal a psychological point of view, recasts the fundamental narrative issues of show and tell. What brings emotional feeling to the spectator in *Yeelen* is the way in which the film transforms Western cinema's stereotypes into human and complex subjects. It valorizes and humanizes Africans and their past systems. In other words, it elevates the *Komo,* which is just another barbaric ritual in anthropological films, to the level of science. Similarly, an old woman (Soumba Traoré) who plays Ninankoro's mother is beautiful, thoughtful, and resourceful. In Western films, such a woman would have looked repulsive with her bare breasts and ugly with holes in her nose and ears.

Like *Yeelen*, Ouedraogo's *Yaaba* is also beautifully filmed. It is about the friendship between Bila, a twelve-year-old boy, and Sana, an outcast old woman. Although the whole village considers Sana a witch and blames her for every accident or illness, Bila calls her *Yaaba*, grandmother in the *More* language, which is also a term of endearment. Sana is thus humanized through the eyes of the young boy who defies the village tradition of staying away from outcasts. Ouedraogo wanted to construct a simple story at all levels of the film: the film was shot on location and "from a cinematic perspective, it was this village, with all its peacefulness, and everything around, that I was interested in. All cinema is about rhythm. I could not make this film with a rhythm that was too fast, nor with shots that were too sophisticated. I wanted the characters, on the one hand, and the sound and the image, on the other, to blend harmoniously together."[17]

The concern with simplicity is translated in Ouedraogo's cinema as a need to let images speak for themselves, and to deemphasize the role of sound in narrative. Ouedraogo tested this hypothesis in his shorter films, *Poko* (1978) and *Issa le Tisserand* (1985), and won praise from critics in Africa and Europe. But the style loses some of its strength when applied to his feature films. Ouedraogo has only been able to deal with simple surface stories in both *Le choix* (1987) and *Yaaba*, leaving aside complex social, political, and historical issues. In *Le choix*, for example, the city and modernization are constructed as evil, while nature is benevolent. Thus people can easily solve their problems with famine and the humiliation of international aid by uprooting themselves and moving to a region of the country where there is water.

There are no villains in *Yaaba*, unlike *Yeelen*, which puts into motion the conflict between father and son that threatens relations established by kinship rules. The overriding philosophy in the film is "Ne jugez-pas les autres, ils ont leur raison" (Let's not judge others, they have their own reasons). With this bourgeois humanist conception of tolerance, which is imported from the big city, the film asks the spectator's sympathy not only for Sana who is an outcast but also for a drunkard and for adulterers within the tight social relations of the village.

Ouedraogo's films are popular in Ouagadougou, where he is from, and with critics, which forces one to respect him as an artist and to think that his simple style reveals more than is discussed here. *Yaaba* won the People's Award of Ouagadougou and was selected for screening and the "Quinzaine des réalisateurs" at Cannes. Perhaps the critics today prefer Ouedraogo's poetry, his construction of a world without conflict, to African films that put into question European neo-colonialism and the African dictatorial regimes. Ouedraogo avoids serious conflicts in his construction of the story of Sana, who resembles the mother in Kaboré's *Wend Kuuni.* But while Kaboré only devotes the first five minutes of his film to it and uses the rest to explore the related issues of sexism, women's liberation, and other social conflicts, Ouedraogo spends the entire film trying to humanize Sana. Her physical appearance also brings to mind the mother in *Yeelen,* and she dies at the end without alerting the spectator to the plight of other outcast women like her. Her history as a particular type of African woman is made transparent while the spectator thinks of her as Bila's friend.

Ouedraogo's last film, *Tilai* (1990), is in my opinion his best film to date. The director's poetic style is supported here with a complex story that concerns the foundations of kinship systems in the *More* tradition. The moment of change, which is thematized in most African films as the transition from tradition to modernity, becomes in *Tilai* the driving force of the narrative. At the beginning of the film, Saga returns from a journey only to find out that his own father has married Nogma, his fiancée. When Saga returns to his village, he blows three times into a horn. This ritual is supposed to restore him in the village tradition. Ironically, his return to the village is not the traditional return of a hero who gets the princess as reward; the order of things has changed; his old fiancée is now his stepmother, and any attempt on his part to refuse this reality would amount to breaking the rules of kinship. Tradition thus sides with the father, who tells Saga that he will forgive him for what took place between him and his former fiancée if Saga makes the first move in that direction.

Saga decides instead to leave the village and see Nogma in secret. When the village finds out, the punishment is death for Saga, and his own brother, Kougri, must carry it out. The viewer of the film realizes at this moment that for this *More* village, adultery is a worse crime than fratricide. Kougri lets his brother escape with the promise that he will never return again. Nogma also escapes and joins Saga in another village, where they get married. Unfortunately for them, Saga hears the news that his mother is dying and he comes back to see her. At the edge of the village he sounds his horn three times, and the people in the village, taking him at first for a ghost, run away. When they find out that he is alive, his father bans Kougri from the village. Frustrated, Kougri picks up a rifle and kills Saga.

Tilai, like *Yeelen* and *Ceddo,* describes the moment of change by siding with the younger generation against tradition. At the end of the film, when Kougri walks away from the village, it is clear that the traditional regime of truth has been condemned. It has been accused of abusing the practice of polygamy and of being too dogmatic toward the youth. Ouedraogo's philosophical views, as seen in *Le choix* and *Yaaba,* are apparent here, too. The notion in *Yaaba* of "Ne juger pas les autres, ils ont leurs raisons," a sort of French liberalism, is deployed in *Tilai* as a philosophy of tolerating others with their desires and weaknesses. Saga, for example, knows that Nogma has had an affair with another man. But he is not consumed with the desire for total love. For Ouedraogo, such an essentialism, with its need to completely possess the objects of desire, is at the root of the destruction of tradition.

In the way he suspends any type of strong judgment in his films, Ouedraogo is part of a young generation of writers and filmmakers in Africa who take a postmodern attitude toward colonialism and nationalism. He is against the "strong thought" and the assigning of the blame on one side. *Tilai* is like a western with an antihero in search of a utopian society. Saga is happy in his aunt's village, where he and Nogma can love each other freely. Thus the aunt's village is Ouedraogo's ideal community and one that he tries to delineate in his films.

Tilai is also postmodern in its nostalgic gesture toward "primitive cinema" and the Oedipus drama. At the end of the film, the poetic way in which Kougri picks up the rifle and shoots Saga brings together film history and the African oral traditions. Because the camera is static and the acting looks clumsy, the shot reminds us of early cinema. But the distance between the characters and the spectator, the refusal to let the spectator into the characters' minds, is also a trait of the oral traditions. We know that we are being told a story by a third person (the griot or the filmmaker), and every shot must be negotiated through that narrator. The end of *Tilai,* like the king's court in *Ceddo* and the *Komo* scene in *Yeelen,* lifts African cinema to a new dimension of cinematic pleasure and magic. The camera, in each of these scenes, obeys the mise-en-scène of the oral tradition.

In conclusion, what can one say about these typologies in African cinema? Taken as a whole it is clear that they reflect Africa in its quest for social and economic justice (social realist), identity (return to the source), and history (confrontation). Given the importance of each of these categories, it is counterproductive to look at form alone and posit it as the criterion for a developed cinema. Thus it is simplistic to single out *Yeelen* or *Tilai,* for example, as the new direction in African cinema and to judge other films by their relative affinities to this film. To convince spectators of the probability of his story, Cissé finds it necessary to use beautiful images to counter the stereotypical images of Africa constructed by Hollywood and Western history. One important task for a return to the source film is therefore to challenge Western cinema on the level of form. *Yeelen* defines its own language by deemphasizing the psychologically based shot/reverse shot and close-ups of Western cinema, and by valorizing long shots and long takes, which through their "natural" feel are destined to describe the characters' relationships to each other and to time and space. In comparison to films like *Yeelen* and *Ceddo,* Western cinema seems to make very little use of space and time to define its characters. The long views that return-to-the-source films use enable them to reveal the rituals under the Baobab tree, the secret spaces in the rooms, man and woman's relation to time, land, water, and sky. In most Western films, this "long perspective" of things disappears, and in its place are establishing shots and close-ups taken out of context. Another challenge facing return-to-the-source filmmakers is to be able to construct narratives that do not fall into the trap of primitivism and simplemindedness as projected onto Africans by Eurocentric historians.

Unlike the return-to-the-source tendency, the other two types of narratives define their Africanness within dominant cinematic forms. They borrow just as much from Hollywood as they do from auteurist European and Third World cinema. For example, the social realist movement, opting for a populist cinema, exposes contemporary problems through dominant narrative forms, as well as through popular African narrative forms, and utilizes stars from music and theater. Because they are under less constraint to invent a film language that is unique to Africa, the filmmakers use whatever form they find suitable to the contents. In Yoruba (Nigeria) popular films, for example, the camera is always fixed on the popular stars, reminding the film student of the early beginnings of cinema. But the static camera does not make the features, with popular stars such as Baba Sala and Chief Ogunde, less popular with spectators who are nonetheless sophisticated admirers of the latest James Bond film, *Close Encounters of the Third Kind,* and Indian melodramas.

Just as it is misleading to fetishize form for the purpose of debunking some films, it is also dangerous to impute quality to a particular film because it is more realistic than others or because it is the only avant-garde film in African cinema. This book has tried to evaluate films by assessing their coherence in the particular discourse they choose to deploy. It is hoped that by delineating different tendencies the reader has been teased to engage in a dialogue about the diversity of movements in African cinema.

notes

Introduction

1. Georges Sadoul, "Le marché africain," *Afrique Action* (May 1961). Report in *Histoire du cinéma mondial* (Paris: Flammarion, 1973), 499–505. This and subsequent translations from French are mine, unless otherwise indicated.

2. Jean Rouch, *Films ethnographiques sur l'Afrique noire* (Paris: UNESCO, 1967), 375–408. This section was first presented in 1961 at a UNESCO round table discussion in Venice. This title is "Situation et tendance du cinéma africain."

3. Med Hondo, "Cinémas africains, écrans colonisés," *Le Monde* (Jan. 21, 1982): 12.

4. Guy Hennebelle, "Entretien avec Sembène Ousmane," *Afrique littéraire et artistique*, no. 49 (1978): 124 (special issue: "Cinéastes d'Afrique noire"). To define the term *mégotage,* the word *mégot* means cigarette butt; therefore, the concept means to make a film by the painful process of putting bits and pieces together. It means waiting—as one waits for a cigarette butt—for European remains such as film stock left over by rich producers. This is why it takes five to ten years to finish a film such as *Samory* by Sembène, *Sarouine* by Med Hondo, or *Yeelen* by Souleymane Cissé.

5. Victor Bachy, "Panoramique sur les cinémas sud-sahariens," *CinémAction*, no. 26 (1982): 25 (special issue: "Cinémas noirs d'Afrique").

6. Férid Boughedir, *Afrique noire: Quel cinéma?* (Paris: Actes du Colloque, Université Paris X, Nanterre, 1981), 31.

I. Anglophone African Production

1. L. A. Notcutt and G. C. Latham, eds., *The African and the Cinema* (London: Edinburgh House Press, 1937), 23.

2. J. Koyinde Vaughan, "Africa South of the Sahara and the Cinema," *Présence Africaine*, no. 14–15 (June–Sept. 1957): 218.

3. Frantz Fanon, *Sociologie d'une révolution* (previously published under the title *L'an V de la révolution algérienne*) (Paris: François Maspero, 1959), 29. See also Albert Memmi, *Portrait du Colonisé, précédé du Portrait du Colonisateur* (Paris: J. J. Pauvert, éditeur, 1966).

4. Frantz Fanon, *Pour la révolution africaine* (Paris: François Maspero, 1964), 92.

5. Paulin S. Vieyra, *Le cinéma africain: Des origines à 1973* (Paris: Présence Africaine, 1975), 103.

6. Michael Raeburn, "Interview with Sam Aryetey," *Afrique littéraire et artistique,* no. 49 (1978): 19.

7. Victor Bachy, "Dictionnaire de 250 Cinéastes," *CinémAction,* no. 26 (1982): 185–201.

8. Mbye B. Cham, "Film Production in West Africa," *Présence Africaine,* no. 124 (1982): 173.

9. Ola Balogun, "Les trois long métrages nigérians," *Afrique littéraire et artistique,* no. 20 (1972): 251 (special issue: "Les cinémas africains en 1972").

10. Michael Raeburn, "Le cinéma piétine encore dans les pays d'Afrique noire anglophone," *Afrique littéraire et artistique,* no. 20 (1972): 254.

11. Hannes Kamphausen, "Cinema in Africa: A Survey," *Cinéaste 5*, no. 2 (Spring 1972): 31.

12. Aryetey defends his film on grounds that it was not made for Europeans, but for Africans only. He concedes, however, that it was "a mistake to have taken sixty-five minutes for a scenario which should not have gone beyond twenty-five minutes." See his interview with Raeburn (note 6).

II. Zairian Production

1. Pierre Haffner, "Entretien avec le père Alexandre Van den Heuvel," *Afrique littéraire et artistique,* no. 48 (1978): 88

2. Ngangura Mweze, unpublished interview with author, University of California, Los Angeles, 1983.

3. *Unir cinéma: revue du cinéma africain,* no. 5 (March–April 1983): 24.

III. France's Contribution to the Development of Film Production in Africa

1. Guy Hennebelle, "Entretien avec Jean-René Débrix," in *Afrique littéraire et artistique,* no. 43 (1975): 82.

2. Paulin S. Vieyra, "Le cinéma au Sénégal en 1976," *Présence Africaine,* no. 207 (1978): 207.

3. Victor Bachy, "Dictionnaire de 250 cinéastes," *CinémAction,* no. 26 (1982): 185–201.

4. Paulin S. Vieyra, "Propos sur le cinéma africain" *Présence Africaine,* no. 23 (1958): 109.

5. Jean Rouch, *Films ethnographiques sur l'Afrique noire,* 21.

6. Ibid., 396. According to Rouch, there is a commercialized version of *Les statues* which Marker and Resnais do not endorse.

7. Georges Sadoul, *Histoire du cinéma mondial,* 499.

8. Jean-René Débrix, "Dix ans de coopération Franco-Africaine ont permis la naissance du jeune cinéma d'Afrique noire," in *Sentiers 1* (1970): 15.

9. Jacques Gerard, *Afrique noire: Quel cinéma?,* 36.

10. Interview with Cissé, recorded by the author, Los Angeles, 1983.

11. "Cinémas sans visa," monthly program, French National Television, FR3, May 1982.

12. Férid Boughedir, *Afrique noire: Quel cinéma?,* 33.

13. Conversation with Gerard Desplanques, who is the new "Chef du Bureau de la Coopération Cinématographique."

14. Pierre Haffner, *Afrique noire: Quel cinéma?*, 33.

15. Victor Bachy, "Panoramique sur les cinémas sud-sahariens," 25; see also Paulin S. Vieyra, in *Le cinéma africain*, 104.

16. Tahar Cheriaa, *Ecrans d'abondances ou cinémas de libération* (Tunis: Editions Sindbad, 1974) and Férid Boughedir, "Cinéma africain et décolonisation," unpublished dissertation, Université Paris III, 1976.

17. Siradou Diallo, "*Jeune Afrique* fait parler Sembène Ousmane," *Jeune Afrique*, no. 629 (1973): 48–49.

18. Emile James, "Entretien avec Sembène Ousmane," *Jeune Afrique*, no. 499 (1970): 41.

19. Cissé, interview with author, Los Angeles, 1983.

IV. The Artist as the Leader of the Revolution

1. Paulin S. Vieyra, "Propos sur le cinéma africain," in *Présence Africaine*, no. 23 (1958): 114–15.

2. Blaise Senghor, "Pour un authentique cinéma africain," *Présence Africaine*, no. 49 (1964): 109.

3. Timité Bassori, "Un cinéma mort-né?" in *Présence Africaine*, no. 49 (1964): 111–14.

4. Jean-René Débrix, "Le cinéma africain," in *Afrique Contemporaine*, no. 40 (Nov.–Dec. 1968): 6.

5. OCAM is an economic and cultural organization grouping the following Francophone African countries: Senegal, Mali, Mauritania, Guinea, Ivory Coast, Upper Volta, Niger, Benin, Toga, Cameroon, Gabon, Chad, and the Central African Republic. For a critique of OCAM, see Brigette Nouaille-Degorge, "OCAM: An Outdated Organization," UFAHAMU 5, no. 2 (1974): 135–47.

6. Férid Boughedir, *Afrique noire: Quel cinéma?*, 63.

7. Pierre Pommier, *Cinéma et développement en Afrique noire francophone* (Paris: Editions A. Pedone, 1974), 153.

8. Férid Boughedir, "La (trop) longue marche des cinéastes africains," *CinémAction* no. 26 (1982): 156–57.

9. Guy Hennebelle, "La charte d'Alger du cinéma africain," *Afrique littéraire et artistique*, no. 49 (1978): 165.

10. Férid Boughedir, *Afrique noire: Quel cinéma?*, 65.

11. Férid Boughedir, "Le nouveau credo des cinéastes africains: Le Manifeste de Niamey," *CinémAction*, no. 26 (1982): 168.

12. Teshome Gabriel, *Third Cinema in the Third World: The Aesthetics of Liberation* (Ann Arbor: UMI Research Press, 1982), 107.

13. Tahar Cheriaa, "Le cinéma africain et les 'réducteurs de têtes,'" *Afrique littéraire et artistique*, no. 49 (1978): 8.

14. Férid Boughedir, "La (trop) longue," 158.

15. Teshome Gabriel, *Third Cinema*, 115.

16. Fernando E. Solanas and Octavio Gettino, *Ciné cultura y decolonizacion* (Buenos Aires: Siglo 21, 1973).

V. The Situation of National and International Film Production in Francophone Africa

1. Jean Rouch, *Film ethnographiques sur l'Afrique noire*, 395.

2. Paulin S. Vieyra, *Le cinéma africain: Des origines à 1973* (Paris: Présence Africaine, 1975), 104–5.

3. See chapter 3 on France's contribution to African film.

4. Jean-René Débrix, "Le cinéma africain," in *Afrique Contemporaine*, no. 38–39 (July–Oct. 1968): 7.

5. On the West German contribution to Ghanaian production, see chapter 1 on production in Anglophone Africa. See also John Collins, "NAFTI Leads the Way: Interview with Kweku Opoku, Director of the National Film and Television Institute in Ghana," *West Africa*, no. 3477 (Apr. 9, 1984): 769–70.

6. Guy Hennebelle, "Entretien avec Jean-René Débrix," *Afrique littéraire et artistique*, no. 43 (1975): 81.

7. Timité Bassori, "Un Cinéma Mort-né?" *Présence Africaine*, no. 49 (1964): 114.

8. I learned this from a conversation at the Cinémathèque de la Coopération with Felix Diagne (filmmaker from Senegal), Joseph Akouisonne (Central Africa), and Evelyn Casnave (Manager of the Cinémathèque).

9. I am not using the word *defy* lightly. Guy Hennebelle agrees: "Only three countries have tried to take the destiny of their cinema in their own hands: they are Guinea, Upper Volta, and Mali." See *Afrique littéraire et artistique*, no. 20 (1972): 197 (special issue on "Les cinémas africains en 1972").

10. Unpublished interview with Mahama Traoré, recorded by the author, Los Angeles, 1983.

11. Férid Boughedir, "Le cinéma africain, pays par pays," in *Jeune Afrique Plus*, no. 6 (April 1984): 72.

12. Paulin S. Vieyra, *Le cinéma et l'Afrique* (Paris: Présence Africaine, 1969), 184.

13. Francophone African directors were forbidden to film Africa by the Laval Decree. See chapter 3.

14. Jean-René Débrix, "Le cinéma africain," in *Afrique Contemporaine*, no. 38–39 (1968): 10.

15. According to Bachy, "The structure of production was lacking everywhere [in Africa]. Filmmakers who, one must admit, were idealists created their own production houses. Besides their courage they had no other means of production, but they counted, partially, on the help of the Coopération Française. Their production companies had as names: Pascal Abikanlou: Abiscal Films in Cotonou; Daniel Kamwa, D.K.7 Films in Douala and Paris; Désiré Ecaré, Les Films de la Lagune in Abidjan; Oumarou Ganda, Cabas Films in Niamey; Philippe Maury, Les Films Philippe Maury in Libreville; Sembène Ousmane, Les Films Domirev in Dakar; Med Hondo, *Les Films du Soleil O* in Paris; and others." See Bachy, "Panoramique sur les cinémas sud-sahariens," *CinémAction*, no. 26 (1982): 27 (special issue: "Cinémas Noirs d'Afrique").

16. Paulin S. Vieyra, "Le cinéma au Sénégal en 1976," *Présence Africaine*, no. 207 (1978): 207.

17. Unpublished interview with Traoré.

18. See chapter 4 on FEPACI. See also Farida Ayari, "Vers un renouveau du cinéma africain: Faut-il dissoudre la FEPACI?" and "L'oeil vert," in *Le Continent* (March 9 and 10, 1981). No page numbers indicated.

19. Paulin S. Vieyra, *Le cinéma africain,* 172. See also p. 187 for more details on censorship in Senegal.

20. Paulin S. Vieyra, "Le cinéma au Sénégal en 1976," 210–17.

21. Unpublished interview with Traoré.

22. Unpublished interview with Gnoan M'Bala, Los Angeles, 1983.

23. Victor Bachy, *Le cinéma en Côte d'Ivoire* (Brussels: Cinémédia, 1982), 27–34.

24. Paulin S. Vieyra, *Le cinéma africain,* 54.

25. *Chemin de fer de la R.A.N.* (16mm), *Kossou III* (16mm). For further information see Bachy, *Le cinéma au Côte d'Ivoire,* 29–30.

26. Guy Hennebelle and Catherine Ruelle in *Afrique littéraire et artistique,* no. 49 (1978): 93.

27. *Anemié* won awards at the Festival of Dinard and at JCC.

28. Unpublished interview with M'Bala.

29. *L'audio-visuel en Côte d'Ivoire—Annuaire 1984* (Abidjan: Ministère de l'education national et recherche scientifique, 1984), 11–53.

30. Guy Hennebelle, in *Afrique littéraire et artistique,* no. 20 (1972): 197.

31. Paulin S. Vieyra, *Le cinéma africain,* 114–15. For more details, see Hennebelle in *Afrique littéraire et artistique,* no. 20 (1972): 197, and Bachy, *La Haute Volta et le cinéma* (Paris: Editions OCIC/L'Harmattan, 1983), 11–14.

32. Hennebelle, p. 197. See particularly Bachy, *Le cinéma au Mali* (Brussels: Cinémédia, 1983), 12–13.

33. For information about films produced by the Malian government, see Bachy, *Le cinéma au Mali.* See below in this chapter for films produced by the government of Upper Volta.

34. Guinea was the first Francophone African country to become independent in 1958. The move so surprised and humiliated General de Gaulle that he vowed to punish the Guineans. The independence did not only result in a revolution of all aspects of life in Guinea, but it also brought about an isolation of the country from its pro-France neighbors. This isolation is at the root of the failure of many economic and development ventures of the country. It is because of this economic boycotting that critics, such as Bachy, blame France for punishing those Francophone countries that attempt to break with her. It is important, therefore, to look at the difficulties in the development of Guinean film production, too, in this light.

35. Rouch, *Film éthnographiques,* 402–3. According to Rouch, Ivory Coast and Senegal were some of the Francophone countries that were ill-advised in the manner they produced their monthly and bimonthly newsreels. They used 35mm facilities to make newsreels that required the laboratories of Paris to be finished. This not only cost a great deal of money, but it also took a long time. In this sense, one can easily see the advantages of the 16mm facilities that Guinea has.

36. See Vieyra, note 3, p. 108. According to Vieyra, Mahomamed Lamine Akin, Costa Diagne, and other filmmakers were accused of plotting a coup

d'etat against the president of Guinea in 1970. They were arrested and put in jail. By 1970, the Guinean president was notorious for his dictatorial and unpredictable behavior.

37. Gilbert Minot, "Toward the African Cinéma," in *UFAHAMU* 12, no. 2 (1983): 47.

38. Bachy, *La Haute Volta et le cinéma,* 13. In the beginning, the SONAVOCI was completely owned by the government. According to Bachy, "Today, the SONAVOCI is an anonymous society with a joint economy. The assets consist of 20 million CFA francs, divided as follows: 74.65 percent for the government and 25.35 percent for different private sources."

39. See also "Interview with Moustapha Ky, Directeur of CINAFRIC," *L'Observateur: Quotidien Voltaïque d'Information,* no. 2520 (Feb. 2, 1982): 10–14.

40. Conversation with Sina Boli (filmmaker for Upper Volta), ATRIA, Paris, 1983.

41. Bachy, *Le cinéma en Côte d'Ivoire,* 23.

42. Bachy, *Le cinéma au Mali,* for further information.

43. Unpublished interview with M'Bala.

44. Rouch, *Films ethnographiques,* 379–81. Rouch said that at the IHEC they insisted that all films be made with 35mm equipment. "However, at the same time, this institute was interested in parallel experiences of young film-makers (1946) with the 16mm" (p. 381).

45. Bachy, *Le cinéma en Côte d'Ivoire,* 73.

46. CIDC files, "Notes sur la fiscalité cinématographique en Afrique noire francophone," Ouagadougou, 1981, 5.

47. Farida Ayari, "Vers un renouveau du cinéma africain" (no page indicated).

48. "Notes sur la fiscalité cinématographique en Afrique noire francophone," 4–6.

49. CIDC files "Fin du colloque sur la production cinématographique," in *Le Sahel* (Niamey, Niger) (May 3, 1982), 2.

50. B. Hubert Pare, "8ème FEPASCO: Symbole de l'Unité Africaine," in *Carrefour Africain* (Ouagadougou, Upper Volta), no. 765 (Nov. 2, 1983): 23.

51. Bachy, *La Haute Volta et le cinéma,* 60.

VI. Film Production in Lusophone Africa

1. For the colonial politics of production in Anglophone countries and Zaïre, see appropriate chapters above.

2. Victor Bachy, "Panoramique sur les cinémas Sud-Sahariens," in *Ciném-Action,* no. 26 (1982): 42 (special issue: "Cinémas noirs d'Afrique").

3. Clyde Taylor, "Interview with Pedro Pimente: Film reborn in Mozambique," in *Jump Cut,* no. 28 (1983): 30.

4. See their important essay, "Toward a Third Cinema," in *Movies and Methods,* ed. Bill Nichols (Berkeley: University of California Press, 1976), 56–58.

5. Gary Crowdus and Udayan Gupta, "A Luta Continua: An Interview with Robert Van Lierop," *Cinéaste* 9, no. 1: 31.

6. "Toward a Third Cinema," in *Movies and Methods,* 61.

7. Paulin Vieyra, *Le cinéma africain,* 42. Although Vieyra admits that the beautiful scenes and framing are not obstacles to the story, he says that the acting was awkward and the dance scene at the end unnecessary. Vieyra's criticism, however, fails to show that Maldoror intentionally used non-professional actors and that the dance scene was supposed to underline the importance of the revolution and prevent identification with the mourners. For Maldoror's response to the esthetic quality of her film, see: Guy Hennebelle, "Interview with Sarah Maldoror," in *Afrique littéraire et artistique,* no. 49 (1978): 90–91.

8. Guy Hennebelle, "Chronologie de la production Africaine pays par pays et par années," *Afrique littéraire et artistique,* no. 49 (1978): 168.

9. Some of the revolutionary countries organized around the AACC were Tanzania, Guinea-Konakry, Guinea-Bissau, Congo Brazzaville, Benin, etc. See Pierre Haffner in *Afrique noire: Quel cinéma?,* 53.

10. Victor Bachy, "Dictionnaire de 250 cinéastes," in *CinémAction,* no. 26 (1982): 192.

11. Jean-Pierre Oudart and Dominique Terres, "Enquête: Super 8 au Mozambique," in *Cahiers du cinéma,* no. 296 (Jan. 1979): 57.

12. Ruy Guerra was born in 1931 in Mozambique. Shortly after his training at the Institut des Hautes Etudes Cinématographiques (Paris), he went to Brazil where he became a founding member of Cinema Novo. His films *Os cafojestes* (*The Beach of Desire,* 1962) and *Os fuzis* (*The Rifles,* 1964) are considered among the best films of Cinema Novo. For more details on Guerra's contribution to Brazilian Cinema Novo, see Guy Hennebelle and Alfonso Gummico-Dagron, *Les cinémas de l'Amérique Latine* (Paris: Editions Lherminier, 1981); Randal Johnson and Robert Stam, *Brazilian Cinema* (Brunswick: Associated University Press, 1982). After the independence, Guerra returned to Mozambique and became head of the Institute of Film.

13. Bachy, "Panoramique," 42. According to Bachy, *Kuxa* means "birth" in Runga, a language of the North Mozambique, and *Kenema* means "image" in Makua, a language of the South.

14. Jean-Pierre Oudart and Dominique Terres, "Enquête: Super 8 au Mozambique," 57.

15. The style of *Mueda* is similar to that of *Os Fuzis* which Guerra made in 1964, at a period considered by critics as the maturation stage of Cinema Novo. Just as the fictional continuity of *Mueda* is often disrupted by interventions of real events, in *Os Fuzis,* too, there is a documentary style which is interrupted by sudden eruptions of fictional characters and events. *Os Fuzis* is considered by Paulo Antonio Parangua as one of the three best films of the maturation era of Cinema Novo. See *Les cinémas de l'Amérique Latine,* 146–48.

16. Pierre Haffner, "Comment filmer la liberté: Entretien avec Jean Rouch," in *CinémAction,* no. 17 (1982): 20 (special issue: "Jean Rouch, un griot gaulois").

17. For more details on the Super 8 program at the Université de Paris X Nanterre, see Haffner, pp. 17–18. See also *Le Monde Diplomatique* (August 1980), p. 23; and *Cahiers du cinéma,* no. 296 (Jan. 1979): 54–59.

18. Louis Marcorelles, "16 et Super 8: De Boston au Mozambique, entretien avec Jean Rouch," in *CinémAction,* no. 17 (1982): 35–37.

19. Pierre Haffner, "Comment filmer la liberté," 21.

20. Jean-Luc Godard, "Le dernier rêvue d'un producteur," in *Cahiers du cinéma*, no. 300 (May 1979/special): 116.

21. Colin MacCabe et al., *Godard: Images, Sounds, Politics* (Bloomington: Indiana University Press, 1980), 138.

22. For more details on Sily-Cinéma, see chapter 5 on Francophone production.

23. See also Jean-Pierre Oudart and Dominique Terres, "Enquête: Super 8 au Mozambique," 59.

24. There is a famous statement by Sembène Ousmane which says that Rouch's camera depicts Africans as insects. Because Rouch works with the French Ministère des Relations Extérieures, the Musée de l'Homme and the Université de Paris X Nanterre, many African filmmakers see him as an imperialist and a neo-colonialist. For more details on how African directors perceive Rouch, see: "Jean Rouch jugé par six cinéastes d'Afrique Noire," 66–76; "Jean Rouch—Sembène Ousmane: 'Comme des insectes,'" *CinémAction*, no. 17 (1982): 77–78.

25. Louis Marcorelles, "16 et Super 8: De Boston au Mozambique," 37; Rouch's comments on framing and mise-en-scène are particularly interesting in this interview.

26. Rouch, too, had argued that the video was not practical compared to the Super 8 because of its small screen. In his interview with Haffner, Rouch said: "The video is limited; you have a small screen, you have fifteen people (watching together). Here (with the Super 8) you have two hundred (people watching) and it's outdoors" (p. 25).

VII. Film Distribution and Exhibition in Francophone Africa

1. Pierre Haffner, "Entretien avec le père Alexandre Van den Heuvel," in *Afrique littéraire et artistique*, no. 48 (1978); see also no. 16 (1970): 89.

2. Jean Rouch, *Films ethnographiques sur l'Afrique noire*, 1–9.

3. Jean-René Débrix, "Le cinéma africain," in *Afrique Contemporaine* no. 40 (Nov.–Dec. 1968): 2.

4. See Inoussa Ousseini, "La fiscalité cinématographique en Afrique noire francophone," in *Film Echange*, no. 17 (Winter 1981): 37–39. See also Gaston Samé and Catherine Ruelle, "Cinéma et télévision en Afrique: De la dépendance à l'indépendance" in *Communication et Société*, no. 8 (1983): 11.

5. See Afrique Noire Francophone report by Pierre Roitfeld for *Unifrance Film* (Sept. 1980): 72. See also Victor Bachy, "La distribution cinématographique en Afrique noire," *Film Echange*, no. 15 (Summer 1982): 36–41.

6. Thomas Guback, "Hollywood's International Market," in *The American Film Industry*, ed. Tino Balio (Madison: University of Wisconsin Press, 1985), 482.

7. Thomas Guback, "American Films and African Market" in *Critical Arts* 3, no. 3 (1985): 6.

8. Tahar Cheriaa, "Film Distribution in Tunisia," in *The Cinema in the*

Arab Countries, ed. Georges Sadoul (Beirut: Interarab Center of Cinema and Television, 1972).

9. Inoussa Ousseini, "Le CIDC," in *L'observateur* (quotidien Voltaique d'information) no. 2035 (Feb. 23, 1981): 11.

10. "La fiscalité cinématographique en Afrique Noire francophone" 39.

11. Manuscrit inédit, Dakar: SIDEC (1975), 262.

12. "La SIDEC est sur la voie de redressement," in *Le Soleil* (Feb. 7, 1977).

VIII. The Present Situation of the Film Industry in Anglophone Africa

1. Paul Lazarus, "Film Production in Kenya," unpublished report to ICDC and KFC (May 1983).

2. Sharad Patel, "The Communication Gap," unpublished paper presented to the Kenya Film Week (Dec. 1986).

3. Janice Turner and Jai Kumar, "Shooting It Out with Rambo," *South* (Nov. 1977): 93.

4. "Video Piracy in Ghana," *West Africa,* no. 3463 (Jan. 2, 1985): 22.

5. Nanabanyin Dadson, "The Bad Old Days," *West Africa,* no. 3655 (Aug. 31, 1987): 1694.

6. Françoise Pfaff, *Twenty-five Black African Filmmakers* (Westport, Conn.: Greenwood Press, 1988).

7. Françoise Balogun, *Le Cinéma au Nigeria* (Paris: Editions OCIC/L'Harmattan, 1983), 20.

8. Saddik Balewo, "Nigerian Film Industry," *West Africa,* no. 3513 (Dec. 1984): 2584.

9. Richard Ikeibe, "Nigerian Film Industry Gets More World Attention," *Daily Times* (May 24, 1980), 7.

10. "Filmmaking in Nigeria: Problems Inherent," *Nigerian Standard* (May 13, 1985): 3.

11. Wole Soyinka, "Theatre and the Emergence of Nigerian Film Industry" in *The Development of the Film Industry in Nigeria,* ed. Alfred E. Opubor and Onuora E. Nwuneli (Lagos: Third Press International, 1979), 102–3.

IX. African Cinema and Festivals

1. *Sidwaya: Quotidien Burkinabé d'Information et de Mobilisation du Peuple (Ouagadougou),* no. 217 (1985): 6–8. For more information on FESPACO, see a series of articles by Omer Ousmane Ouedraogo "Si le FEPACO m'était conté," in *Sidwaya,* no. 217–22 (1985).

2. One of the most important events in the development of African cinema took place in 1970 when Upper Volta nationalized its movie theaters. It signaled a historic break between African cinema and the two monopolist companies, COMACICO and SECMA, and the beginning of national production subsidized by revenues from distribution and exhibition.

3. *9ème FESPASO: Cinéma et Libération des Peuples* (Ouagadougou: Secrétariat Général des Festivals Cinématographique, 1985), 24.

4. On the theories and practice of Third Cinema, see Gabriel Teshome, *Third Cinema and the Third World: The Aesthetics of Liberation* (Ann Arbor: UMI Research Press, 1982).

5. *El Moudjahid* (Algiers), March 16, 1985.

6. Quoted in *Sidwaya,* no. 217.

X. African Cinema Today

1. See Laurence Gavron, "Ouedraogo et sa 'grand-mère' d'Afrique," in *Liberation* (May 12, 1989): 35: "When dealing with the problems of production and distribution, one must take into account the experiences of other countries and other film industries. But the tendency here is to proceed as if we were still in the sixties; to continue to magnify things that no longer need to be magnified; and we forget that the struggle is hard and that we have many shortcomings. We ghettoize ourselves in a miserable position of inferiority. It is a sign of maturity that, this year, a look at the films at FESPACO, good or bad, reveals a diversity of styles and a sense of professionalism in the production" (my translation).

2. Unpublished interviews with Med Hondo (March 1989, in Dakar), and Cheick Oumar Sissoko (March 1989, in Ouagadougou) by the author.

3. See Manthia Diawara and Elizabeth Robinson, "New Perspectives in African Cinema: An Interview with Cheick Oumar Sissoko," in *Film Quarterly* 41, no. 2 (1987/88): 43–48.

4. Sapeur refers to a new generation of fashion conscious youth in Zaire, Cameroon, and Gabon. They take pride in wearing the most expensive clothes and shoes, and parading on the sidewalks of the capital cities.

5. Fatou Sow, "Senegal: The Decade and Its Consequences," trans. Anne C. Rennick and Catherine Boone, in *Issue: A Journal of Opinion* 17, no. 2 (Summer 1989): 32.

6. Lédji Bellow, "Cinéma: Le sérail en folie," in *Jeune Afrique,* no. 1473 (March 29, 1989): 57 (my translation).

7. Fatou Sow, "Senegal: The Decade and Its Consequences," 35.

8. Serge Daney, "Ciné-bilan Ouaglais," in *Libération* (March 8/9, 1987): 30 (my translation).

9. Kofi Anyidoho, "Heritage Africa," in *Uhuru* (Feb. 1989): 6.

10. See my essay "Film in Anglophone Africa: A Brief Survey," in *Blackframes: Critical Perspectives on Black Independent Cinema,* ed. Mbye B. Cham and Claire Andrade-Watkins (Cambridge: Celebration of Black Cinema/ MIT Press, 1988), 37–49.

11. Françoise Kaboré, "Heritage Africa: Rupture avec la patrie," in *Sidwaya,* no. 1223 (March 1, 1989): 4 (my translation).

12. Manthia Diawara, "Souleymane Cissé's Light on Africa," in *Black Film Review* 4, no. 4 (1988): 13.

13. See my essay "Oral Literature and African Film: Narratology in Wend Kuuni," in *Présence Africaine,* no. 142 (1987): 36–49; reprinted in *Questions of Third Cinema,* ed. Jim Pines and Paul Willemen (London: British Film Institute, 1989).

14. See Françoise Pfaff, "Oumarou Ganda," in her *Twenty-Five Black African Filmmakers* (Westport, Conn.: Greenwood Press, 1988), 131.

15. See Laurence Gavron, "Ouedraogo et sa 'grand-mère' d'Afrique," 35. See also Serge Daney, "Ciné-bilan Ouaglais."

16. Thérèse-Marie Deffontaines, "Le 11e festival de Ouagadougou: Toutes les images de l'Afrique," in *Le monde* (March 16, 1989): 22 (my translation).

17. Laurence Gavron, "Ouedraogo et sa 'grand-mère' d'Afrique," 35.

bibliography

Afrique littéraire et artistique. Special issue: "Les cinémas africains en 1972." No. 20 (1972).

Afrique littéraire et artistique. Special issue: "Cinéastes d'Afrique noire." No. 49 (1978).

Afrique noire: Quel cinéma? Paris: Actes du Colloque, Université Paris 10 Nanterre, December 1981.

Albertini, Rudolf Von. *Decolonization: The Administration and Future of the Colonies, 1914–1960.* Trans. Francisca Garvie. New York: Africana Publishing Co., 1982.

Althusser, Louis. *Pour Marx.* Paris: François Maspero, 1975.

Amin, Samir, J. Nyerere, and D. Peren. *Le dialogue inégal: Écueil du nouvel ordre économique international.* Geneva: Editions Cetim, 1979.

D'Arthuys, Jacques. "Les indépendants du cinéma direct," in *Le monde diplomatique* (Aug. 1980): 23.

L'audio-visuel en Côte d'Ivoire—Annuaire 1984. Abidjan: Ministère de l'education National et recherche scientifique, 1984.

Aumont, Jacques. "Entretien avec Désiré Ecaré." *Cahiers du cinéma,* no. 203 (Aug. 1968): 21–22.

Ayari, Farida. "Vers un renouveau du cinéma africain: Faut-il dissoudre la FEPACI?" *Le Continent* (March 9 and 10, 1981).

———. "L'oeil vert," *Le Continent* (March 10, 1981).

Bachmann, Gideon. "In Search of Self-Definition: Arab and African Films at the Carthage Film Festival." *Film Quarterly* 26, no. 3 (1973): 48–51.

Bachy, Victor. "Le cinéma du Cameroun." *Revue du Cinéma, Image et Son,* no. 351 (June 1980): 87–94.

———. "Dictionnaire de 250 cinéastes," *CinémAction,* no. 26 (1982): 185–201.

———. *La Haute Volta et le cinéma.* Brussels: Cinémédia, 1982.

———. *Le cinéma en Côte d'Ivoire.* Brussels: Cinémédia, 1982.

———. *Le cinéma au Mali.* Brussels: Cinémédia, 1983.

———. "Panoramique sur les cinémas sud-sahariens." *CinémAction,* no. 26 (1982).

Balogun, Françoise. *Le cinéma au Nigeria.* Paris: OCIC/L'Harmattan, 1983.

Baudry, Jean-Louis. "Ideological Effects of the Basic Cinematographic Apparatus." *Film Quarterly* 28, no. 2 (1974–75).

Bazin, André. *What Is Cinema?* 2 vols. Berkeley: University of California Press, 1967.

Bever, L. Van. *Le cinéma pour africain.* Brussels: G. Van Campenhout, 1952.

Beye, Ben Diogaye. "Situation du cinéma Africain." *Cinéma* (Paris), no. 221 (May 1977): 64–69.

Binet, Jacques. "La nature dans le cinéma africain." *Afrique littéraire et artistique,* no. 39 (1976): 52–59.

———. "Classes sociales et cinéma africain." *Positif,* no. 188 (Dec. 1976): 34–43.

———. "The Contribution and the Influence of Black African Cinema." *Diogènes,* no. 110 (1980): 66–82.

Bonitzer, Pascal. "Ousmane Sembène: *Le Mandat.*" *Cahiers du Cinéma,* no. 209 (Feb. 1969): 57–58.

Bosseno, Christian. "Le cinéma en Algérie." *Revue du Cinéma, Image et Son,* no. 327 (April 1978): 55–96.

Boudjedra, Rachid. *Naissance du cinéma Algérien.* Paris: François Maspero, 1971.

Boughedir, Férid. "La (trop) longue marche des cinéastes africains." *CinémAction,* no. 26 (1982).

———. "Le nouveau credo des cinéastes africains: Le manifeste de Niamey." *CinémAction,* no. 26 (1982): 168.

———. "Le cinéma africain, pays par pays." *Jeune Afrique Plus,* no. 6 (April 1984): 72.

Boulanger, Pierre. *Le cinéma colonial: De l'atlantide à Lawrence d'Arabie.* Paris: Editions Seghers, 1975.

Burch, Noel. *Theory of Film Practice.* Trans. Helen R. Lane. New York: Praeger, 1973.

Cabral, Amilcar. *National Liberation and Culture.* Trans. Maureen Webster. Syracuse: Syracuse University Program of Eastern African Studies, 1970.

———. *L'arme de la théorie.* Paris: François Maspero, 1975.

Caughie, John, ed. *Theories of Authorship.* London: Routledge and Kegan Paul, 1981.

Caute, David. *Frantz Fanon.* New York: Viking Press, 1970.

Césaire, Aimé. *Discours sur le colonialisme.* Paris: Présence Africaine, 1955.

Cham, Mbye B. "Film Production in West Africa." *Présence Africaine,* no. 124 (1982): 168–87.

"Charte d'Alger du cinéma africain." *Afrique littéraire et artistique,* no. 35 (1975): 100–101.

Cheriaa, Tahar. "Film distribution in Tunisia." In *The Cinema in the Arab Countries,* ed. Georges Sadoul. Beirut: Interarab Center of Cinema and Television, 1972.

———. *Ecrans d'abondances ou cinémas de libération.* Tunis: Editions Sinbad, 1974.

———. "Le cinéma africain et les 'réducteurs de têtes.'" *Afrique littéraire et artistique,* no. 49 (1978).

CIDC files. "Notes sur la fiscalité cinématographique en Afrique noire francophone." Ouagadougou. 1981.

CIDC files. "Fin du colloque sur la production cinématographique." *Le Sahel* (Niamey, Niger) (May 3, 1982): 2–4.

Cinémaction, no. 14 (1981), Special issue: "Cinémas du Maghreb."

CinémAction, no. 17 (1982), Special issue: "Jean Rouch, un griot gaulois."

CinémAction, no. 26 (1982), Special issue: "Cinémas noirs d'Afrique."

Cluny, Claude Michel. "Actualité du cinéma arabe." *Cinéma* (Paris), no. 222 (June 1977): 31–40.

————. "Les nouveaux cinémas arabes." *Cinéma* (Paris), no. 240 (Dec. 1979): 41–53.

Collins, John. "NAFTI Leads the Way: Interview with Kweku Opoku, Director of the National Film and Television Institute in Ghana." *West Africa,* no. 3447 (April 9, 1984): 769–71.

Crowdus, Gary, and Udayan Gupta. "A Luta Continua: An Interview with Robert Van Lierop." *Cinéaste* 9, no. 1 (1978–79): 26–31.

Dadson, Nanabanyin. "The Bad Old Days." *West Africa,* no. 3655 (August 31, 1987).

Daney, Serge. "Ceddo." *Cahiers du Cinéma,* no. 304 (Oct. 1979): 51–53.

Débrix, Jean-René. "Le cinéma africain." *Afrique Contemporaine,* no. 38–39 (July–Oct. 1968): 7–12.

————. "Le cinéma africain." *Afrique Contemporaine,* no. 40 (Nov.–Dec. 1968): 2–6.

————. "Dix ans de coopération Franco-Africaine ont permis la naissance du jeune cinéma d'Afrique noire." *Sentiers* 1 (1970): 15.

————. "Situation du cinéma en Afrique francophone." *Afrique Contemporaine,* no. 81 (Sept.–Oct. 1975): 44–49.

Diallo, Siradou. "Jeune Afrique fait parler Sembène Ousmane." *Jeune Afrique,* no. 629 (1973): 44–49.

Diawara, Manthia. "Oral Literature and African Film: Narratology in *Wend Kuuni.*" *Présence Africaine,* no. 142 (1987).

————. "Popular Culture and Oral Traditions in African Film." *Film Quarterly* 41, no. 3 (1988).

————. "Souleymane Cissé's Light on Africa." *Black Film Review* 4, no. 4 (1988).

————. "The Tales of African Cinema." *Discourse* 11, no. 2 (1989).

Diawara, Manthia, and Elizabeth Robinson. "New Perspectives in African Cinema: An Interview with Cheick Oumar Sissoko." *Film Quarterly* 41, no. 2 (1987–88).

Diop, Cheick Anta. *Les fondements économiques et culturels d'un Etat Fédéral d'Afrique.* Paris: Présence Africaine, 1974.

Dubois, W. E. B. *The Souls of Black Folk.* Chicago: A. C. McClung, 1903.

Eisenstein, Segei. *Film Form.* Ed. and trans. Jay Leyda. New York: Harcourt Brace, 1949.

Enckell, Monique, and Smail Benassin. "*Noua,* un chef-d'oeuvre du cinéma djidid algérien." *Afrique littéraire et artistique,* no. 28 (1973): 88–94.

Fanon, Frantz. *Peau noire, masques blancs.* Paris: Editions du Seuil, 1952.

————. *L'an V de la révolution algérienne.* Paris: François Maspero, 1958.

————. *Les Damnés de la terre.* Paris: François Maspero, 1961.

————. *Pour la révolution africaine.* Paris: François Maspero, 1964.

Foucault, Michel. *L'archéologie du savoir.* Paris: Editions Gallimard, 1969.

Gabriel, Teshome H. "Xala: A Cinema of Wax and Gold." *Présence Africaine,* no. 116 (1980): 202–14.

————. *Third Cinema in the Third World: The Aesthetics of Liberation.* Ann Arbor: UMI Research Press, 1982.

————. "Teaching Third World Cinema." *Screen* 24, no. 2 (March–April 1983).

Garcia Espinosa, Julio. "For an Imperfect Cinema." *Afterimages,* no. 3 (Summer 1971).

Geismer, Peter. *Fanon: The Revolutionary as Prophet.* New York: Grove Press, 1971.

Gendzier, Irene. *Frantz Fanon: A Critical Study.* New York: Pantheon, 1973.

Gerima, Haile. "On 3000 Year Harvest." *Framework,* no. 7/8 (Spring 1978): 30–35.

Ghali, Noureddine. "Entretien avec Moumen Smihi." *Cinéma* (Paris), no. 205 (Jan. 1976): 92–101.

———. "Ousmane Sembène." *Cinéma* (Paris), no. 208 (April 1976): 83–95.

Godard, Jean-Luc. "Le dernier rêve d'un producteur." *Cahiers du cinéma,* no. 300 (May 1979/special): 70–129.

Gutsche, Thelma. *The History and Social Significance of Motion Pictures in South Africa.* Cape Town: Howard Timmis, 1972.

Haffner, Pierre. "Entretien avec le père Alexandre Van den Heuvel, pionnier d'un 'cinéma missionaire.' " *Afrique littéraire et artistique,* no. 48 (1978): 86–95.

———. *Essai sur les fondements du cinéma africain.* Abidjan: Les Nouvelles Editions Africaines, 1978.

———. *Palabres sur le cinématographe.* Les Presse Africaines, 1978.

———. "Comment filmes la liberté: entretien avec Jean Rouch." *CinémAction,* no. 17 (1982).

Haustrate, Gaston, et al. "Le cinéma algérien." *Cinéma* (Paris): no. 207 (March 1976): 36–92.

Haustrate, Gaston, and Claude Michel Cluny. "Le cinéma Tiers mondiste." *Cinéma* (Paris), no. 242 (1979): 59–65.

Hennebelle, Guy. "Sembène Ousmane: Pour moi le cinéma est un moyen d'action politique, mais . . ." *Afrique littéraire et artistique,* no. 8 (1969): 73–83.

———. "Table ronde: Pour ou contre un cinéma africain engagé?" *Afrique littéraire et artistique,* no. 19 (1971): 87–93.

———. "Recontre à Dinard avec des responsables de la Fédération Panafricaine des Cinéastes." *Afrique littéraire et artistique,* no. 24 (1972): 92–98.

———. "Entretien avec Jean-René Débrix." *Afrique littéraire et artistique,* no. 43 (1975): 77–90.

———. "Entretien avec Mahama Traoré." *Afrique littéraire et artistique,* no. 35 (1975): 91–106.

———. "Deux films sénégalais de Ben Diogaye Beye." *Afrique littéraire et artistique,* no. 41 (1976): 92–97.

———. "Où va le cinéma algérien, que devient le cinéma djidid?" *Afrique littéraire et artistique,* no. 40 (1976): 83–97.

———. "Entretien avec Sembène Ousmane." *Afrique littéraire et artistique,* no. 49 (1978): 125.

———. "Cinémas de l'emmigration." *CinémAction,* no. 8 (1979/special).

———. "The Adventure of Political Cinema." *Cinéaste* 10, no. 2 (1980): 20–25.

———. *Les cinémas de l'Amérique Latine.* Paris: Editions Lherminier. 1981.

———. "Le tiers monde en films." *CinémAction* (1982/special).

Hennebelle, Monique. "Sambizaga." *Afrique littéraire et artistique,* no. 28 (1973): 77–88.

———. "Coup de tonnerre dans le cinéma algérien: Le cinéma djidid fait irruption." *Afrique littéraire et artistique*, no. 29 (1973): 1–40.

———. "Mass Média et Culture traditionelle en Afrique Noire: *Le cinéma* une thèse de Mohamed Diop." *Afrique littéraire et artistique*, no. 33 (1974): 74–78.

Hondo, Med. "Med Hondo." *Framework*, no. 7/8 (Spring 1978): 28–30.

———. "Cinémas africains, écrans colonisés." *Le Monde* (Jan. 21, 1982): 12.

Huanou, Adrien. "Sembène Ousmane, Cinéaste et écrivain." *Afrique littéraire et artistique*, no. 33 (1974): 24–29.

———. "*Xala:* Une satire caustique de la société bourgeoise sénégalaise." *Présence Africaine*, no. 103 (1977): 145–58.

Jalee, Pierre. *L'imperialisme en 1970*. Paris: François Maspéro, 1970.

James, Emile. "Entretien avec Sembène Ousmane." *Jeune Afrique,* no. 499 (1970): 41.

Jinadu, Adele L. *Fanon: In Search of the African Revolution*. Enugu: Fourth Dimension, 1980.

Johnson, Randal, and Robert Stam. *Brazilian Cinema*. Brunswick: Associated University Press, 1982.

Kamphausen, Hannes. "Cinema in Africa: A Survey," *Cinéaste 5*, no. 2 (Spring 1972): 28–41.

Kamwa, Daniel. "Dans *Pousse Pousse,* je dénoncerai la pratique de la dot au Cameroun." *Afrique littéraire et artistique,* no. 33 (1974): 69–74.

Khlifi, Omar. *Histoire du cinéma en Tunisie*. Tunis: Société Tunisienne de Diffusion, 1970.

Lazarus, Paul. "Film Production in Kenya." Unpublished report to ICDC and KFC, May 1983.

Legum, Colin. *Pan-Africanism: A Short Political Guide*. London: Pall Mall Press, 1962.

Leprohon, Pierre. *L'exotisme et le cinéma*. Paris: Editions J. Susse, 1945.

MacCabe, Colin, et al. *Godard: Images, Sounds, Politics*. Bloomington: Indiana University Press, 1980.

Marcorelles, Louis. "16 et Super 8: De Boston au Mozambique, entretien avec Jean Rouch." *CinémAction*, no. 17 (1988).

Martin, Guy. "Fanon's Relevance to Contemporary Political Thought." *UFAHAMU* 4, no. 3 (Winter 1973).

Maynard, Richard A. *Africa on Film: Myth and Reality.* Rochelle Park: Hayden, 1974.

McBean, James Roy. *Film and Revolution*. Bloomington: Indiana University Press, 1975.

Memmi, Albert. *Portrait du colonisé précédé du portrait du colonisateur*. Paris: Editions Buchet, 1957.

Minot, Gilbert. "Towards the African Cinema." UFAHAMU 12, no. 2 (1983): 37–43.

Mitry, Jean. *Dictionnaire du cinéma*. Paris: Larousse, 1963.

Moore, Carrie D. "Evolution of an African Artist: Social Realism in the Works of Ousmane Sembène." Ph.D. dissertation, Indiana University, Bloomington.

"Moustapha Ky, Director of CINAFRIC." *L'observateur: Quotidien Voltaique d'Information* (Feb. 2, 1983): 10–14.

Nichols, Bill, ed. *Movies and Methods*. Berkeley: University of California Press, 1976.

———. *Ideology and the Image*. Bloomington: Indiana University Press, 1981.

Nkrumah, Kwame. *Neo-colonialism: The Last Stage of Imperialism*. London: Heinemann, 1965.

Notcutt, L. A., and G. C. Latham. *The African and the Cinema: An Account of the Bantu Educational Cinema Experiment during the Period March 1935 to May 1937*. London: Edinburgh House Press, 1937.

Nouaille-Degorge, Brigette. "OCAM: An Outdated Organization." *UFAHAMU* 5, no. 2 (1974): 135–47.

Oladitan, Olarere, "Une lecture fanoienne du roman africain: Vue d'ensemble d'une approche." *Présence Africaine*, no. 104 (1977).

Opubor, Alfred E., and Onuora E. Nwuneli, eds. *The Development and the Growth of the Film Industry in Nigeria*. Lagos: Third Press International, 1979.

Oudart, Jean-Pierre, and Serge Daney. "Entretien avec Sidney Sokhona." *Cahiers du Cinéma*, no. 285 (Feb. 1978): 48–54.

Oudart, Jean-Pierre, Serge Daney, and Dominique Terres. "Enquête: Super 8 au Mozambique." *Cahiers du Cinéma*, no. 296 (Jan. 1979): 54–59.

Oyekunte, Segun. "The Promises of Mogadishu." *West Africa* (Dec. 19–26, 1983): 2938–40.

Paquet, André. "Toward an Arab and an African Cinema: The 1974 Carthage Film Festival." in *Cineaste* 7, no. 1: 119–26.

Pare, B. Hubert. "8ème FESPACO: Symbole de l'Unité Africaine." *Carrefour Africain*, no. 765 (Nov. 2, 1983): 23.

Pearson, Lyle. "Four Years of African Films." *Film Quarterly* 26, no. 3 (1973): 42–47.

———. "Four Years of African Films." *Film Quarterly* 26, no. 4 (1973): 19–26.

Perry G. M., and Patrick McGilligan. "Sembène Ousmane." *Film Quarterly* 25, no. 3 (1973): 36–42.

Pfaff, Françoise, "De quelle moisson s'agit-il? Dialogue avec Haile Gerima." *Positif*, no. 198 (Oct. 1977): 53–56.

———. "Entretien avec Ousmane Sembène." *Positif*, no. 235 (Oct. 1980): 54–58.

———. *The Cinema of Ousmane Sembène: Pioneer of African Film*. Westport, Conn.: Greenwood Press, 1984.

———. *Twenty-five Black African Filmmakers*. Westport, Conn.: Greenwood Press, 1988.

Pommier, Pierre. *Cinéma et développement en Afrique noire francophone*. Paris: Editions A. Pedone, 1974.

Pouillade, Jean-Luc. "L'emblème (sur *Ceddo*). *Positif*, no. 235 (Oct. 1980): 50–54.

Prédal, René, ed. "Jean Rouch, un griot gaulois." *Cinémaction*, no. 17 (1982/special).

Présence Africaine. "Le rôle cinéaste Africain dans l'éveil d'une conscience de᷄ civilisation noire." no. 90 (1974/special).

Raeburn, Michael. "Entretien avec Sam Aryetey." *Afrique littéraire et artistique*, no. 49 (1978): 19.

Rouch, Jean. *Films ethnographiques sur l'Afrique noire*. Paris: UNESCO, 1967.

Sadoul, Georges. *The Cinema in the Arab Countries.* Beirut: Interarab Center
    of Cinema and Television, 1966.
———. *Histoire du cinéma mondial.* Paris: Flammarion, 1973.
Salmane, Halor, ed. *Algerian Cinema.* London: BFI, 1976.
Sarris, Andrew. *The American Cinema: Directors and Directions 1929–1968.*
    New York: Random House, 1968.
Sartre, Jean-Paul. *Search for a Method.* Trans. Hazel Barnes. New York:
    Random House.
"Sembène Ousmane: Filmmakers Have a Great Responsibility to Our People."
    Cinéaste. 45, no. 1 (n.d.): 26–31.
Senghor, Blaise. "Pour un authentique cinéma africain," *Présence Africaine,*
    no. 49 (1964): 104–10.
Senghor, Leopold S. *Liberté II: Nation et voie africaine du socialisme.* Paris:
    Editions du Seuil, 1971.
Sokhona, Sidney. "Notre cinéma." *Cahiers du Cinéma,* no. 285 (Feb. 1978):
    55–57.
Solanas, Fernando E., and Octavio Gettino. *Ciné Cultura y Decolonizacion.*
    Buenos Aires: Siglo 21, 1973.
Sumo, Honoré de. "Génèse et avenir du cinéma camerounais." *Afrique lit-
    téraire et artistique,* no. 39 (1976): 59–63.
Taylor, Clyde. "Film Reborn in Mozambique." *Jump Cut,* no. 28 (1983): 30–
    31.
Timité, Bassori. "Un cinéma mort-né?" *Présence Africaine,* no. 49 (1964):
    114–15.
Touré, Sékou. *L'action politique du parti démocratique de Guinée en faveur de
    l'émancipation de la jeunesse guinéenne.* Vol. 8. Konakry: Imprimerie
    Patrice Lumumba.
Traoré, Mahama. "Cinema in Africa Must Be School." *Cinéaste* 6, no. 1: 32–
    35.
Turner, Janice, and Jai Kumar. "Shooting It Out with Rambo." *South* (Nov.
    1987).
Unir cinéma: revue du cinéma africain, no. 5 (March–April 1983): 24.
Vaughan, J. Koyinde. "Africa South of the Sahara and the Cinema." *Présence
    Africaine,* no. 14–15 (June–Sept. 1957)
Vauthier, Claude. *L'Afrique des africains: Inventaires de la négritude.* Paris:
    Editions du Seuil, 1964.
Vieyra, Paulin S. "Propos sur le cinéma africain." *Présence Africaine,* no. 23
    (1958).
———. *Le cinéma et l'Afrique.* Paris: Présence Africaine, 1969.
———. *Sembène Ousmane cinéaste.* Paris: Présence Africaine. 1972.
———. *Le cinéma africain: Des origines à 1973.* Paris: Présence Africaine,
    1975.
———. "Le deuxième congrès de la FEPACI." *Présence Africaine,* no. 97
    (1976): 165–74.
———. "Le cinéma au Sénégal en 1976," *Présence Africaine,* no. 207 (1978):
    207–17.
Zahar, Renate. *L'oeuvre de Frantz Fanon.* Trans. Roger Dangerville. Paris:
    François Maspero, 1970.

index

MANTHIA DIAWARA is Professor of English and Associate Director of the Center for the Study of Black Literature and Culture at the University of Pennsylvania, Philadelphia.